THE POWER BROKERS

The Tory Party and Its Leaders

Robert Shepherd

HUTCHINSON

London Sydney Auckland Johannesburg

This edition first published in 1991 by
Hutchinson

Random Century Group Ltd
20 Vauxhall Bridge Road, London SW1V 2SA

Random Century Australia (Pty) Ltd
20 Alfred Street, Milsons Point, Sydney, NSW 2061, Australia

Random Century New Zealand Ltd
PO Box 40–086, Glenfield, Auckland 10, New Zealand

Random Century South Africa (Pty) Ltd
PO Box 337, Bergvlei, 2012, South Africa

BRITISH LIBRARY CATALOGUING-IN-PUBLICATION DATA
Shepherd, Robert
The power brokers: The Tory Party and its leaders.
I. Title
324.24104

ISBN 0–09–174995–6 *Hardback*
ISBN 0–09–175028–8 *Paperback*

Typeset by Speedset Ltd, Ellesmere Port
Printed and bound by Butler and Tanner Ltd,
Frome, Somerset

Contents

Illustrations

Introduction

Iain Macleod, the politician whose oratory and radical Tory* ideals inspired the young John Major, suffered few illusions about the party for which he fought with such vigour. As Macleod used to observe, the Conservative Party exists to maintain or win office. This insight provides the key to understanding one of the great dramas of modern British politics – how Margaret Thatcher, the United Kingdom's longest-serving twentieth-century prime minister, was forced to resign in the mid-term of a Parliament in which she commanded a Commons majority approaching three figures and after she had just won the support of a majority of Tory MPs in the first ballot of the party's leadership contest.

The aim of the opening three chapters of this book is to tell the story of what really happened in the Tory Party during the autumn of 1990, and why. This account is based on extensive interviews, including numerous conversations held before and during the leadership contest, with many of those who were most closely involved. In this section of the book the non-attributable basis of many of my interviews precludes me from disclosing all my sources. I should, however, like to thank all those who agreed to help and also the ministers, MPs, peers and advisers who have discussed the Tory leadership with me over the past few years.

The events of the autumn of 1990 are only one instalment in the long story of the Conservative Party and its leaders. No other party in the world can claim the same continuity, stretching back to the days before democracy had come into existence. In Europe, revolution and war have repeatedly disrupted the continuity of constitutions and parties alike. Although various ideological strands can be traced over the centuries, none of the major continental parties possesses the same clear, con-

---

* Although from the late nineteenth century until Baldwin's leadership in the 1920s Conservatives were usually referred to as Unionists, I follow common usage and often refer to the Conservative Party as the Tory Party and to Conservatives as Tories.

tinuous lineage. In the United States of America, parties developed as a result of democratic elections and did not precede them. The British Conservative Party has outlasted its oldest rival, the Liberal Party, which formally merged with the Social Democrats, and long pre-dates the Labour Party.

This book sets recent events in the context of relations between the Conservatives and their leaders since the 1830s, when Sir Robert Peel became the first modern leader of the party. The impact of Thatcher's leadership and the prospects for Major are also viewed in this longer perspective. As the book shows, the onus rests on the party leader to fulfil the party's rationale, and win or maintain office. The leader can demand enormous loyalty as long as this basic requirement is met; but the party is ruthless in dealing with failure.

I am particularly grateful to Frank Delaney, whose interest first sparked the idea for this book; to Richard Cohen and Michael Shaw for their advice and encouragement; and to Gillian Shepherd for her invaluable help with the research.

ROBERT SHEPHERD
London, March 1991

He Who Wields The Dagger

'The time has come for others to consider their own response to the tragic conflict of loyalties with which I have myself wrestled for perhaps too long.'
Sir Geoffrey Howe, QC, MP, on his resignation from the government,
House of Commons, 13 November 1990

I

Rarely has a politician who has resigned from cabinet exercised his right to make a personal statement in the House of Commons to such effect as Sir Geoffrey Howe in November 1990. 'Devastating' was the immediate verdict of the most hard-bitten Conservative MPs. And devastating it proved to be. Nine days later the prime minister, Margaret Thatcher, announced that she would resign.

'Geoffrey Howe's speech tore away the veils,' a Tory MP from the northwest observed; 'it showed that the talk about divisions in the party was true and that it wasn't the poll tax, it wasn't Michael Heseltine, it wasn't Europe, it was her.' One of Thatcher's closest advisers later admitted that she had been 'deeply hurt' by her former deputy's criticism, coming as it did from somebody who had worked at her side since she became leader of the party fifteen years earlier.

However, in large part it was a hurt that she had brought on herself. She dared not risk sacking Howe but treated him appallingly. At the last two cabinet meetings before his resignation she had openly displayed her impatience with him when he spoke, 'rolling her eyes and looking at the ceiling', according to one minister. Their relationship had steadily deteriorated since 1983 when Thatcher moved him from the Treasury to the Foreign Office, where his incipient sympathy for closer European union became a source of irritation. As they fell out of step on policy she became increasingly annoyed with what one Thatcher loyalist called Howe's 'shuffling' and 'sleepiness'. At cabinet, his mumbled presentation of the Foreign Office's weekly review of foreign affairs barely reached the ears of his colleagues at the far end of the table. On one occasion when Malcolm Rifkind, then a minister of state at the Foreign Office, deputised in Howe's absence, a minister was heard to comment as cabinet ended, 'I hadn't realised until now that we had a foreign policy.'

Howe had considered resigning on at least three occasions before he finally went. In the summer of 1989 the Prime Minister had agreed to accept the conditions for sterling's entry into the European Exchange- Rate Mechanism, the so-called 'Madrid conditions', only when Howe and Nigel Lawson, the chancellor, threatened to resign. A month later, Howe considered resigning when Thatcher exacted her revenge by moving him from the Foreign Office and appointed him Leader of the House and 'deputy prime minister'. As soon as he had agreed to accept the post, Thatcher's aides stressed that his title as her deputy was purely nominal.

He found himself in an impossible position. He was denied any respect by Thatcher, lacked authority among ministers and was left without any role. His humiliation was made complete as he was reduced to concerning himself in his duties as Leader of the House with such business as dealing with MPs' complaints about the Commons cafeteria. In the summer of 1990 he again considered resigning but was dissuaded by friends. His eventual decision to quit on the last day of the parliamentary session had the air about it of a resignation which had long been coming.

In the twelve days between his resignation and his Commons statement, a period extended by the six days' break between the end of the parliamentary session and the state opening of another, he had become increasingly annoyed by the line that he had left office over nothing more than a difference of style. 'Don't let them belittle your resignation,' he was advised by friends and political colleagues. One wrote to warn him against wasting his resignation speech with a damp squib of a statement, as Anthony Eden had done after quitting the Foreign Office in February 1938 over Neville Chamberlain's conduct of foreign policy. In the event, Howe's demolition of the 'official' version of his resignation was telling: 'If some of my former colleagues are to be believed, I must be the first minister in history to resign because he was in full agreement with government policy.'

History will not find Howe guilty of repeating Eden's error, but he does stand accused of Thatcher's political assassination – 'Sir Geoffrey the Assassin' as the *Daily Mail* proclaimed the day after his speech. As after any assassination, conspiracy theories abound: that Howe was in cahoots with his fellow Welshman Heseltine; that he was acting alone but wanted to be Heseltine's kingmaker – after all, he later declared himself to be a Heseltine supporter; that he wanted to flush out Heseltine and force him to stand, expecting Heseltine to lose but to wound Thatcher mortally, thereby enabling Howe to seize the crown, possibly in the spring of 1991. It was also said that Howe's wife, Elspeth, coveted the tenancy of Number 10, and that her alleged venom for Thatcher had been increased by the Howes' loss of their official residence at Chevening in the July 1989 reshuffle. There were also references to Lady Howe as Lady Macbeth, 'passing the dagger to her husband who was fool enough to take it and use it', in the words of one Thatcherite ultra-loyalist.

Howe's increasingly miserable predicament at the Prime Minister's hands and the alleged anger of his wife gave credence to the cruel jibe which gained currency among Tory MPs after Howe's resignation speech that it 'took him ten years to deliver what it had taken his wife ten minutes to write'. But the notion of his being egged on by his wife appeals to the party's Misogynist Tendency. A better insight is provided by Tories who saw Howe before his speech and suspect that he did not realise its full potential. The assassin was motivated not by guile but by a characteristic-ally dogged determination to set out the facts fully and argue a reasoned case, whatever the political consequences. He was blinkered rather than bloody-minded. It was a trait that had marked his entire career: his presentation, as Solicitor-General, of the Heath government's industrial relations legislation during 1970–71 had provoked particular hostility on the Labour benches. The same approach had typified his four years as Thatcher's chancellor from May 1979, when the monetarist case was argued with legalistic precision while Britain suffered its deepest recession since the 1930s and fellow Tories despaired of his lack of political touch. The late Earl of Stockton, the former Harold Macmillan, had implored him at a Tory gathering to 'do something political, Geoffrey'.

When Howe searched for a precedent for his resignation speech he recalled the emergency Commons statement which he had had to make as foreign secretary immediately after the killing of three suspected IRA terrorists by the security forces on Gibraltar in March 1988. He had been acutely aware then that the Crown's case in any subsequent legal proceedings would rest on what he said that day. Likewise, his resignation statement would be consciously designed to withstand the test of time. His final draft, completed with an hour to spare, was intended to be compact and comprehensive, and as measured and durable as possible.

Howe's purpose was twofold: to put his version of events on the record and to make his Tory colleagues think again about how the government was being run. The conjunction of the two proved explosive for a party already in a high state of nerves as a result of Howe's departure, had by-election defeats at Eastbourne and Bradford North and frenzied speculation that Thatcher would be challenged for the Tory leadership later that month, as she had been by Sir Anthony Meyer the previous year under the rules which require annual re-election. The forensic exactitude with which Howe presented his account of events provided an irresistible manifesto for the increasing number of Tory MPs anxious to remove Thatcher before the next election. Howe's reputation for not being devious, his unrivalled record of service with Thatcher – as he recalled in his speech '700 meetings of Cabinet or Shadow Cabinet over the last eighteen years, some 400 hours alongside each other and more than thirty international summit meetings' – and his widely recognised patience over the years in the face of his leader's undermining of agreed policy through 'some casual comment or impulsive answer', all served to confirm his departure as a touchstone of how bad things had become in the government.

Within moments of Howe's call in his speech to colleagues to consider where their true loyalties lay, many Tory MPs were approaching Heseltine and urging him to challenge Thatcher for the party leadership. One friend who sought to dissuade Heseltine was told by him that after Howe's speech 'she's finished'. Yet the battle for Tory leadership was not at the time of Heseltine's choosing: he was being forced to enter the lists, partly through pressure from his allies, partly through the efforts of his political enemies and partly through his own miscalculation.

II

Ever since Michael Heseltine resigned over the handling of the Westland affair in January 1986, walking out of the cabinet in the style of Joseph Chamberlain one hundred years earlier, he had met all enquiries about his leadership ambitions by religiously repeating that he could not foresee the circumstances in which he would challenge Margaret Thatcher for the leadership of the Conservative Party. This carefully constructed formula was his armour against the charge of public disloyalty to the party leader, a treasonable offence in the Tory Party, as long, that is, as the leader remains in power. Significantly, however, the formula ruled nothing out: circumstances have a habit of being unforeseen.

His leadership ambition burning bright through the coded armour, Heseltine hit the campaign trail in 1986 like an American presidential candidate and with the independent means to match. He had amassed a personal fortune as a co-founder of a magazine-publishing firm, Haymarket, and it was from a modest office owned by the company in a red-brick building in Victoria Street, Westminster, that Heseltine's policy ideas spilled forth in articles, interviews, speeches and two books, *Where*

There's a Will and *The Challenge of Europe*. As the words deluged the media and sustained their interest in him, Heseltine began working the electoral college for Tory leadership elections – that is, the Tory parliamentary party – for all he was worth, which was an awful lot.

Before his resignation, Heseltine had been a 'doer'. He had been appointed a front-bench Tory spokesman within three years of first being elected to the Commons in 1966 and remained on the front bench for the next seventeen years, in government and opposition. Not a naturally clubbable man, he preferred to cultivate his landscape garden near Banbury. Resisting the advice of his political associates, he refused suddenly to spend more time round the Commons, telling them that 'it would look too transparent'.

Heseltine, however, came to realise soon after Westland that he had no alternative but to abandon his aloofness. Discarding his previous disdain for the gossipy company of backbenchers, he started being seen around the Commons, chatting in the tearoom, exchanging the odd word in the corridors and around the lobbies. He enthusiastically accepted invitations to speak in Tory MPs' constituencies, clocking up hundreds of thousands of miles and consuming innumerable local party-association dinners on what is patronisingly called the 'rubber chicken circuit'. He was building up credit with MPs from all wings of the party and, although local party activists have no vote in the electoral college, it would do no harm if they were singing his praises to their MPs. At by-election after by-election he was the star turn, invariably attracting the largest audiences and impressing the party faithful with powers of political speechmaking, unequalled among his Tory contemporaries. Surely no politician had ever given a clearer demonstration of his willingness to serve the party in whatever capacity he was asked? And if his colleagues were to ask, no doubt he would even be ready to lead the party. Not, of course, that he could foresee such circumstances.

Ever vigilant against the charge of disloyalty, Heseltine resolutely refused to sanction anything which, were it to leak, could be portrayed as evidence that he was running a leadership campaign. During the summer of 1990, MPs who wanted to help him and suggested concerting their efforts were turned away. Heseltine continued to rely on his closest, long-standing unofficial aides in the Commons: Michael Mates, a former regular soldier, and Dr Keith Hampson, a former academic. He also vetoed the idea of compiling any sort of list of Tory MPs to whom he had spoken, whose constituency he had visited, who were for him or against. Fearing that such a list would be bound to leak, he would respond that 'the only list that matters is in my mind'. And indeed, when the time came, he impressed his aides by 'churning out like a computer' the details of his constituency visits, his contacts with Tory MPs and what they had told him.

The strategy achieved its first, all-important objective. Not since Winston Churchill in the 1930s had a former minister, consigned to the political wilderness of the Tory backbenches, succeeded in commanding such attention. Heseltine had kept himself centre stage while other possible contenders for the leadership fell by the wayside, including John Moore, who had the looks of an American presidential candidate and Thatcherite credentials but who lacked the staying power; Norman Tebbit, who was more Thatcherite than Thatcher; and Peter Walker, whose coded speeches of dissent from within the cabinet during the 1980s began to pall. The full glare of the spotlight swung on Heseltine after the summer of 1989. In the election for the European Parliament in June, the Tories polled only 34.2 per cent of the national vote.

In July, Tory unease was increased by a botched cabinet reshuffle, which pushed Howe to the brink of resignation when Thatcher sacked him from the Foreign Office and embarrassed Douglas Hurd, the home secretary, whose job Thatcher at one point offered to the disgruntled Howe. It seemed that Thatcher was losing her political touch as well as her electoral appeal.

She had replaced Howe with John Major as foreign secretary, giving the first public signal that he was her heir-apparent, but her putative successor had only had two years' experience in the cabinet as chief secretary. Thus with Howe humiliated, Hurd languishing at the Home Office and nobody else seemingly in serious contention for the leadership, Heseltine was widely seen as the frontrunner to succeed Thatcher.

Through the autumn of 1989, the spotlight on Heseltine barely dimmed. In his address to a fringe meeting at the party conference in Blackpool – no longer a minister, he had been unable to deliver a full-length speech to the conference proper since 1985 – Heseltine uncompromisingly listed the elements that set his brand of Tory radicalism apart from Thatcher's. But neither Heseltine nor anybody else expected the leadership issue to come to the boil as quickly as it did. Within weeks of the Tories having gathered at Blackpool under the slogan 'the right team', one of their key players, the chancellor of the Exchequer, Nigel Lawson, resigned over the role which his captain accorded her economics adviser, Sir Alan Walters, although the deep disagreement between chancellor and prime minister over exchange-rate policy had been common knowledge for months.

In retrospect, one of the most remarkable aspects of Lawson's departure was the speed with which it was discounted by Tory MPs. But in its immediate aftermath the dramatic exit of one of the chief architects of her economic policies from the mid-1970s seemed a potentially mortal blow to Thatcher's authority. It was quite impossible for her to dismiss it as one of those 'little local difficulties' in the nonchalant style of Harold

Macmillan's reaction in January 1958 to the resignation of his chancellor, Peter Thorneycroft, and two treasury ministers, Enoch Powell and Nigel Birch.

Lawson's resignation, on the eve of a new session of Parliament, could scarcely have come at a more inopportune moment for Thatcher. Her discomfort stemmed from the revision to the rules for choosing the leader of the Conservative Party which had been introduced when she defeated the incumbent leader, Edward Heath, in February 1975. Before 1975 the decision to hold a leadership election had remained at the leader's discretion. Following the two election defeats of 1974, however, a growing number of Tory MPs wanted to remove Heath as leader, but under the rules as they stood an unpopular leader might choose to ignore the pressure on him to go. Heath accepted that there should be a review of the rules and agreed to various revisions which included the provision for an annual leadership election by the parliamentary party. Tory MPs were given an opportunity to choose a leader within twenty-eight days of the opening of each new session of Parliament.

Until 1989, the annual leadership election had always been a formality, with Thatcher being returned unopposed on each occasion. However, in November that year, Sir Anthony Meyer, a 69-year-old baronet and old-style, independent-minded, paternalist Tory with strongly pro-European views, broke with precedent and declared himself a candidate. Meyer, who had been a critic of the Falklands war, argued that he was standing in order to allow the party a choice. There was never any prospect of his being elected leader. The real issue was how much damage he would do Thatcher in terms of the number of votes withheld from her, and whether he would prove an effective 'stalking horse' for another, as yet undeclared, contender who might emerge if the Prime Minister was mortally wounded.

Heseltine was not party to talks with Meyer or anybody else about running a stalking horse and expressly forbade his lieutenants, Mates and Hampson, from joining any such plan. But with the party about to enter the uncharted waters of the first formal challenge to Thatcher's leadership Tory MPs anxiously tried to estimate how many would withhold their vote from her and at what level of withheld votes her leadership would be fatally undermined. Pessimists feared that Meyer might attract as many as 80 votes, and set 120 votes as the 'crisis level' for Thatcher in a total electorate of 372 MPs.

This prompted renewed discussion among those who were determined that Heseltine should never lead the party, disliking, as one of them would later say, 'the sound of the crack of the whip on leather'. Renewed, because during the Westland affair in 1986, Chris Patten, John Patten (no relation) and William Waldegrave, three of the brightest members among those first elected to the Commons in 1979 and by then all ministers of state, had approached Douglas Hurd, the then Home Secretary, saying that if Thatcher fell they wanted him to succeed her. Hurd's unsought supporters were founder members of the 'Blue Chip' group, drawn mainly from the 1979 intake, who regularly dine together and who in 1979–81 had elegantly encapsulated the leftish Tory, or 'wet', orthodoxies in their pamphlet *Changing Gear*.

Those who approached Hurd were acting on their own initiative, fearful of the impact on the party of Heseltine's incipient authoritarianism. By contrast, Hurd, an old Etonian and ex-diplomat, appeared a 'gent', in the style of generations of Tory MPs, which his father and grandfather had been. His advocates felt that after Thatcher's leadership Hurd's traditional Toryism would be balm for the party. But nothing further was done apart from Hurd's name being pushed in the press by his acolytes in the early part of 1986 as a potential leadership contender whose stock was rising.

The talks among Tory ministers and MPs at the time of Meyer's challenge in late 1989 barely merit the description 'contingency planning'. But the risk of irreparable damage being inflicted on Thatcher prompted those who opposed Heseltine to review the alternatives in the event of Thatcher being forced to stand down. There was a paucity of choice. Howe was nominally deputy prime minister but was seen as 'expended', and it was reckoned that Heseltine 'would beat the pants off him'. Major's move to the Exchequer, after only three months at the Foreign Office, marked him as a longer-term leadership prospect, but he was still too inexperienced to warrant serious consideration. Easily the most credible 'stop Heseltine' candidate at this stage was Hurd, whom Thatcher had finally had to appoint foreign secretary in the changes forced on her by Lawson's departure, despite her suspicion of his pro-European sentiments.

Hurd was drafted as a potential contender despite himself. Possessed of a strong sense of constitutional rectitude, he had not sought to push his claim. But Hurd's support had spread from his natural allies on the left to include Alan Clark, the minister of state for defence and one of the most senior members of the right-wing '92 Group' of Tory MPs so called because their meetings were initially held at 92 Cheyne Walk, then the home of a founder-member, the former Tory MP Major Patrick Wall. Clark was fiercely determined that Heseltine should never become party leader. As a Thatcher loyalist who would never join any plot to undermine her, Clark would always fight with Thatcher to the last. But he was enough of a realist to appreciate that she was not invincible, and that it might become necessary, post-Thatcher, to mobilise against Heseltine. So a 'mothball fleet' was being formed for Hurd with vessels of every description but, as events a year later were to prove, no battle plans were ever discussed.

Meyer attracted enormous media coverage but his challenge never proved a serious threat for Thatcher's campaign manager, George Younger, the former Scottish and defence secretary and a reassuringly centrist figure. When the result of the first ballot was declared on Tuesday 5 December, Thatcher had an easy victory, winning 314 votes to Meyer's 33, with 24 abstentions or spoilt papers and one MP absent through ill-health. In all, 58 MPs, or 16 per cent of the parliamentary party, had failed to support the Prime Minister, a total well below the private fears of some Thatcher loyalists.

However, the challenge had set a precedent. Immediate suggestions that the rules be redrawn to discourage further contests were quickly seen to be maladroit, and the only revision was that in future the names of a candidate's proposer and seconder would be made public. The contest had also established a yardstick against which to measure Thatcher's future standing with Tory MPs. And, significantly, up to thirty MPs had voted for Thatcher in December 1989 only on the assurance from Younger that she would change her style and run a more collective government.

III

Suggestions during the winter of 1989–90 that the leadership crisis would not recur before the next general election were soon proved wrong. Increasing inflation and higher interest rates were gnawing deep into Tory support, particularly among former Thatcherite converts in the lower middle and skilled working class. Tory MPs privately voiced their alarm that the economic cycle was slipping irretrievably out of kilter with the political timetable; it looked as if economic recovery would come too late to help them at the polls, since they would prefer not to postpone an election until the latest possible date in July 1992 and risk losing the initiative. Added to these worries on the Tory benches was an immediate and mounting anxiety at the impact of the community charge, or poll tax, which in April would replace local domestic rates in England and Wales and was already making the Tories unpopular in Scotland, where it had been introduced the previous spring.

Tory MPs desperately wanted a good tune to whistle. In the March 1990 debate on the economy Heseltine took his cue. Tories rushed from the tearoom as he displayed a reassuring grasp of industry's problems and excited Tory centrists and right-wingers with his proposal to privatise the Bank of England and create a monetary authority on the lines of the German Bundesbank, independent of government and therefore free from manipulation by politicians. 'A genuine case of spontaneous combustion', one of his allies claimed as Heseltine's leadership prospects were re-ignited.

The excited response from Tory MPs set alarm bells ringing behind the iron gates of Downing Street. Thatcherite loyalists in the press rallied with striking similarities of phraseology, which betrayed all the signs of an orchestrated campaign. The Lords Stevens and Wyatt in the *Daily Express* and *The Times* respectively were among the most notable contributors to a fusillade of newsprint which denounced the man and his policies, condemning Heseltine's alleged personal impetuosity and economic interventionism – 'Lego-Keynesianism' was one of the more exotic phrases dreamed up for the occasion.

Major's March budget combined a common-sense style of presentation with an imaginative initiative to encourage saving (the TESSA scheme) and included further relief to ease the burden of the poll tax in its first year of implementation in England and Wales. But in a crass oversight the Scots, who had virtually completed their first year of poll tax, were given no comparable backdated relief. Such was the ferocity of reaction in Scotland that within two days the Government was forced to make a U-turn, and announced a four-million-pound package of concessions to Scottish poll taxpayers. Thatcher's cabinet was again in a shambles. The loss, in the same week, of the Mid-Staffordshire by-election, with the biggest swing from the Tories to Labour in more than fifty years, renewed speculation about Thatcher's leadership. In April 1990, Thatcher's popularity as prime minister slumped to the lowest ever recorded. She was increasingly seen as an electoral liability by Tory MPs.[1]

As the shock-waves from the first poll-tax demands were felt across the country, triggering mass demonstrations in the Shires and prompting resignations from the party by local councillors, Tories braced themselves for disastrous results in May's local elections. The poll tax was proving unpopular in constituencies where the Party would be defending small majorities against Labour. Some couples whose rates had been £150–£200 were presented with poll-tax bills totalling £750–£800. Initial estimates of the likely levels of the poll tax, although causing anxiety to Tories, had encouraged some to feel that the new system would be defensible. But in a town like Bury, where the Tories hold its two seats with majorities of only 2,679 and 6,911, an estimated figure of around £250 was transformed into a final charge of £373. With every extra pound the number of losers from the poll tax increased and the number of gainers decreased. In general the final charge was significantly higher than the average level of rates on small terraced houses. Voters on whose support Thatcher had built three general-election victories – typically, skilled workers – felt that their bills had risen too much, too quickly, and at a time when they were already being hit by rising inflation and high interest rates.

The last comparable district-council elections in England and Wales had been held in 1986, also a bad year for the Tories. It was therefore easier for the Tories to present the 1990 results as not being as bad as had been feared, a ploy assisted by Labour's ill-advised campaign that the elections were a referendum on the poll tax. When the London boroughs of Ealing, Wandsworth and Westminster showed sweeping gains for the Tories, Kenneth Baker, chairman of the Conservative Party Organisation, achieved a remarkable triumph of political presentation in portraying isolated successes against the national trend as proof that the Government was on the road to political recovery.

Heseltine was eclipsed as suddenly as he had dazzled at the time of his March speech on the economy. At his post mortem after the May local elections, he was advised that he had succeeded in keeping himself on the Tory stage since Westland and that the spotlight would find him again as it had done before. Heseltine, though not convinced, had little option but to continue with his strategy of the previous four years.

Opponents of Heseltine seized on his loss of momentum and throughout the summer of 1990 pushed the line that he had missed his chance, an impression which he inadvertently reinforced when he ventured into the political minefield of the poll tax. He had promised to outline his proposed reform of the poll tax after the local elections, and did so in the form of a well-publicised article in *The Times*. On the eve of the publication his plans were being rubbished at Westminster by Tories who had been primed to go on the attack before the article had even appeared. Heseltine's approach was not to scrap the poll tax but to seek to improve its working. His suggestion that councils who overspent should be subject to re-election was, however, ill-considered and vindicated his critics.

On 2 August, Iraq's invasion of Kuwait seemed bound to transform the political landscape. A change of prime minister would be out of the question with war imminent in the Persian Gulf and British troops heavily committed. Although it was uncertain when the crisis would be resolved, the next election was possibly only a year away and the Tory Party would not be in a mood to consider any change of leader. Heseltine chose to deliver a traditional rallying speech at his fringe meeting at October's party conference in Bournemouth. Emphasising his full backing for the British and American position on the Gulf, he devoted much of his speech to party-political knockabout. He won a standing ovation, but the occasion seemed strikingly different from Blackpool a year earlier. There was a sense that time was passing him by.

Thatcher's mockery in her party-conference speech of the Liberal Democrats as the 'dead parrot' of British politics displayed dangerous hubris. Nemesis was swift. Within a fortnight the Liberal Democrats had won the Eastbourne by-election, overturning the late Ian Gow's majority of 16,923. At the Rome European Community summit at the end of the month, Thatcher's hard-line opposition to political and economic union isolated her from other heads of government. Although her subsequent statement in the Commons adhered to the text agreed with the more pro-European foreign secretary Hurd and her chancellor Major, she appeared to adopt a tougher line in her replies to questions, seeming to be more of a soul mate of Nicholas Ridley (who had resigned from her cabinet in July following his indiscreet anti-German remarks) than of her senior cabinet colleagues. Her deputy, Howe, who was sitting alongside the Prime Minister during her statement, was appalled.

Two days later, at six o'clock on the evening of Thursday 1 November, Howe called on the Prime Minister in her study at Number 10 to inform her that he could no longer serve in her government. The last remaining member from her May 1979 cabinet had quit, and had done so in circumstances which revived memories of Lawson's departure twelves months earlier and expunged any impression that she might, as promised, have changed her style of government since Meyer's challenge. Thatcher was vulnerable.

IV

Heseltine had long before planned to use the interval in early November between the end of the old parliamentary session and the start of the new one to visit Israel and Jordan. He was due to leave London on Saturday 3 November. After a dinner engagement on the evening of Howe's resignation, he faced a hectic day on Friday 2nd and had still to complete the preparations for his trip and the speech he was due to deliver in Israel.

Heseltine had very little time in which to consider his response to Howe's resignation. He had an article to write for that weekend's *Sunday Times*, and was anxious to reinforce Howe's stand both on the way the government was being run and on Europe. Heseltine completed his draft by early Friday morning. It was a powerful statement. But he was also being pressed by other journalists for his reaction and he decided that it would be better to release his text before he left for the Middle East, although he placed a press embargo on it until Saturday evening.

Lacking any suitable speaking engagement, Heseltine resorted to a device much favoured by other MPs and ministers, including, most notably, Howe. This method involves sending a letter to the chairman of the MP's own constituency Conservative association and releasing the text to the press. Before leaving for Israel, therefore, Heseltine phoned the chairman of Henley Conservatives to warn him what to expect, and assured him that no reply was required. Neither of them realised that the letter would become a *cause célèbre*.

'It was a terrible mistake,' a Heseltine supporter later admitted. Thatcher loyalists seized the opportunity to savage Heseltine, her press secretary Bernard Ingham[2] feeding the media with the topical line, as Bonfire Night approached, that Heseltine had 'lit the blue touch-paper and then retired out of the country'. The press also heard that Thatcher had nothing but 'contempt and disdain' for Heseltine. Some Tory MPs reported an irritated response to Heseltine's letter among their constituency activists, who felt they were 'slogging away trying to win the next election' but all they heard from Westminster was 'endless squabbling'. Others echoed the Ingham message, angry that Heseltine was 'stirring it up again and then sodding off out of the country'. Worst of all from Heseltine's point of view was that his own constituency association became involved.

Few MPs addressing what is, in practice, a press release to their local chairman expect a reply. But after Heseltine had released his letter, his local party officers found themselves being asked by the press for their response. At a meeting attended by the Conservative Central Office agent for Wessex area, Donald Stringer, an experienced party professional, they decided to draft their own letter in a reply. When the Henley letter appeared it was widely seen as a damaging rebuff to their MP. Comparing Heseltine's plight with that of a player in a board game, one senior Tory quipped that the hapless former minister 'had gone down a snake'.

Other Tories, even among Thatcher's staunchest loyalists, were anxious at what they saw as 'the stitching-up' of a local party by Conservative Central Office. Stringer, however, claims that replying to a letter is usual, denies that he was advised to attend the meeting by Central Office, and says that he went at the suggestion of the local Henley officers and had no hand in drafting the reply. Kenneth Baker too, the party chairman, who himself had been a leadership contender but whose star had waned and whose smile had come to look more strained as the party's troubles mounted, maintains that he played no part in organising Henley's response. Although opinion was divided among the Henley officers, they believed that their final draft was 'neutral'. But in the circumstances virtually any reply from them short of a slavish endorsement of Heseltine was likely to be seized on by the press as criticism of him, a reaction exacerbated by the importance attached to it by Thatcher loyalists and the gloss, or 'spin', which they imparted as they talked to the media.

Thatcher's supporters say that among her closest advisers there was a division between hardliners, who were generally not MPs but who had close contact with the press, like Bernard Ingham, and more cautious loyalists, mainly MPs and ministers like Cecil Parkinson. The hardliners would be happy to see Heseltine defeated once and for all, one of them commenting that 'an election in which she smashed him would clear the air'. But the cautious loyalists realised that tough words risked provoking a head-on clash in which Heseltine was bound to attract more support than Meyer the previous year, with potentially fatal consequences for Thatcher's leadership.

Talk of running another stalking-horse candidate in the leadership election due in the first month of the new parliamentary session had been rekindled by Howe's resignation. There was some discussion among members of the 'Lollards', the Tory left-wing equivalent of the 92 Group, so called because a founding member, the former Tory MP Sir William van Straubenzee, was a church commissioner with a flat in the Lollards tower at Lambeth Palace, where the group used to meet. But Heseltine, who was not a Lollard, remained insistent that neither he nor his close supporters should be involved. Although a stalking horse was unlikely to attract sufficient support to remove Thatcher in the autumn, some Tory left-wingers argued that another converted leadership election would serve to demonstrate the decline in her support. As economic recession deepened in the New Year and spring 1991's local elections loomed, the pressure on her to step down would become irresistible. But some of Thatcher's most implacable critics on the Tory left, like Sir Ian Gilmour, rejected any notion of a stalking-horse candidate. Others felt that the Gulf crisis precluded any such challenge.

Even without the Gulf crisis, the notion of a stalking horse would have been fraught with dangers. As Meyer had discovered, many MPs are reluctant to vote for a candidate who is not a serious contender for the leadership. Moreover, Meyer's local party had subsequently deselected him and therefore any MP wishing to stand at the next general election was virtually ruled out. Rumours that Sir Dennis Walters, a senior Tory MP who had announced his retirement at the next election, might emerge as the stalking horse was met with derision. 'Dennis who?' was the riposte from MPs among the 1987 intake, an effective taunt although it revealed their ignorance (not least of one of the better Tory memoir writers).

The party hierarchy, however, was taking nothing for granted and was anxious to prevent a stalking horse challenge because of the electoral damage already being wrought by Tory disunity and the danger that another contest would undermine Thatcher's authority. One way to reduce the likelihood of a challenge would be to bring forward the date for any contest, allowing less time for a stalking horse campaign to be organised. Under the rules for leadership elections, any contest must be held within twenty-eight days of the start of a new parliamentary session, but 'the actual date will be determined by the Leader of the Party in consultation with the Chairman of the 1922 Committee'. When Thatcher met Cranley Onslow, chairman of the 1922 Committee of Tory backbenchers, a bluff character in the tradition of fishing-and-shooting Tories down the ages, they agreed that the date for any leadership election should be brought forward to 20 November, only a fortnight after the state opening of the new session and a fortnight earlier than the contest had been held in 1989.

Morale among Tory MPs was low as Thatcher stumbled from one blunder to another. The decision not to uprate child benefit caused a storm, but the government's climbdown, increasing the benefit for the first child by a small amount, was criticised by Tory MPs for achieving the worst of both worlds – failing to restore the value of the benefit yet undermining the hard-nosed Tory argument that it was wrong to make concessions which helped the rich as well as the poor. To make matters worse, in the Bradford North by-election on Thursday 8 November, the Tories suffered a poor result in a seat which they had previously held and which they had only narrowly lost at the 1987 election.

Despite the increasing gravity of the Gulf crisis, the dominant issue at Westminster was whether Heseltine would run against Thatcher or not. It was unlikely that any stalking horse would emerge unless he was sure that Heseltine was committed to entering the fray after the first ballot. The pressure was mounting inexorably on Heseltine to put his name forward. Back from his Middle East visit, he sounded out MPs around the corridors and tearoom. Some now told him that they would vote for him. He was also warned that this might be his last chance to challenge Thatcher; that it was 'now or never'. Among this latter group were ministers and MPs who were not enamoured at the prospect of Heseltine as leader but who were convinced that Thatcher had to go because she would lose the next election. Their interest lay in persuading Heseltine to stand, sensing that he would mortally wound Thatcher but not win the Tory crown. Some favoured Hurd, others Major. Heseltine was, in effect, their stalking horse.

What amounted to an unholy alliance also developed between Tories who believed that Thatcher had to be ousted and Thatcher's hardline loyalists. Tories whose motive was to remove Thatcher sought to foster the notion that Heseltine was facing a test of his virility, hoping that this challenge to his pride would force him to stand. Thatcherite hardliners pushed the line that Heseltine should 'either put up or shut up', hoping either that they would wrong-foot him and expose him as lacking courage if he decided to defer, or that he would be 'smashed' if he forced a contest.

Cranley Onslow's reaction to these pressures revealed an underlying Tory suspicion of elections. 'This isn't some golf club where you can have a contest and it does not matter,' he fumed. 'This is really a very important matter, and it has to be taken seriously and people have to make serious decisions. This is not the time to fool around with the luxury of dissent.'

'STALKING HORSE: SPORTSMEN OFTEN USED TO CONCEAL THEMSELVES BEHIND HORSES, AND GO ON STALKING STEP BY STEP TILL THEY GOT WITHIN SHOT OF THEIR GAME.'

By pressing Heseltine to launch a direct challenge against Thatcher, Tory MPs would cast him as a 'stalking horse'.

Notwithstanding Onslow's dire warnings, Heseltine faced intense media pressure. Over the weekend of 10–11 November, his allies contacted potential supporters, asking them two questions. Should he stand? And if he did, would he have their support? By early the following week, over a hundred MPs, including some ministers, were saying that he should run and that they would support him. Heseltine had also met with the officers of his local party in Henley. Thatcher's loyalists had made the mistake of placing too much importance on the Henley officers' reply when in fact the officers were divided and Heseltine was able to extract a ringing endorsement from them. After having disappeared 'down a snake', Heseltine 'went back up a ladder'.

It was known that Howe planned to take an opportunity in the Commons early in the week of 12–16 November to set out his reasons for resigning. On Monday evening Thatcher launched her own pre-emptive strike against both her former deputy and any potential leadership rivals. In the unlikely setting of the Guildhall, where she was delivering the prime minister's annual speech at the lord mayor's banquet, she declared that anyone bowling bouncers at her would be 'hit for six'. The following day, Tuesday 13th, Howe retorted in kind in his resignation speech, arguing that her attacks on her chancellor's 'hard ecu' proposals had been 'like sending your opening batsman to the crease only to find that the bats have been broken before the game by the team captain'.

Heseltine had returned from a speaking engagement in Hamburg on Tuesday 13th still undecided whether to challenge Thatcher. The pressure on him to stand and fight was enormous. Although an eventual war in the Gulf was looking more likely, by November it seemed less imminent. Tory MPs were preoccupied with their own electoral prospects. Warnings by Tom King, the defence secretary, and Lord Lewin, chief of the defence staff during the Falklands War, that it was not the time, while British troops were committed in the Gulf, to contemplate a change of leader, backfired. Howe's speech and the reaction of other Tories finally convinced Heseltine that he would have to throw down the gauntlet.

'He would have been too badly damaged if he had not stood at that time,' one Heseltine ally explained; 'we were forced to go, that was the problem'. According to another, 'If Howe had said simply that Thatcher had achieved great things, the policies were fine, but there was just this problem of Europe, then Michael would simply have stayed with his old formula on the leadership.' Instead Howe had gone much further, and in Heseltine's mind raised the very issues over which he himself had resigned. 'People always tend to scoff at Michael when he gets on to the constitutional issues over Westland,' one of Heseltine's friends explains 'but with Howe's speech all that side of it came flooding back. It was impossible for him not to run.'

Westland had rocked the government almost five years earlier. Thatcher was nearly brought down by the issue when her closest staff were implicated in an attempt to discredit Heseltine by leaking confidential advice provided by the Solicitor General, and Heseltine claimed that he was denied the opportunity to argue his case in cabinet. Ever since, she had resolved that Heseltine would not succeed her. Howe's speech finally brought the two protagonists into open combat.

V

The trouble with elections, as the Soviet foreign minister Molotov reputedly observed, is that you can never be sure who will win. Anxiety is inherent, but in few elections do the rules give rise to such uncertainty as those under which the Conservative Party chooses a new leader. The key to understanding the contest between Heseltine and Thatcher is to remember three crucial facts: the conditions required for achieving an outright win; the secrecy of the ballot; and the timescale of the contest.

First, the rules require that in order to win outright on the first ballot a candidate must secure an overall majority of the votes of those entitled to vote *and* receive 15 per cent more of the votes of those entitled to vote than any other candidate. If no candidate satisfies both conditions, a second ballot is held. Since there were 372 Tory MPs at the time of the November 1990 election, Heseltine or Thatcher needed to achieve 187 votes *and* at least 56 votes more than the other in order to win outright on the first ballot. Thus, Thatcher would win outright if she secured 187 votes provided that Heseltine did not receive any more than 131, since this result would give her both an overall majority and a clear majority over him of 56 votes (in this illustrative example 54 MPs abstained). But *she* would not win even if she secured as many as 213 votes provided that Heseltine received 159 votes and there were no abstentions, since this result would give her an overall majority but would deny her the necessary 15 per cent majority over him.

Second, the secrecy of the ballot enables some MPs to promise their support to one candidate but vote for another, and others to make pledges to more than one candidate – the total of the pledges made to the contenders invariably far exceeds the total number of Tory MPs in the Commons. The so-called 'fib factor' is a threat to all candidates but particularly to the incumbent leader as there is every incentive for MPs, however they intend to vote, to promise their support to the current source of patronage.

Finally, there are only five days between the deadline for nominations at noon on a Thursday (although Heseltine declared his intentions to stand a day earlier) and voting on the following Tuesday, which begins at 11.00 am and continues until 6.00 pm. But the weekend intervenes and many MPs are in their constituencies by Friday, leaving Thursday as the key day for approaching them. Although MPs are canvassed by phone over the weekend, many have made up their minds by that stage. The Monday before voting is effectively limited to persuading any remaining don't knows, the doubters and the waverers.

As was widely predicted in the papers on Wednesday 14 November, Heseltine formally announced later that morning his decision to stand in the first ballot due to be held the following Tuesday for the leadership of the Conservative Party. He was proposed by Sir Neil MacFarlane, a former minister, and Sir Peter Tapsell, a former front-bench spokesman in opposition who had resigned from the shadow Treasury team before the 1979 election because he disagreed with the monetarist policy which the Tories were then advocating. Macfarlane's emergence as one of Heseltine's sponsors caused consternation inside Number 10, since he had assisted Thatcher's campaign when she won the leadership in 1975 and he was one of Denis Thatcher's golfing friends. Heseltine's oft-repeated formula about not being able to foresee the circumstances in which he would challenge Thatcher was explained away, quoting a figure of 100 Tory MPs who had called on him to put his name forward.

Heseltine was in fact not exaggerating, and this figure should have served as a warning to Thatcher of the seriousness of the threat he offered.

Heseltine's campaign had momentum from the word go. The pressure on him which had built up over the previous fortnight and the informal soundings by his allies before his declaration gave him a flying start. On the Wednesday morning at his Victoria Street office, he finally sanctioned an analysis of the electoral college. Enlarged photocopies of lists of the names of Tory MPs were pinned on a board and Heseltine, from memory, began pooling his formidable intelligence of the 372-strong electorate and comparing notes with his parliamentary lieutenants, Hampson and Mates.

Volunteers immediately rallied to the Heseltine flag. Prominent among his supporters were Peter Temple-Morris, a senior backbencher, John Lee, a former minister from the 1979 intake, and William Powell, who entered the Commons in 1983. They reflected Heseltine's core support on the left and among MPs with marginal seats in the Midlands and the north. Temple-Morris is a key figure in the leftish-inclined Lollards group; Lee had resigned his ministerial post in order to concentrate on defending his marginal Lancashire seat of Pendle, where his majority over Labour is 2,639; and Powell holds the Northamptonshire seat of Corby with a majority over Labour of only 1,805.

About twenty MPs actively canvassed for Heseltine, although more wanted to be involved. There is a danger in having too many on the campaign team, since canvassing needs to be co-ordinated if it is not to risk being counter-productive – no MP wants to feel pestered. But the failure to include more people in the campaign team on the first day was later regretted in the Heseltine camp. The campaign headquarters remained at Heseltine's office in Victoria Street, with daily meetings held at the House of Commons in Interview Room J, the basement room used by Willie Whitelaw's campaign team during the 1975 leadership contest. Heseltine usually chaired the daily meetings – often held late in the evening after the ten o'clock vote in the Commons – at which he and his campaigners compared notes for the day.

By the weekend, Heseltine's support had built steadily. According to an estimate given privately at the time by a member of his campaign team, Heseltine was set to receive a vote well in excess of his starting point. After adjusting this estimate to make allowance for the fib factor, a vote of at least 130–40 seemed likely. This was significant, since it indicated that unless there were few abstentions Thatcher would probably secure an overall majority on the first ballot but might fail to achieve the required 15 per cent lead of 56 votes over Heseltine.

Whereas Tory MPs described Heseltine's team as 'assiduous' during the vital first few days of the contest, Thatcher's campaign 'never really materialised' and was rated as 'unimpressive'. 'Disastrous' is the word most commonly applied to every aspect of the Prime Minister's campaign, from her strategy to the day-to-day tactics. It is easy with hindsight to be critical, and some MPs attack the strategy but defend the team while others defend the strategy but attack the team. Certainly anxious voices were raised during the campaign but were reassured by her key campaigners.

The impression was that she was out of touch with her parliamentary party, and this was further confirmed by her choice of campaign team, which one of her cabinet loyalists described as 'curious'. Her manager was nominally George Younger, a Tory of eminent reasonableness and centrist reputation, who had calmly defused the threat from Meyer the previous year. But he was not called upon to do much by Thatcher's closest aides. His assurance to doubters in 1989 that Thatcher would change her ways had been demolished by Howe's resignation, and he now gave the impression that his heart wasn't in it. Younger's role as chairman-designate of the Royal Bank of Scotland meant also that he was less in touch with back-bench feeling. Among Thatcher's other campaigners were former cabinet ministers Norman Tebbit and John Moore. Tebbit worked tirelessly, although fellow Thatcher supporters sensed that his hard-right credentials 'raised as many hackles as he won votes'. Not much had been seen of Moore at the Commons since he had left the cabinet two years earlier, and little was seen of him during the campaign, when he seemed to canvass mainly by phone. Michael Jopling, who had valuable experience as Thatcher's first chief whip, was supposedly on her campaign team but was not asked to help. Three others quickly joined the team – Michael Neubert, a former minister and whip; Gerry Neale, a respected figure on the back benches; and Ian Twinn, a member of the 'No Turning Back' ginger group of right-wing MPs drawn mainly from the 1983 intake. Fellow backbenchers reckon that Neale, Neubert and Twinn prevented a catastrophe.

In practice, much depended on the efforts of Peter Morrison, Thatcher's parliamentary private secretary. Views about Morrison, a younger son of Lord Margadale, formerly John Morrison, a past chairman of the 1922 Committee and considerable landowner, are divided to a remarkable degree. Some regard him as a shrewd and effective operator, but others are unimpressed and genuinely baffled that anybody could rate him highly. His demand during the 1989 leadership contest that Tory MPs should be required to take a 'loyalty oath' to the prime minister had irritated many MPs and did not suggest that he would be the ideal person to rally support for Thatcher.

Thatcher's own strategy was to play the prime-ministerial card. It had worked the previous year against Meyer and would help portray Heseltine as divisive. The fact that her proposer was the foreign secretary,

Hurd, and that her seconder was the chancellor of the Exchequer, Major, boosted the prime-ministerial image, but their signatures on her nomination paper were the result of an astute ploy by Morrison. The convention had been that the leader's nomination was signed by the chief whip and his deputy, but that had been in the days when the names of a candidate's proposers were kept secret. Morrison realised the opportunity provided by the rule change and procured Hurd's and Major's signatures on Thatcher's nomination paper, which would need to be submitted even if her re-election proved to be a formality, as it had been every year up to 1989. Hurd's aides certainly feel that he was 'bounced'. Morrison had asked, at very short notice, to see Hurd at the Foreign Office. When he arrived, he requested Hurd's signature on the prime minister's nomination paper, saying that Major had already agreed. Hurd duly signed, and only wondered afterwards whether he should have done so. His aides were horrified.

The decision to hold the first ballot as early as possible meant that Thatcher would be attending the summit on European security in Paris during the campaign's final stages, but she was scarcely seen around the Commons even at the beginning of the contest. If Thatcher and her cabinet had actively canvassed MPs this might have suggested a lack of confidence and given credibility to Heseltine's challenge, but in the event Tory backbenchers complained that 'she hadn't even been tearooming before the first ballot'. Ministers campaigned vigorously on her behalf in media interviews, and she planned to give a few press interviews before leaving for Paris on Monday 19 November, the day before the first ballot, where her appearance would remind the electoral college of her prowess on the world scene. But Heseltine was bound to pose a more serious threat than Meyer. And for Thatcher to be above the media battle during the early part of the campaign was not quite the same thing as allowing her, in effect, to be taken out of the battle where it mattered most, among Tory MPs at Westminster.

Arguably, the decision to run a prime-ministerial campaign fatally constrained the canvassing for Thatcher; but even so this was widely seen as 'third-rate'. MPs found the approaches 'so indirect and oblique' that they weren't sure whether or not they had been canvassed. One MP was approached three times by Heseltine's team, but heard nothing from Thatcher's. Another was astonished to discover that what he had thought was a casual chat was in fact part of the Thatcher canvass. He was even more surprised when he learned that he had been registered as a 'don't know', since no further effort was made to persuade him to back the Prime Minister.

Offers of assistance were not taken up. Tristan Garel-Jones and Richard Ryder, two ministers renowned for their knowledge of the parliamentary party, tried to volunteer their services to Morrison but could not find him and later received a message saying that their help was not required. After the first few days of the contest, Thatcherites in the 'No Turning Back' group sensed that the Thatcher campaign was in serious trouble. Michael Brown, the MP for Brigg and Cleethorpes, prepared his own list of the electoral college and began a 'private enterprise' campaign for the Prime Minister. When concerned Thatcher loyalists expressed their qualms to her PPS, they were told not to worry. Thatcher would win outright on the first ballot. Morrison was not expecting Heseltine to win more than 120 votes.

Heseltine spent Thursday evening speaking for the Tory candidates at the Paisley by-elections and all day Friday touring neighbouring constituencies. But otherwise he was constantly seen around the Commons, and many MPs were impressed when he took the trouble to have five or ten minutes heart-to-heart with them. His Paisley visit, television interviews and articles in the press complemented his canvassing at Westminster. A cabinet minister summed up the difference between the two campaigns:

> Heseltine was around everywhere at the Commons, grabbing people whenever he could. And that place is an absolute gossip-shop, so it only needed a few MPs to see that he was active and the word spread around like wildfire, it didn't need much for the whispering campaign to get going – that Thatcher's team are taking it all for granted, and that Heseltine is here, there and everywhere. And the trouble was that there were plenty of ministers and MPs popping up on TV saying that they were loyal to the Prime Minister . . . but MPs rarely watch the TV: what mattered was what was being done around the Commons.

By the weekend, Thatcher's campaign was in trouble. She spent Friday far removed from the fray on a visit to Northern Ireland, where she was escorted by Richard Needham, the minister whose comment about Thatcher, made during an intercepted phone call to his wife, that it was about time 'that cow' resigned had been leaked to the press the previous week. On Friday morning, while visiting Yorkshire Conservatives, Hurd had said that Thatcher's victory would be 'the best result for the party and the country'. But when asked by journalists to say whether there were no circumstances in which he would stand, he replied 'Against her', a response which implied doubt about her prospects in the first ballot and seemed to suggest his own readiness to stand if she were forced to withdraw.

By Friday lunchtime, Heseltine had seized on Hurd's choice of words, arguing on *The World at One* on BBC Radio Four that voting for him was 'the most likely way of ensuring that Douglas (Hurd) has a chance on any subsequent occasions'. On Saturday morning, the front-page lead story in the *Daily Telegraph* was headlined 'Hurd is ready to stand if Thatcher falters'. Thatcherite loyalists were furious, claiming that Hurd's comment had weakened Thatcher's position and caused a further loss of support. Hurd was depressed during the weekend at this being read into what he had said.

Major, who entered hospital at the weekend for a wisdom tooth operation, had issued a statement on the Friday calling on all Tories to support the Prime Minister. Interviewed on *Channel 4 News* he avoided questions about the leadership, but admitted that there had been 'very heated discussions' with her over policy towards Europe. He also revealed his disagreement with her comment that his planned common European currency, the 'hard Ecu', would not be widely used. 'But she may be wrong and other people may take a different view', he commented. It was clear that Thatcher was unable to restore unity on European policy, which had already caused the departure from her cabinet of Heseltine, Brittan, Lawson, Ridley and Howe.

Before leaving for Paris, Thatcher gave three interviews: to Michael Jones, political editor of the *Sunday Times*; to Charles Moore, associate editor of the *Sunday Telegraph*; and to Simon Jenkins, editor of *The Times*. Since these occasions concerned the leadership contest, a Conservative Party matter, Bernard Ingham's usual place was taken by Thatcher's political secretary, John Whittingdale. In the Sunday papers she floated the idea of a referendum before Britain could accept a single currency, which gave fresh substance to Howe's complaint at her habit of making policy without consulting her ministers. In *The Times* the following morning she launched an aggressive attack on her rival, smearing Heseltine's policies as being 'more akin to some of the Labour Party policies: intervention, corporatism, everything that pulled us down'. On Monday Thatcher left to join other world leaders in Paris, where she would display the prime-ministerial image, but already the mask was slipping. Yet the most significant items in the weekend press had been the opinion polls showing that the Tories would re-capture their lead over Labour if Thatcher was replaced by Heseltine as prime minister. These reports had a profound impact on Tory MPs anxious about their prospects at the next election.

At 10.30 am on Tuesday 20th, in Thatcher's absence, her closest advisers gathered in the Prime Minister's room at the House of Commons. Voting was due to begin upstairs in Committee Room 12 in half an hour's time, and there was little more that could be done in the campaign. Their task was to consider what Thatcher would say in Paris in response to different permutations of the result. Among those present were Morrison, who would be flying out to Paris that afternoon to be with the Prime Minister and relay the result to her; John Wakeham, the energy secretary, a former chief whip and trusted confidant of Thatcher's;

Baker, the party chairman; Younger, her campaign manager; Tebbit, another confidant and member of her campaign team; and Whittingdale. They considered the various drafts prepared by Morrison to cover all possible outcomes.

The trickiest issue was how Thatcher would respond in the event of winning an overall majority but failing to secure the required 56-vote majority over Heseltine. How clearly ought she to say that she intended to fight on and stand in the second ballot before she had been able to consult opinion in London? Baker, who had already prepared a cautious response which had been passed to Thatcher's advisers and to Hurd in Paris, was concerned that she should consult on her return, and nothing should be said which would appear to rule that out. He wanted the Prime Minister to say something along the lines that she was glad that she was so far ahead on the first ballot, that she would make her position known in London when she returned and would consult, but that it was her intention to go ahead. Wakeham, however, felt that she would need to sound more resolute in order to gain time to consult and reach a proper judgement. Most of those present agreed.

Approval was therefore given to a firm statement by the Prime Minister, with no explicit reference either to waiting until she had returned to London or consulting before any decision was made. The idea was that this would be implicit in what she said. But 'a concession' was made to the concern expressed about her making a forthright declaration – one of the participants recalled, 'We put in the word "intention".' In the final draft, to be delivered by Thatcher in the event of her failing to meet both electoral conditions, she would therefore confirm that it was her 'intention' to let her name go forward for the second ballot. The aim, according to those involved in drafting her words, was that she would sound resolute and yet 'soothe people's fears' about any lack of consultation.

That afternoon, having cast Thatcher's proxy vote and voted himself, Morrison left for Paris with the draft statements for the Prime Minister and his estimates of the result. He reckoned that she might win 250 votes, expected her to receive 240, but advised her that she would win 230 votes. Even on his most pessimistic estimate she would win outright on the first ballot, securing both an overall majority and the necessary 56-vote lead. As many as 50 or 60 Tory MPs might abstain, which would leave Heseltine with fewer than 100 votes. Thatcher was expected to win convincingly.

2

The Queen is Dead

'It's a funny old world.'
Margaret Thatcher to her cabinet ministers, 21 November 1990

I

'Michael Heseltine 152 votes, Margaret Thatcher 204 votes'. In the first ballot Thatcher had failed by four votes to secure the required 56-vote majority over Heseltine for an outright win. Only sixteen Tory MPs had abstained. Under the procedure for Tory leadership elections, a second ballot would have to be held a week later, on Tuesday 27 November.

Within moments of the result being announced at about 6.25 pm, TV viewers watched as John Sergeant, BBC chief political correspondent, reported from Paris, his back to the steps of the British embassy where the Prime Minister was in her room and had, so everybody assumed, just been told the figures. Suddenly, visible to everybody except the hapless Sergeant, the familiar figure of Thatcher was seen heading full tilt down the steps, accompanied by Bernard Ingham. 'The Prime Minister is behind you, John,' Peter Sissons cried from the London studio, alerting Sergeant to his unexpected guests. Ingham demanded a microphone, pushing Sergeant aside. Thatcher then declared:

I am naturally very pleased that I got more than half the parliamentary party, and disappointed that's not quite enough to win on the first ballot, so I confirm it is my intention to let my name go forward for the second ballot.

Within minutes, she had returned inside the embassy.
The scene appeared to be a Thatcher cameo: a peremptory statement

accompanied by Bernard Ingham's manhandling of the press. Few people noticed the supposedly qualifying word 'intention' in her statement, except Wakeham, who was watching the television to check whether she kept to the text agreed by her key advisers that morning. Satisfied that she had delivered the text as drafted, he decided to assess the reaction of Tory MPs at the Commons.

To many MPs told of Thatcher's statement, it seemed even more peremptory than it had done on television. Because of confusion in the arrangements for announcing the result, many had gathered in Committee Room 12, where the voting had taken place. But the votes had been counted in Committee Room 10 and it was there that Cranley Onslow, chairman of the 1922 Committee, declared the result. MPs waiting in Room 12 were angry at the mix-up. By the time they finally heard the result, 'word was coming in within seconds' that Thatcher had declared her intention to fight on. One backbencher, quicker off the mark than most, had already left to give a press interview over the phone, saying that he thought the cabinet would be consulted before any decision was made about the second ballot. As he later recalled, 'there was real shock horror' when he and other MPs suddenly learned of Thatcher's announcement.

Thatcher's Paris statement was in fact less instantaneous than it seemed. She had kept word-for-word to the draft agreed by her advisers in the event of her not securing an outright win. Contrary to the impression gained by everybody watching television and by Tory MPs, she had not dashed straight out to the media within moments of first learning of the result.

At 6.15 pm Thatcher's political secretary, Whittingdale, had established an open line from the Prime Minister's room at the House of Commons to Morrison, her parliamentary private secretary with her at the British embassy in Paris. They chatted for a few minutes before Ian Twinn, one of Thatcher's canvassers who was a scrutineer at the count, rushed into the Prime Minister's room. He had run from the committee floor above with the result, which had not yet been announced, and gave it to Whittingdale, who then read out the figures to Morrison. The result meant that the Prime Minister would select the 'fight on' option from the draft statements.

Thatcher's receipt of the result in the British embassy at least five minutes earlier than was generally realised and her keeping to the agreed text shows her to have been less impetuous than was thought. But the seeming speed of her reaction and the firmness of her statement failed to meet the concern at the root of many MPs' anger at her reaction. They immediately saw it as yet another instance of her characteristic refusal to consult her cabinet. Although she had spoken with Hurd who was with her at the embassy, he had not seen the text of her prepared statement, and heard of the line that she would take from one of her staff. In the words of one observer she had 'scuttled out' while her foreign secretary was taking a prearranged call from his PPS, Tim Yeo, who relayed the reactions of Tory MPs immediately after the vote. As Yeo spoke, he could see a television screen and was astonished to see Thatcher suddenly emerge from the embassy. But he could not take in exactly what she was saying as he was still talking to the foreign secretary.

After Hurd had been told of the immediate reaction to the result in London, he asked Morrison if it would help if he were to make a statement. Morrison said that it would, but they agreed that Hurd should not take any questions. Twenty minutes after Thatcher's appearance on the embassy steps, Hurd emerged and delivered a terse statement, saying that the Prime Minister continued to have his 'full support' and that he was 'sorry that this destructive, unnecessary contest should be prolonged in this way'. Hurd was also in regular contact by phone with Major, who was in Huntingdon convalescing from his dental operation, and the chancellor also passed on a message to the press that he would support the Prime Minister in the second ballot.

Thatcher's statement was designed to appear 'resolute' while giving her time to consider her position. As a holding operation this resoluteness achieved its objective, but it signally failed to reassure Tory MPs about consultation. Its delivery so swiftly after the result, and the circumstances in which it was received by Tory MPs, contributed to the mood of anger and dismay sweeping through the parliamentary party. 'The mix-up over announcing the result seemed typical of the way everything was being messed up,' recalled a Tory backbencher who had waited in the wrong room. Others commented that 'her immediate announcement symbolised everything that was going wrong' and felt that 'everything was a shambles'.

Their reaction reflected shock at Thatcher's failure to win outright. Morrison had overestimated the Prime Minister's support and seriously exaggerated the probable number of abstentions. Thatcher received 26 fewer votes than the 'pessimistic' forecast which he had given her, and there were between 35 and 45 fewer abstentions than he expected. By contrast, Heseltine was told by Mates that he would receive 154 votes, only two more than his actual total, with 14 abstentions, two fewer than the final outcome. Mates accurately predicted Thatcher's total vote.

Why was Morrison's estimate less accurate than Mates's? Judgement and the reliability of the information relayed by the canvassers obviously played a part. But it is instructive that, as in 1975, the incumbent leader's campaign team were the more vulnerable to the fib factor. As with Heath, so with Thatcher: many MPs who voted against the leader would never dream of admitting their intention in advance to one of the leader's advisers

Shortly after Thatcher's announcement in Paris, Heseltine emerged on the front step of his Belgravia home accompanied by his wife, Anne, to announce that he too would fight on. He looked to all the world like the victor. Yet the figures showed that he had lost: Thatcher 204 votes, Heseltine 152. In the answer to that contradiction, which puzzles many people including a good many Tories, lies the explanation of events over the next, crucial forty hours.

II

Within minutes of hearing the result and leaving the chaos of the committee room floor, seasoned and senior Tory MPs were echoing Heseltine's judgement following Howe's speech exactly a week earlier: 'It's all over, she's finished.' But their view was not shared universally by fellow Tory backbenchers.

The party was in turmoil. The Commons buzzed with debate and rumour throughout Tuesday night and all day Wednesday. Groups of Tories huddled in the lobbies and corridors, or rushed to meetings in committee rooms or ministers' rooms: others hurried to gatherings beyond the Palace of Westminster. At times, the language became distinctly unparliamentary, 'traitor' and 'wanker' being among the epithets hurled.

Support ebbed from Thatcher. Some MPs had advised Thatcher's canvassers and the Tory whips even before the ballot had closed at six o'clock that although they were voting for Thatcher on the first ballot they would not continue to back her if she failed to win outright. After the result, more MPs went to tell the whips that they had voted for Thatcher, but would not do so again. Others said the same openly to colleagues.

Some Thatcherite die-hards later alleged that reports of MPs deserting Thatcher were part of a bluff organised by Heseltine's camp. They claimed that MPs who had voted for Heseltine went into the lobby after the result and lied to their colleagues and the press, saying that they had voted for Thatcher but would no longer do so. The ploy was supposedly used to persuade waverers to switch to Heseltine on the second ballot. Designed also to fool Thatcher's cabinet and her whips, it was said to have convinced some of her key supporters that she would not win on the second ballot because of the apparent haemorrhage in her vote.

Evidence from different sections of the party does not substantiate these claims. Too many MPs cite Thatcher loyalists among their close circle of trusted colleagues and friends who genuinely concluded that she had been mortally wounded on the first ballot. A Thatcher loyalist who had offered his services to her campaign team on the first ballot but who had been turned away with the assurance that 'everything was fine', dismissed the claim of a Heseltine-inspired plot as 'absolute nonsense'. He conducted his own straw poll among twenty or thirty friends and colleagues around the House on the Tuesday night and found that it was 'a very nasty experience indeed'. Although it 'grieved him', he detected a clear slide in Thatcher's support. He knew that other MPs were 'finding the same thing' and therefore went to see the whips and told them that 'it looked as though the Prime Minister was not the best person to fight the second ballot.'

Heseltine's supporters, who obviously deny any plot, claim that within about half an hour of the result, MPs who would have rated as copper-bottomed Thatcher loyalists on anybody's list were saying that they would not vote for Thatcher on the second ballot. Significantly, when this intelligence was phoned through to Heseltine during Tuesday evening, he sensed that the extent of the slippage in Thatcher's support might cause her to withdraw and that new candidates would come forward to challenge him for the next round. But Thatcher's performance in Paris convinced most of his team that 'he'd got it'.

A further key factor was the importance of the so-called 'payroll' vote – ministers, whips and parliamentary private secretaries, although PPSs are unpaid and serve as their ministers' eyes and ears in the Commons. The 'payroll' vote numbers around 120 MPs, almost one-third of the electoral college, who are appointed to office either directly by the prime minister or with reference to the prime minister's wishes. In general, ministers and PPSs had not been actively canvassed on the first ballot because it would have been 'destabilising'. If Thatcher's team were seen to be asking members of her government about their loyalty, word would have spread that she was in serious trouble. Their support as beneficiaries of her patronage was largely taken for granted at least on the first ballot, and rightly so: Heseltine's canvassers found 'an amazing degree of loyalty to Thatcher, even from people on the left of the party'.

But once members of the payroll vote had discharged their duty to the Prime Minister in the first ballot and the issue became the future of the party, many felt no longer bound by the loyalty requirement. Ministers and PPSs were soon among those telling the whips and Thatcher's campaign team that they would no longer support her. One minister, a Thatcher loyalist not in the cabinet, confirms that there was 'an immediate stampede' from Thatcher throughout the party. Even a PPS regarded as a 'through-and-through party man' told him in the division lobby that night that he would no longer support the Prime Minister. At that moment the minister saw 'with absolutely clarity' that Thatcher 'had become a liability' and that it would be vital 'to maximise the vote' of another candidate if Heseltine was to be stopped.

Some of the government whips were drawing the same conclusion. One of Hurd's supporters was advised by a whip to warn Hurd against signing Thatcher's nomination paper for the second ballot. But by the time the embassy was contacted, the foreign secretary had already left for the evening banquet at Versailles. However, one of Hurd's officials at the embassy said that the foreign secretary had not signed any paper. Yet, later in the evening, a minister, who had called Paris to express his doubts about the Prime Minister's prospects in the second ballot, was telling colleagues that the message from Charles Powell, her private secretary, was that Hurd had already signed her nomination paper. The impression being conveyed to waverers from her entourage in Paris was that the matter was settled, which only served to confirm the worst suspicions of Tory doubters at Westminster about her statement on the embassy steps.

As Tuesday evening wore on, the debate among ministers, PPSs and MPs raged at meetings and across dinner tables. The No Turning Back group, the Thatcherite praetorian guard, was split, and initial exchanges between members were vituperative. Among the die-hards were the ministers Michael Forsyth (Scottish Office), Michael Portillo (Local Government) and Edward Leigh (Trade and Industry); Michael Brown, a PPS at Trade and Industry; and Neil Hamilton, a government whip. Among those taking a more cautious line were Peter Lilley, secretary of state for Trade and Industry, and Francis Maude, financial secretary to the Treasury. Earlier, some had attended a farewell party at the Department of Trade and Industry for Douglas Hogg, who had been moved to the Foreign Office in the reshuffle necessitated by Howe's resignation. One of them recalls that he felt his stomach turn over when he first heard the result on the television.

The No Turning Back group met that evening in a room on the lower ministerial conference floor before the ten o'clock vote at the Commons. As they gathered, Waldegrave, the leftish-inclined cabinet minister, happened to walk past the door. 'What do you make of it all, Willie?' Tebbit called to him. Waldegrave delivered what one of his largely unsympathetic audience recalled as a 'rather impressive' response to the effect that what had happened was a tragedy but it did seem that the curtain was coming down on the end of an era.

As Thatcherite loyalists, most of the group were shocked at the result of the first ballot. They were 'on a short fuse' as they began to consider what to do 'when our candidate returned from France'. One participant reported 'blood on the carpet' as some members admitted that they thought that Thatcher's position was irretrievable. These doubters, or realists, were later caricatured by the ultra die-hards as a minority of 'contrary siren voices'. The group was split down the middle, although those who felt that Thatcher's position was impossible tended to be less vociferous. One of the realists walked out of the meeting because the ultras were becoming so 'emotional and hysterical' and he thought that it was useless to argue with them any longer, but eventually he returned.

The ultra die-hards countered the arguments of the realists by denying that there was any hard evidence of a slide of support away from Thatcher. The ultras were talking themselves into the role of 'storm-troopers', but, as a realist commented, although the No Turning Back group were good at convincing one another of the correctness of their cause, any idea that they were effective in persuading other Tories was nonsense: 'they cut no ice at all with other tranches of opinion in the party'. The fierce loyalty of ultra die-hards to the Prime Minister resulted from their conviction that no other viable candidate would be remotely comparable to Thatcher in carrying forward the radical torch. They found the possibility of change too awful to contemplate.

Angered at the abysmal failure of her campaign team, the ultras reviewed their own canvassing returns, which had predicted Thatcher's majority of 52 but had assumed 40 abstentions. They set about identifying the doubters, and sent Hamilton to Number 10 with a message for Thatcher's staff: 'We're the footsoldiers there to be employed, and make sure that this time you use us.' As an ultra die-hard recalls, they wanted to see Thatcher come out fighting before the second ballot, with the cabinet actively canvassing for her and any doubters being 'hauled in to see the Prime Minister' and confronted by her 'withering stare'. The No Turning Back discussion was interrupted by the division bell for the ten o'clock vote, and when members reassembled they were joined by Thatcher's political secretary, Whittingdale. By this stage, however, the tone was more one of sorrow than of anger.

Discussions among other Thatcher loyalists followed similar lines. Die-hards castigated those who feared that Thatcher was doomed. Talk of a collapse in her support was dismissed as 'hype'; she had failed to win outright only by a whisker and a more aggressive campaign would bolster her position and send Heseltine to his final defeat. Doubting loyalists began to sense that such discussions were a waste of time. They felt that the die-hards were 'doing the maths' but, as one minister recalled, 'they hadn't got their finger on the pulse or even had their eyes open to what was going on around the Commons'.

'Maths' and 'mood' were at the nub of the debate within the Tory parliamentary party that night. Die-hard Thatcherites disbelieved un-favourable reports of the Prime Minister's support and were convinced that with a different strategy she could still win, particularly since only an overall majority (187 votes) was needed on the second ballot. Doubters were sensitive, however, to the 'mood' of the party, fearing that an aggressive campaign for Thatcher, even if it brought her an overall majority on the second ballot, would shatter any hopes of restoring party unity. More probably, Thatcher's continued candidacy would guarantee victory for Heseltine, and many of the doubters were still die-hards when it came to the need to deny Heseltine the leadership.

These conflicting views reflected different interpretations of the election result. Die-hards protested that on the first ballot Thatcher had only failed to win outright by four votes – if only two MPs who had voted for Heseltine had voted for Thatcher she would have been re-elected without any need for a second ballot. Doubters were more conscious that 45 per cent of Tory MPs (Heseltine's 152 votes plus 16 abstainers) had not supported the Prime Minister. This was a sizeable disaffection, and already more MPs were saying that they would not support her on the second ballot. It was difficult to see how she would ever restore her authority. The analogy, though not precise, was with Neville Chamberlain in May 1940, who resigned as prime minister following the debate on the Norway campaign when a large back-bench revolt reduced the government's majority from over 200 to 81. Although the government had not been defeated, Chamberlain resigned as prime minister because he had lost his authority.

These were the judgements being weighed by Tory MPs that night. As they milled around the lobby, Tristan Garel-Jones, a minister of state at the Foreign Office and a former deputy chief whip, talked about the first ballot with ministerial friends. Like many others he had been gauging the mood of the party and, taking up a suggestion from several friends, invited colleagues to join him for a drink at his home in Catherine Place, near Buckingham Palace. Garel-Jones frequently entertains fellow Tories at his home, one of his most regular guests being John Major. Thus was born what some of the press and die-hard Thatcherites allege was the 'Catherine Place conspiracy'.

This 'conspiracy' casts Garel-Jones as the instigator and his guests as co-plotters. Garel-Jones is an archetypal whip, earmarked as such by his cronies in the Blue Chip dining club from the day they entered the Commons together in 1979. He seemed so much at home during his long service in the government whips' office throughout most of the 1980s that he personifies to many Tory MPs the aura of smoke-filled rooms. His Blue Chip colleagues attract from fellow Tories a milder form of the double-edged respect which used to be accorded to Iain Macleod. Tories like having clever people in their party but never seem entirely at ease with them. Macleod was described by Lord Salisbury in 1961 as being 'too clever by half' and although, unlike Macleod, Blue Chip ministers have never been professional gamblers nor attempted anything as radical as demolishing Britain's African Empire, they are undeniably clever fellows. Other bright ministers, not Blue Chip members, who visited Garel-

Jones's house that evening, have also been implicated as conspirators.

From about 10.30 pm onwards ministers began arriving at Catherine Place. Some were already leaving by the time others arrived. Several had no idea how many others had been invited. In all ten ministers appeared, five from the cabinet – Norman Lamont (Treasury), Tony Newton (Social Services), Chris Patten (Environment), Malcolm Rifkind (Scotland) and William Waldegrave (Health) – plus Alan Clark (Defence), Douglas Hogg (Foreign Office), Alan Howarth (Education), John Patten (Home Office), Garel-Jones, and also Richard Ryder (Treasury) who arrived much later than anybody else. Also present was Tim Yeo, Hurd's PPS. They tried to contact Kenneth Clarke, the education secretary, but could not find him – he was appearing on BBC television's *Newsnight*. Four of those present were founder members of the Blue Chip Group (Garel-Jones, Chris Patten, John Patten and Waldegrave) and the others represented a cross-section of party opinion. As members of the 'payroll' vote it can be assumed that most had voted for Thatcher earlier that day.

The two Pattens and Waldegrave had long favoured Hurd as party leader in the event of Thatcher's resignation. According to one version of the conspiracy theory, a combination of Garel-Jones's supposedly black arts of persuasion and the sheer intellect of other Blue Chip members suborned their ministerial colleagues into agreeing that Thatcher had to be removed and an alternative candidate recruited who would be capable of blocking Heseltine. But this version collapses when the list of ministers invited is scrutinised. Not everyone was able to attend – among ministers invited was Francis Maude of the No Turning Back group, who was in a meeting at the Commons at the same time. And to those who know the men who did attend, the idea of, say, Hogg or Clark or Ryder being gullible or taking anything at face value is laughable. The suggestion that Hurd's backers overlooked Major's claims is also mistaken, although they were indeed later to underestimate his support.

During the discussion at Garel-Jones's that night it became clear that nobody thought that Thatcher was certain of winning sufficiently conclusively on the second ballot for her authority to survive. They began considering which of the potential alternative candidates would block Heseltine. Only Lamont said that he would definitely back Major in the event of Thatcher not fighting on. Chris Patten was Hurd's strongest advocate. Others were less committed. But at that stage they assumed that either Hurd or Major would stand in the second ballot, not both of them. This raised the awkward problem of how to decide which of the two potential candidates should run and which one should not. There was a suggestion of assessing opinion at the Commons the next day, but their immediate concern was 'What do we do now?' The cabinet ministers decided collectively to advise the whips that Thatcher ought not to stand on the second ballot. They therefore left at about 11.30 pm for the

Commons to convey their conclusion to the government chief whip, Tim Renton, while the others stayed talking with Garel-Jones for another hour or so. After Yeo finally left, he phoned Hurd at about 1.00 am (2.00 am) in Paris and briefed him on the meeting.

As the Cabinet Ministers made their way from Catherine Place into the Commons, they bumped into John Wakeham, who was leaving for the night in order to prepare for his launch, next morning, of the privatisation of the electricity-supply industry. The five ministers did not discuss their views with him, but said that they were on their way to see the chief whip. Wakeham told them that they also ought to see John MacGregor, the Lord President of the Council and Leader of the House of Commons, because he was seeking opinions within the cabinet.

Earlier in the evening, Wakeham had been taking his own soundings at the Commons. He knew that on her return from Paris Thatcher would need advice on the mood of the party and he felt that she was entitled to know the views of her cabinet. He had therefore seen MacGregor and told him that if he himself had not been busy with electricity privatisation he would have canvassed the cabinet and assessed their views and, in so far as was known, those of their junior ministers.

There was an ulterior motive in Wakeham's concern that the cabinet should be consulted. As one of Thatcher's most loyal and trusted confidants, he wanted to provide her with independent verification of whatever she was told by Renton. The chief whip's relative inexperience was less of a worry than one of those peculiar twists of fate which complicate relationships at the most inconvenient moments, for he was a close friend and political associate of Howe, whose resignation had triggered the leadership crisis. Wakeham realised that Thatcher would find it particularly difficult to accept bad news from Renton because of his links with Howe, and was therefore anxious to ensure that any bad news was corroborated. But even his scheme would have complications.

Meanwhile, the five cabinet ministers from the Catherine Place gathering saw the chief whip and expressed their collective view that Thatcher ought not to stand in the second ballot. As they left Renton they were met by Baker, the party chairman and Thatcher loyalist, who had heard of their deputation to see the chief whip and hoped to catch a word with them. As one of them commented, during the leadership crisis Baker was 'all over the place', saying how awful it was but urging everybody to stay calm. His advice to his five cabinet colleagues that night was that they should sleep on it. They were unimpressed.

III

At 6.20 the following morning, Wednesday 21 November, Alan Clark, one of the ministers who had attended the discussion at Garel-Jones's house late the previous night, telephoned Peter Morrison, Thatcher's PPS, at the British embassy in Paris (it was 7.20 in France). He told Morrison to warn the Prime Minister that when she returned to Number 10 later that morning she would be told she would lose in the second ballot and must step down. Clark's own message was that, even though she would lose, she should fight: she must go down in history as never having thrown in the towel. Clark's purpose in phoning had been to ensure that Thatcher heard the bad news from a loyal supporter, and in telling her to fight on he was hoping to make the essential message of certain defeat more palatable.

By breakfast-time in London those charged with assessing party opinion were presented with further evidence of the weakness of Thatcher's position. Renton, the chief whip, consulted Viscount White-law, the great party elder, whose loyalty as deputy prime minister had been unquestioned. Whitelaw had come to the view that if Thatcher fought on she risked being humiliated.

MacGregor, the Leader of the House, was busily contacting the cabinet, his purpose being not to ask whether they supported the Prime Minister – as members of her cabinet their loyalty was not questioned – but to establish whether she ought to continue to stand in the second ballot, on the basis of their estimates of the numbers who had switched support. Although MacGregor spoke with Hurd and Major (who was convalescing in Huntingdon), he did not seek their views since they were her proposer and seconder. MacGregor's exercise would become the cause of considerable controversy later in the day.

As the morning wore on, MPs and ministers began gathering at the Commons, repeating the pattern of Tuesday night, some huddled in groups around the corridors and lobbies and others visiting one another's rooms. Tory MPs in the tearoom feared Labour's attack at the next election if Thatcher stayed on: if 45 per cent of Tory MPs would not vote for Thatcher, why should the British people support her? In renewed soundings Alistair Burt, PPS to Baker, the party chairman, confirmed his impression that 'there was a strong hard-core of support for her, which was coming through loud and clear, it was strong, die-hard and loyal. But there had been a drift away, and Heseltine was gaining.' But the party chairman remained adamant in believing that Thatcher should fight on, and Burt soon ceased working as his PPS.

During the morning, as part of Thatcher's holding operation, Hurd and Major agreed the wording of a joint statement confirming their willingness to continue as the Prime Minister's proposer and seconder respectively for the second ballot. Heseltine's nomination had already been submitted, but crucially Thatcher's would not be completed until she had returned and consulted on the position in the parliamentary party. Late in the morning, Major was phoned by a senior backbencher and former minister who expressed his horror that the party should be denied a wider choice on the second ballot. He told Major that in interviews during the day he proposed to say that Thatcher ought not to stand on the second ballot and that the party needed a wider choice. But if Major had strong objections to his saying this publicly, he would not do so. Major did not demur.

Shortly before noon Thatcher returned to Number 10, where she consulted her campaign team and heard their assessment of opinion in the parliamentary party. But beforehand she had a word with Norman Tebbit and John Wakeham, her trusted confidants. Earlier that morning, while Wakeham had been launching the electricity privatisation at the Cumberland Hotel at Marble Arch, he received a call saying that Thatcher wanted to see him on her return from Paris. He arrived in Downing Street at around 12.30 pm and went straight upstairs, where he joined Thatcher and Tebbit.

Had it not been for the electricity-privatisation launch, Wakeham would have consulted the cabinet by this stage. But now, lacking their collective judgement, his advice to Thatcher was twofold: first, that even if she lost there would be no disgrace or dishonour in fighting for something in which she believed. If she decided to fight on, Wakeham would support her. Second, since her party advisers, the 'men in grey suits', all shared her policies and believed that these would be best perpetuated by her or by one of her cabinet and not by someone who had walked out and had been outside it for four years, she should listen to what they had to say courteously. In plain language, she should not interrupt. She should then ask each of them a single question: 'Do you have a better plan?'

Over a working lunch in the cabinet room, with sandwiches and sparkling water (not beer, but wine was on offer), Thatcher consulted the 'men in grey suits'. This definition is imprecise but those attending on this occasion included Renton (government chief whip), Cranley Onslow (chairman of the 1922 Committee), Baker (party chairman) and MacGregor (Lord President and Leader of the House), Tebbit, Wakeham, Morrison and Whittingdale. They were all supporters of the Prime Minister, either through their position in her government or through personal loyalty, but their roles differed: some would offer impartial advice on opinion in the party, others were clearly Thatcher's partial supporters or staff. The numbers present and this combination of roles would cause a serious problem.

Renton reported that on the whips' estimates she had suffered a net loss of 25 votes, reducing her support from 204 on the first ballot to 179. His analysis was later described by one of those present as 'a grim and accurate' picture. She had fallen below the target for winning on the second ballot, which was 187, an overall majority. Opinion in the Whips' Office was divided, but Renton's advice was that despite the initial loss of support she could probably win if she fought on. The gist of his message, however, seemed to be that the best that she could hope for would be a narrow victory.

Cranley Onslow, reporting on the views of backbenchers, was in a difficult position because the 1922 Committee's officers and Executive committee, who are elected by backbenchers, were divided. The challenge of reconciling the opposing views of his fellow officers proved beyond Onslow's stolid Toryism. He waffled about the absurdity of there having been an election at all and gave no clear line, appearing to avoid saying that she ought to stand down while at the same time suggesting that the party would welcome a wider choice.

MacGregor had been placed in an awkward position also, although for quite different reasons. Concerned that relaying the cabinet's confidential advice to the Prime Minister be handled in a manner she would think correct, he decided not to reveal their views in a meeting attended by several who were not members of her cabinet – especially since the cabinet had judged, by a majority of two to one, that on the second ballot Thatcher would either lose, or at best, win by too narrow a majority, and so had concluded that she ought to step down.[1] He had found it impossible to have a word with Thatcher beforehand and therefore he simply hinted at their concern and insisted that she ought to consult them.

Baker, on the other hand, reported that Thatcher continued to enjoy the overwhelming support of the party in the country, with around 90 per cent of constituency parties still backing her. However, the mood of the parliamentary party was markedly different and Baker must have been aware, from his experience as Heath's campaign manager in the 1975 leadership election, that even a leader who had led the Tories into two general election defeats had received a similar level of support from the party activists. None the less, he strongly urged Thatcher to fight on, believing that she would be able to defeat Heseltine, and that her resignation would shatter party morale.

But Baker also pressed for a more dynamic campaign. Despite his encounter with the five cabinet ministers who had expressed their reservations to the chief whip late the night before, he had said on the radio that morning that the Prime Minister would fight the second ballot on a ticket of cabinet unity. He also urged her to campaign actively and to talk to MPs. The message from one participant at the lunchtime meeting recalled the party chairman's insisting that Thatcher could 'out-Heseltine Heseltine'. After Baker's contribution, Tebbit said little.

In the discussion that followed, the strong consensus was that she was the best candidate but that it would need to be a very different campaign. The point already forcibly pressed by her die-hard supporters, notably the No Turning Back group, that the cabinet would need to be actively involved was accepted. This decision reinforced MacGregor's earlier insistence that she ought to consult her cabinet. Although MacGregor had proposed this step for different reasons, it was seen by Thatcher loyalists as a necessary foundation on which to build her campaign on the second ballot. And Younger, who must very shortly assume his full responsibilities as chairman of the Royal Bank of Scotland, would be replaced as her campaign manager.

The Prime Minister left in order to prepare her statement in the Commons that afternoon on the European security summit. As Tories at Westminster pondered the likely outcome of her lunchtime meeting, some wondered 'whether the men in grey suits had any balls'. During the lunchhour a rumour spread that Thatcher would announce her intention to resign during the afternoon, and former cabinet ministers were hurriedly ferried to television studios ready to give their reactions and pass instant judgement on Thatcher's premiership.

By the early afternoon, however, word was out that she would fight on. The worst fears of Tory doubters were confirmed. Many ministers and MPs who had been anxious to remain loyal to Thatcher were appalled at the consequences for the party of a fight to the death. They were disturbed to hear that 'the gents', like Younger, were being sacked from her team, that the likes of Tebbit would be calling the shots, and that Thatcher was reportedly planning to see every MP who was thought to be wavering. At least one Tory doubter made plans to go to ground from Thursday night until the following Tuesday, the day of the second ballot, warning his constituency chairman to do likewise for fear that Thatcher's new campaign team would track him down through his local party. Others caricatured the 1922 Committee as 'a bunch of political eunuchs' following Cranley Onslow's uncertain advice. They dubbed the lunch-time meeting a 'fiasco' and regarded the change in the campaign team as being on a par with changing generals in mid-battle.

Two groups of Tories were delighted at what they heard – the Thatcherite die-hards and Heseltine's supporters. The former felt that the new campaign team and more aggressive strategy would give Thatcher a better chance of victory. The latter felt more confident that Heseltine would be the next Tory leader. The rumours that Thatcher would fight on also came as heartening news to Labour MPs, many of whom believed that their best chance of winning the next election lay in Thatcher continuing as Tory leader. The Labour front bench had sought to unite the Tories in support of Thatcher by tabling a motion of no confidence in the government for debate the following day.

Shortly before 3.10 pm Thatcher left Number 10 for the Commons, declaring, 'I fight on. I fight to win.' But her aides were discovering that the foundations on which her new campaign strategy would supposedly rest were distinctly shaky. A plan to recruit Kenneth Clarke, the no-nonsense education secretary and one of politics' pugilists, to run Thatcher's campaign for the second ballot was short-lived. He was called by Morrison, ostensibly to congratulate him on his continued defence of the Prime Minister on *Newsnight* the previous evening, but when Thatcher's lunchtime decision to fight on was mentioned, Clarke was appalled. Before the first ballot, he had gained the impression from Thatcher's confidants that her prepared statement, in the event of her failing to win outright, was merely designed to hold the line until she returned to London. On this understanding he had agreed to give media interviews. He was later reported by colleagues to be 'fuming' during Wednesday afternoon, but the real cause of his anger was his sense of having been misled.

Wakeham took on the job as Thatcher's new campaign manager. News of his appointment cheered some doubters, who recalled his days as chief whip when he had never shied away from telling Thatcher home truths. As he struggled to recruit a new campaign team, he realised how seriously her support had been eroded. He was told by Garel-Jones and Ryder that her position was hopeless.

After completing her statement in the Commons on the Paris summit, Thatcher returned to her room. She visited the tearoom with her closest supporters in an effort to revive her flagging support. She had decided, after the lunchtime meeting at Number 10, to seek the advice of her cabinet ministers as soon as possible by consulting them individually at the Commons. She happened to see Francis Maude, the junior Treasury minister and one of the doubters among the No Turning Back group, as he had gone to her room looking for Morrison to discuss the campaign for the second ballot. MacGregor finally managed to have a brief word with the Prime Minister and she therefore learned, only shortly before she began consulting her cabinet one by one, that most of them thought she ought not to continue. It soon became clear that Thatcher did not realise how vulnerable her position had become.

IV

Geography had a hand in the dramatic events of late Wednesday afternoon and early evening. The prime minister's room at the Commons is located in a corridor behind the Speaker's chair, on the same level as the chamber. Immediately outside the prime minister's room are two small anterooms, which serve as waiting rooms. One floor above, and reached by a nearby staircase, are the rooms allotted to cabinet ministers, located along either side of a fairly narrow corridor.

Immediately after the Prime Minister's statement, ministers began gathering behind the Speaker's chair, congregating in groups of between three and six, going to and fro between one another's rooms and clustering along the ministerial corridor. The proximity of the prime minister's room and their own rooms, the crowding together and mixing between one group and another, tended to confirm their collective role. The eventual outcome would probably not have altered, but, had the cabinet been summoned individually to Number 10, the atmosphere would undoubtedly have been different. As it was, any hope which the Prime Minister might have entertained of being able to pick off her critics in cabinet one by one was effectively dashed.

'Distraught', 'very steamed up', 'hopping up and down with rage', 'tearing our hair', 'end of an era stuff' are phrases used by those involved to capture the atmosphere as they waited to see the Prime Minister. Now that the 'men in grey suits' had failed to deliver their lines, it fell to the cabinet ministers to give their individual verdicts to the Prime Minister. But what exactly ought they to say?

Most of the cabinet were doubters – Thatcher loyalists in the first ballot who thought that she ought not to continue in the second. Some felt that the best that the Prime Minister could hope for would be a close result in the next round, but many feared that it would be a lot worse. Since the previous evening their PPSs and other ministers had been giving them various estimates of how badly Thatcher might fare. Junior ministers like Garel-Jones and Ryder tried to eliminate any double-counting in the calculations, which some cabinet ministers suspected might be inflating the claims about the number of MPs saying they would no longer support Thatcher. But all the forecasts pointed in the same direction. One of the more reliable estimates indicated that she would lose the backing of at least 30 to 40 MPs, reducing her total vote to around 160–70 votes. Another source, which seemed improbably gloomy, predicted that she would receive a mere 90 votes.

In the discussions among ministers, Kenneth Clarke and Chris Patten, supported by Malcolm Rifkind, the Scottish secretary, expressed their determination to be candid with the Prime Minister. They maintained that the likelihood of Heseltine's victory was so strong that she must stand down and let other candidates come forward. Because they were convinced that her fighting on would be a mistake for the party, they would not be able to enter wholeheartedly into any second-ballot campaign for Thatcher. Some of their colleagues questioned what this would mean if she won – would they continue to serve in her cabinet? The issue was not finally resolved. Other ministers who agreed that Thatcher was in serious risk of defeat, or who felt that the vote would be too close to call, were more inclined to set out what they regarded as the facts to the Prime Minister but to allow her to reach her own judgement on what she should do. They justified their guarded advice by saying that Thatcher would be more inclined to listen to those who she felt would remain totally loyal. At around 5 pm Thatcher began consulting close colleagues in her room while other ministers debated outside her door. Shortly before 5.30 pm she left for her weekly audience with the Queen at Buckingham Palace. On her return she began seeing her cabinet one by one at about 6.15 pm. 'This is an important moment in history,' Wakeham told ministers as they waited to enter the prime minister's room. 'You owe it to her to tell her the truth.'

'It's a funny old world,' Thatcher commented to her ministers. She had won three general elections and believed that she retained the overwhelming support of the Conservative Party in the country. She had not lost a motion of confidence in the Commons and the first ballot still showed that she commanded the support of a majority of Conservative MPs. Yet her future as prime minister was now cast in doubt. What did they think?

The first few ministers who were called in to see her felt that she had not realised the strength of feeling in her cabinet. At first she was trying to 'jolly' them along and stop them being so defeatist. But gradually the message began to sink in as one minister after another warned her that she risked defeat and a divided party if she stood on the second ballot. Those ministers who saw her later were told by Wakeham to be firm but not too tough. They found her 'gracious', but her self-control did not prevent some ministers from feeling that this was the most unpleasant meeting of their lives. As they returned to their discussions in the corridor above, anxious colleagues asked them what they had told Thatcher.

Among the first to see the Prime Minister, Hurd reassured her of his continued support. But he was also concerned that her campaign on the second ballot should not become a personalised attack against Heseltine, as had occurred in the last few days before the first ballot. He therefore advised her to keep to the issues. Major was not consulted, but he and Hurd were in regular contact by phone, and like Hurd he would continue to support the Prime Minister if she decided to fight on.

From Clarke, Patten and Rifkind, the Prime Minister heard the same basic argument which they had been putting to their colleagues upstairs. They believed that it would be an act of folly for her to fight on – one maintained that it would be as disastrous as the Charge of the Light

Brigade. The cabinet had all supported her on the first ballot, but regrettably it was clear that in the second ballot she would lose. They had campaigned for her and still bore the scars of battle, but they would find it hard to do so again before the second ballot. By fighting on she would risk dividing the party hopelessly and breaking the authority of the government. Their advice was that she must release other ministers to stand on the second ballot if Heseltine was to be defeated. The party wanted a wider choice. They did not threaten to resign. But one demanded that if she was still thinking of fighting on there should be a cabinet meeting that evening so that the position could be discussed collectively.

If theirs had been the only voices advising her that she was finished, she would 'simply have told them to push off as she would have expected that sort of thing from them', one of her aides later claimed. Their arguments were unlikely to prove decisive with Thatcher, but the existence of even a small minority of ministers who were unwilling to campaign for her had already dented any idea that the cabinet's strong backing could remain a central feature of her appeal for support in the second ballot.

A much more serious problem for the Prime Minister was the fact that the cabinet's gloomy judgement was confirmed by other ministers, including centrist figures like Tom King and John Gummer. The latter retained a strong personal loyalty to Thatcher but he too was horrified at the prospect of her fighting on. And the same doubts came even from those ministers whom Thatcher regarded as the most ideologically sound members of her cabinet – Norman Lamont, Peter Lilley and Michael Howard. Their voices were the most influential because, along with Gummer, they would have fought 'like tigers' if Thatcher had decided to stand in the second ballot.

As her one-to-one talks continued, she was told that her supporters were 'deserting in droves'. One minister told her that he would put himself at her disposal and would not utter a word in public about his doubts, but he thought that she would lose. A close ideological ally was so determined to give her the clearest message about her predicament that he feared afterwards that he had been 'too brutal'. At least one minister was in tears. Another told her that it was the worst thing that could ever have happened, that it should never have happened, but that she was going to lose. Some ministers asked her to consider the consequences if she won on the second ballot, but only by a narrow majority, as she would be leading a deeply divided and demoralised party into the next general election.

Only Baker and Parkinson remained die-hard loyalists. Peter Brooke, the Northern Ireland secretary, was not closely in touch with the mood of the party because of his duties in the province but if she stood again she would have had his support. David Hunt, the Welsh secretary, who was on official business abroad, sent a telegram saying that if she fought on he would back her.

'She's not a kamikaze where the party's concerned,' observed a loyalist minister who had been ready to campaign for Thatcher but who advised her that she faced defeat or at best victory by a small majority. He was confident, even before seeing her, that she would not fight on once she realised the implications for the party. What struck him most about the Prime Minister's reaction was her concern to safeguard their achievements as a government over the previous eleven and a half years and to unite the party and win the next election. 'There was a certain bewilderment about how this had happened, but it wasn't to do with her personal feelings,' he recalls, 'it was all about the party, preserving their successes, that's what she was asking about.'

Others among the throng for much of the afternoon and evening included the deputy chief whip, Alastair Goodlad, and Alan Clark, the Thatcher loyalist who had come to the conclusion that she ought not to stand on the second ballot. Clark had phoned Thatcher's PPS, Morrison, first thing that morning to warn him of the advice that Thatcher would receive. Determined that Heseltine must be stopped at all costs, Clark now attempted to make a grim message palatable. 'I will vote for you as long as you fight,' he told Thatcher, 'but I think that we will perish like Leonidas at Thermopylae.'

Whether or not Thatcher fully grasped Clark's classical allusion to the Spartan king and his 300 who were overwhelmed by the Persians, his message was clear. She remained composed, but by this stage appeared already to have accepted the inevitable. Preserving her place in history by fighting on and perishing in glory was one thing, but allowing Heseltine to win was quite another.

V

There was no single moment at which Thatcher realised that she must resign. It was more an impression that developed as she talked with her ministers. But by 7.30 pm her doubts were clear to those who saw her, including her closest supporters Baker, Moore, Morrison, Tebbit and Wakeham. Until her mind was finally made up, they would maintain the line that she was fighting on but privately they knew otherwise.

At the same time, die-hard loyalists among the No Turning Back group were again meeting in the lower ministerial conference room at the Commons to organise their resources before seeing Wakeham, her new campaign manager. Immediately afterwards, those who also belonged to the right-wing 92 Group attended a meeting in an upstairs committee room of around fifty MPs, at which in a desperate last ditch bid to rally her, the group's main organiser, George Gardiner, accompanied by John Butcher, Edward Leigh and Michael Portillo, was delegated to see the Prime Minister and urge her to fight on. Plunging past Morrison and Baker, they entered Thatcher's room to find her 'white and tearful'. She admitted that she was 'coming under a lot of pressure'.

While the final scenes of the drama were being played out in the prime minister's room at the Commons, her political secretary, Whittingdale at Number 10, was acutely aware of time ticking by. It had not yet been possible to start organising Thatcher's nomination papers for the second ballot. Arranging Hurd's signature had been no problem because he was in London, but Major's enforced absence in Huntingdon presented a more serious difficulty. Already it was early evening, and nothing had been done to collect Major's signature in good time before the noon deadline the next day (Thursday). The nightmare loomed of Thatcher eventually deciding to fight but her nomination papers not being submitted in time.

Whittingdale called the chancellor's private office at the Treasury. Would they be sending a box to the chancellor in Huntingdon? The day's box had already been sent. Furthermore the Prime Minister's private office confirmed that it would be impossible to send a government car on party business. The last hope appeared to be Morrison's personal chauffeur, but he could not be found. In some desperation, Whittingdale was explaining the problem to Morrison's secretary when into his office walked the former Tory MP and deputy party chairman and best-selling novelist, Jeffrey Archer.

Archer, who undertakes numerous speaking engagements for local parties, had been called to Number 10 on 'a constituency matter'. As he heard Whittingdale's anxiety, he realised that he would be able to help. The Majors' constituency home is relatively near Archer's Cambridge-shire house and Major and Archer know one another well – Archer had spent the previous day with Major, who was suffering the after-effects of his dental operation. Archer had an engagement in Morden that evening, but his driver would be able to take Thatcher's nomination paper to Huntingdon to collect Major's signature, then return to collect Archer, who would deliver it personally to Number 10. A relieved Whittingdale entrusted the nomination paper to Archer.

As Whittingdale prepared to leave Number 10 at around 7.30 pm for something to eat, he was told by one of the Prime Minister's private secretaries, 'It's not looking too good.' While Whittingdale and Robin Harris, from the Number 10 Policy Unit, had a quick meal at Pizzaland in Whitehall before returning to work on Thatcher's speech for the no-confidence debate, Tory doubters leaving the Commons to dine at outside engagements and gentlemen's clubs were 'extremely depressed' at the

END OF THE COLD WAR

Garland

"I'M JUST GOING OUTSIDE, I MAY BE SOMETIME."

Thatcher leaves the epoch-making European security conference in Paris to face the possibility of defeat in the Tory leadership contest.

prospect that Thatcher might fight on. 'The party faced Armageddon', according to one such doubter, who believed that Heseltine would win but Thatcher's die-hard approach would prevent him restoring party unity.

Cabinet ministers had continued discussing their predicament after they had each seen the Prime Minister. They debated who should stand in the event of Thatcher's withdrawal, but not all of them were confident that she would decide to step down. They knew that the Thatcherite die-hards were mobilising in an attempt to persuade her to fight on to the bitter end and were concerned that the cabinet would have no opportunity of tackling her collectively until the weekly cabinet meeting scheduled for the following morning. If she waited until then to announce her decision, they feared that she would be able to 'bounce' the cabinet into backing her again – there would be too little time before the noon deadline to organise the nomination of an alternative candidate. And it would not be the first time that her cabinet had been 'bounced'.

During the evening, Kenneth Clarke, accompanied by Goodlad, the deputy chief whip, told Wakeham that unless Thatcher announced her readiness to stand down there should be a meeting of the full cabinet at 11.00 pm. Clarke was persuaded not to persist in his demand by Wakeham's reassurance that it would not be necessary, and also because the morning's scheduled cabinet was brought forward to nine o'clock. But ministers like Clarke and Chris Patten were still not completely convinced that the Prime Minister would go and were prepared to raise the issue when the cabinet gathered, if necessary. They had not threatened resignation earlier but now realised that they might be left with no alternative.

By eight o'clock, however, the message that she might not fight on after all began to spread as cabinet ministers chatted with colleagues and PPSs after leaving their ministerial rooms. MPs dining at the Commons were astonished when they were told that Thatcher might resign. A PPS who had voted for Heseltine was told that 'it was not all over yet', she had seen her cabinet individually and 'it's gradually sinking in on her'.

At about 8.30 pm Wakeham suggested that she should go across to Number 10 and talk with her husband, Denis, before working on her speech for the next day. She would sleep on her decision. Wakeham stayed in her room at the Commons to see ministers and MPs who were still arriving at Thatcher's door, including Tim Raison, the former minister for overseas development, delegated by a dozen of his fellow doubters from the One Nation group of Tories, who happened to be holding a dinner at the House that evening and believed that the party should be given a wider choice on the second ballot.

'It's all over,' Whittingdale was told when he returned to Number 10 with Harris shortly before nine o'clock. When Thatcher returned from the Commons, she saw Denis upstairs before coming down to draft what she would say in the no-confidence debate. His advice, reported by friends, that he did not want her to be humiliated confirmed what she had already heard from her ministers. Gummer and Tebbit joined the speechwriting team. Thatcher looked terrible but quickly settled into her work and began to behave 'as if it was another confidence debate and she had a majority of 150 or so'.

Tebbit had fought a fierce rearguard campaign throughout the evening, holding the line in television interviews that Thatcher would stand on the second ballot. He was Leonidas's lieutenant – in Alan Clark's classical allusion – providing a glimpse of how glorious but also how bloody the defeat would have been. As a colleague of Tebbit's observed, 'although he was probably losing her votes in the process it was magnificent stuff'.

The No Turning Back group, who met in Lord North Street, a stone's throw from Parliament, for one of their regular dinners, were shocked when John Butcher, one of their members, arrived with the warning that unless they acted it would be too late. Three of the junior ministers present, Forsyth, Portillo and Michael Fallon, were dispatched to Number 10 with the message that Thatcher should not listen to the cabinet's advice because it did not reflect the view of backbenchers. As one die-hard minister claimed, the cabinet were acting on 'duff information'. A message that they had arrived was brought to those conferring on Thatcher's speech, but her advisers knew that there was nothing that would be achieved by their seeing her and thought it better that she was not disturbed any more. But before they departed, Forsyth left a note for the Prime Minister.

The letter was shown to Thatcher much later in the evening, as she was completing her speech. Of course she would see them. At around midnight, the three No Turning Back ministers returned, accompanied by Neil Hamilton, also a member of the group and a government whip. Forsyth, Portillo and Hamilton saw the Prime Minister, while Fallon remained outside. Her mind had been made up for some hours but she listened to their pleas 'rather reflectively, in a calm way'.

It was after one o'clock. Her speech completed and the last of the series of talks on her future at an end, Thatcher finally called it a day. At lunchtime she had thought that she had a good chance of continuing as prime minister. But less than twelve hours later, as she climbed the stairs to the flat in which she and Denis had lived for the previous eleven and a half years, she knew that her days in Downing Street were numbered.

VI

Shortly after 6.30 on the morning of Thursday 22 November, Charles Powell, Thatcher's private secretary, already at work in Number 10, received a call from the policeman on duty outside. There were two men with him, called Brown and Leigh, saying that they were MPs and wanted to see the Prime Minister.

Powell recognised them as Michael Brown and Edward Leigh, two of the most enthusiastic members of the No Turning Back group. He told the policeman to allow them in. Powell had not yet seen the Prime Minister himself since she had not long risen and was preparing for what would be an emotionally trying day. Powell listened sympathetically as Brown and Leigh berated him, claiming that their own canvass returns showed that Thatcher would win on the second ballot. When Morrison, Thatcher's PPS, arrived shortly before 7.30 am, Brown and Leigh berated him also. They refused to leave until they had seen the Prime Minister, and for the time being were provided with newspapers and coffee in a ground-floor waiting room.

At 7.30, Thatcher informed Morrison and her private secretary, Andrew Turnbull, that she would stand down. Other senior staff, including Bernard Ingham, were told a few minutes later and Buckingham Palace was informed. When Wakeham arrived at 8.30 am, the news which he had been expecting since the previous evening was confirmed. Around the same time, Thatcher began her regular preliminary briefing for that afternoon's question time in the Commons. This was a difficult occasion, because she had not yet informed the cabinet of her decision to resign. Some officials at the meeting were unaware of the dramatic turn of events since the previous afternoon.

From early that morning, ministers and PPSs who had sensed the change in mood within the Thatcher camp during Wednesday evening were calling one another. Some were told that 'there's still an outside chance that we're in business'. One minister returned from his early-morning ride to receive an urgent message from his PPS. Others conferred anxiously about the prospects for the morning. Little more than three hours remained until nominations for the second ballot closed. But some ministers were still unsure whether or not the Prime Minister would resign.

Brown and Leigh, still sitting in the waiting room at Number 10 and oblivious to the events unfolding around them, heard a crescendo of voices as nine o'clock approached. Cabinet ministers who put their heads round the door were puzzled to see two members of Thatcher's praetorian guard reading the papers. Suddenly there was an eerie silence. Usually, ministers continue to chat among themselves as the Prime Minister appears. But on this occasion they fell quiet the moment they saw her and gazed at her as she walked past them and into the cabinet room, where she spent two or three minutes alone. Then they were summoned and silently trooped in. 'It was awful,' a member of the Number 10 staff recalled, 'they almost seemed terrified of her.'

Thatcher was 'red-eyed' and opened the cabinet meeting by informing her colleagues that she would shortly be issuing a statement. She then began to read but she faltered halfway through and broke down. 'I have never done that before,' she said, and then proceeded to read the statement from the beginning for a second time. Ministers found it excruciating. Several were in tears. She said that having consulted widely among colleagues, she had concluded that party unity and Conservatives' prospects of victory at the next election would be better served if she stood down in order to enable cabinet colleagues to enter the leadership contest. The Lord Chancellor, Lord Mackay, replied on behalf of the cabinet, expressing their gratitude for all she had achieved. Hurd added a short impromptu statement, recording the courage and grace shown by the Prime Minister in Paris over the last few days, particularly at the Versailles banquet after she had received news of the vote in the first ballot. The cabinet moved on to other business, including deployment of British troops in the Gulf. As one minister observed, as soon as Thatcher was able to deal with the business of government she was 'splendid'.

As the cabinet meeting proceeded, Brown and Leigh went to see Whittingdale in his office. 'I suppose that's it,' said Brown. Whittingdale was unable to confirm that the Prime Minister was resigning until the official announcement had been issued. But his demeanour was eloquent confirmation. Brown and Leigh prepared to leave, but a barrage of press and cameras hovered in Downing Street and Whittingdale led them through the adjoining offices and into Whitehall, tears in their eyes.

At 9.33 am, with the cabinet meeting still in progress, Number 10 officially announced that later that day Thatcher would inform the Queen of her intention to tender her resignation as prime minister. At the conclusion of government business, when officials left the cabinet room, ministers resumed their discussion of the leadership contest. Thatcher hoped that members of the cabinet would work to ensure that one of their number was elected to succeed her. The meeting ended at 10.15 am. Ministers emerged from the cabinet room looking dazed. 'It was as if they did not know what they had done,' a Number 10 insider said. They sat around having coffee and chatting for ten to fifteen minutes. Thatcher returned to her speech-writing. Ministers trooped from Number 10 to their ministerial cars, still looking shell-shocked. Baker, who had remained a staunch supporter to the end, made a brief statement to the press in Downing Street. 'She is an outstanding leader,' he said. 'We will not see her like again.' Thatcher saw the Queen immediately before lunch, informing her that she intended to resign when a new leader of the Conservative Party had been elected the following week.

Her worst ordeal would come that afternoon in the Commons. Tactics for question time were discussed at her second briefing session. Opposition MPs were expected to be very hostile. 'I can take that,' she said. 'It's the sympathy that I'll find the hardest.' Extraordinary scenes greeted Thatcher's arrival in the Commons shortly before 3.15 pm. As she made her way to her place near the dispatch box, back-bench Tory MPs stood, many cheering and waving their order papers. Loyalists, doubters and opponents joined in expressing a mixture of emotions – admiration, relief, respect, sadness. Fifty years earlier, in May 1940, Tory MPs had cheered Neville Chamberlain when he entered the chamber for the first time after his resignation as prime minister – although he at least had continued as their party leader. Thatcher had asked Wakeham to sit beside her during question time and her speech in the no-confidence debate. She had dreaded expressions of friendliness, and her most testing moment came when Elaine Kellett-Bowman, who had been at Oxford with her forty-five years earlier, expressed her gratitude at all that the Prime Minister had done for her country and her party.

Later that afternoon, when she replied to the opposition's motion of no confidence, Thatcher gave a 'bravura performance', as Paddy Ashdown, the Liberal Democrats' leader, acknowledged. Her advisers felt that the speech was not particularly good, but it was transformed by her delivery. When Dennis Skinner, the Labour MP for Bolsover, characteristically intervened to suggest that Thatcher might become head of a new European central bank, she retorted, 'What a good idea!' and, as the cheers and laughter subsided, added, 'I'm enjoying this.' Afterwards, as friends congregated in the prime minister's room to congratulate her on her speech, she was heard to ask, 'What would we do without Skinner?'

VII

Adversarial debate had long been Thatcher's meat and drink. Shortly before becoming prime minister she had declared that a cabinet led by her would not 'waste time having any internal arguments'. It struck her colleagues at the time as improbable and so it quickly proved to be when, on entering Downing Street, she appointed a cabinet in which the majority opposed her 'conviction' style of politics. 'She loves an argument,' Lord Prior, a former Cabinet wet, observed, 'as long as she wins.'[2] She argued and mostly she won.

No single factor caused Thatcher's downfall. Without the concurrence of pressures and events in the autumn of 1990, she might have continued to serve as prime minister for some years. Her length of service as prime minister is unparalleled in the twentieth century. Only David Lloyd George in 1922, Stanley Baldwin in 1937 and Harold Wilson in 1976 had resigned, like her, while still in good health and without being defeated at an election or suffering serious loss of support in a vote on the floor of the House. Baldwin and Wilson went at the time of their own choosing and Lloyd George fell as a result of a vote by Tory MPs. The previous longest single period of continuous rule by Conservative governments, the thirteen years from 1951 to 1964, brought four prime ministers: Churchill, Eden, Macmillan, Home. The fourteen years of Conservative-dominated coalitions between 1931 and 1945 also saw four prime ministers: Ramsay MacDonald, Baldwin, Neville Chamberlain and Churchill. In the eleven and a half years of Tory rule since May 1979, only Thatcher had been prime minister. With Howe's resignation, she had become the last remaining member of her original cabinet.

As Enoch Powell has observed, over time a prime minister's sheer length of service increases the extent of his or her already formidable power over other ministers.[3] Thatcher's domination of the government was without modern parallel. But British government is not presidential: it remains rooted in the cabinet and the parliamentary party. Patronage is a double-edged weapon. The numbers of the neglected and the rejected in the party tend to increase the longer any leader remains in office. And for too long Thatcher had regarded loyalty as a one-way street. She presumed that ministers would remain loyal to her, even though there were many occasions when she appeared to show little loyalty towards them. She allowed herself to become out of touch with her parliamentary party. Her personal staff at Number 10 came to be seen as courtiers, a role which some seemed to relish rather than reject – one minister commented after her resignation that the man who had brought her down had not been Howe or Heseltine, but Bernard Ingham, whose off-the-record briefings had faithfully conveyed Thatcher's views of her ministers.

Thatcher was eventually undermined by her inability to manage people and her reluctance to manage issues in a collective fashion. She had scattered critics within the cabinet 'like skittles to the wind' as one of her former ministers put it – not only Norman St John Stevas, Ian Gilmour, Francis Pym, Jim Prior and the rest of the wets, but by the end also Lawson and Howe, architects of her supposed 'economic miracle'. From her days in opposition she had settled policy by launching personal *démarches*, for example on immigration and pay policy. The poll tax, which contributed to her undoing, became government policy only through her single-minded determination. Her inflexibility had created no-go areas for any discussion of policy.

Among die-hard Thatcherites the belief persists that she would have won had she fought on the second ballot – they argue that simply by going into the tearoom she would have collected an extra ten votes, and that by casting her gaze on the remaining waverers she would have rallied them. Estimates of her likely support can be argued ad infinitum and no doubt will be. The motives of some ministers are also questioned, notably those who emerged as the strongest supporters of Hurd and Major, but the evidence suggests that ministers and MPs who became doubters did so as a result not of prior allegiances but of genuine soundings among many different groups of parliamentary acquaintances and colleagues. Some ministers' estimates of the result of the second ballot may have been wrong, but Heseltine was certainly confident of victory, and it seems unlikely that they were all wrong. In any case, it was a matter not only of arithmetic but also of weighing the impact on party unity of a no-holds-barred fight on the second ballot, whether Thatcher won or lost; and, crucially, the damage already inflicted on her authority as leader by the numbers who had failed to vote for her on the first ballot. At the end of the day what had counted was the collective judgement of the cabinet. Thatcher had come to be seen by Tory MPs as an electoral liability, and her ministers judged that she had lost the authority required to retrieve her position.

Thatcher's resignation had thrown open the succession. Who would seize the Tory crown?

3

Long Live the King

'It is a very exciting thing to become leader of the Conservative Party, particularly exciting to follow one of the most remarkable leaders the Conservative Party has had.'

John Major, Downing Street, 27 November 1990

I

On Wednesday afternoon, while the Prime Minister was consulting cabinet colleagues about her future, Heseltine asked his campaign manager, Michael Mates, what he ought to do the following day. They had previously feared that Thatcher would stand down, so her pledge after the lunch-time meeting at Number 10 that she would 'fight on' was music to their ears. Mates told Heseltine that there was nothing more to be done. They checked his diary for the next morning, Thursday 22 November, and discovered that he had a long-standing commitment to plant acorns at London Zoo in Regent's Park, accompanied by children and an elephant. Heseltine would go but was advised to cancel the elephant, thus at least respecting half of W. C. Field's dictum about never appearing with children and animals.

As Heseltine was driven to the zoo on the Thursday morning, he was contacted on his car phone and told that Thatcher would resign. Mates was called as he relaxed in his bath. Ten minutes later he arrived at Heseltine's office and began organising the campaign for the second ballot.

Hurd was told the news of the Prime Minister's decision first thing in the morning, having gone to bed the night before thinking that she might well fight on. But Major, as he has since acknowledged, 'was telephoned and told late in the evening', that is, on Wednesday night [1]. When a ministerial colleague called Major in Huntingdon at around breakfast-time on Thursday morning, the Chancellor confided the news, saying that he wanted to travel to London and attend that morning's cabinet to share in whatever happened. His colleague discouraged him, arguing that he was not expected to be there as he was convalescing and besides, if there was to be any 'blood-letting', he was better advised to stay away. Major was reluctant to agree, but the cabinet's nine o'clock start effectively settled the argument.

Major had another pressing reason to leave Huntingdon for London. He planned to declare himself a candidate for party leader before the noon deadline for nominations. He heard official confirmation of Thatcher's intention to resign on the car radio as he headed south from Huntingdon.

After the result of the first ballot on Tuesday evening, a growing number of ministers and Tory MPs had been demanding that the party should be given a wider choice. During the subsequent twenty-four hours they had become increasingly 'desperate and depressed', convinced that the party was 'shooting itself in the foot'. But it was to prove almost as difficult to decide who should stand in Thatcher's place as it had been to persuade her to resign. Some ministers felt that it was not until she had posed the question 'Who's it to be if it's not me?' that what had previously been for them a hypothetical debate 'really began to gel'.

By late Wednesday afternoon, cabinet ministers were therefore finally forced to confront the question of the succession to Thatcher. With the exception of the Welsh secretary, David Hunt, who was to emerge as a supporter of Heseltine's before the second ballot, their imperative was how to prevent Heseltine, who had been outside the cabinet since 1986, seizing the prize which virtually all of them felt must go to one of their own number. The widespread assumption had been that the task of blocking the 'outsider' demanded a single 'unity' candidate from the cabinet. The foreign secretary, Hurd, had served in the political firing line as Northern Ireland secretary from 1984 to 1985, and Home Secretary from 1985 to 1989. He had been a favoured choice to block Heseltine for some time, at least since Meyer's challenge to Thatcher the previous year, and since 1986 in some quarters on the left of the party.

During the autumn of 1990, Major too emerged as a potential 'unity' candidate. His joint pre-eminence with Hurd over their cabinet col-leagues had, in effect, been endorsed by Morrison's shrewd recruitment of them as the Prime Minister's proposers, although in the immediate aftermath of the first ballot it had seemed, for an awkward period, that this joint role might rule them out for the second ballot. But how had Major, who had been first elected to the Commons a mere eleven years previously, and appointed to the cabinet only after the 1987 election, emerged as a leadership contender so quickly and so forcibly?

Major's own realisation that he might one day be a contender for the Tory leadership had crystallised during 1986, in the summer after the Westland crisis, while Major and Robert Atkins, the Tory MP for South Ribble, and their wives, Norma and Dulcie, were taking a holiday aboard a narrow boat cruising through the English countryside. Major and Atkins had been friends since their days twenty years earlier in the Greater London Young Conservatives when they were both elected as borough councillors in the Tory local election landslide of 1968 – Major in Lambeth, Atkins in Haringey. As their wives sat at the bow of the narrow boat, Major and Atkins chatted at the stern, steering and listening to the ball-by-ball radio commentary on the England versus New Zealand test match. Atkins recalls that they were talking over their prospects when they suddenly realised that Major 'was in the frame' and 'John first saw the possibility that he might become the prime minister one day'.

Neither of them thought that it was other than a distant prospect, possibly at the earliest in around six years' time, i.e. 1992. And certainly they could not have foreseen the extraordinary turn of events which would transform Major from an outsider into a front-runner for the leadership. There was no planning or formal discussion but they talked over Major's prospects from time to time. It was not until late 1989, and then only very informally, that Atkins discussed Major's chances with David Mellor, the MP for Putney. Mellor had known Major since the 1970s. They had both applied for and had been shortlisted as the Tory candidate for Putney before Major withdrew in the hope of being selected as candidate in the 1976 Carshalton by-election. After their election in 1979, they got to know one another better, joining the 'Guy Fawkes' dining club of Tory MPs and as soccer fans sometimes attending Chelsea's home games at Stamford Bridge. But any conversations about the leadership remained very casual. Like most of their colleagues, Major, Atkins, and Mellor simply 'didn't expect things to move that quickly'.

At the time of his narrow-boat conversation with Atkins, Major had risen only as far as the relative obscurity of junior minister at the Department of Health and Social Security. But he had already caught Thatcher's eye in an incident during his spell between 1983 and 1985 as a government whip, when he had 'patiently explained' to her the thinking of Tory MPs although it was at odds with her own. At the DHSS, dealing with social security, a potential minefield for ministers where the devil is in the detail, he developed a reputation for mastering his brief and presenting an assured, calming impression at the dispatch box.

Rewarded in the 1987 reshuffle by being appointed chief secretary to the Treasury, Major was the first of the 1979 intake to gain cabinet rank.

He was surprised, as the height of his expectation at that stage had been the post of chief whip, a powerful position which would have allowed him to attend cabinet but without being accorded cabinet status. The role of chief secretary attracts little public attention but carries with it responsibility for overseeing the annual spending round, ensuring that Departments' bids are brought as close as possible to the amount previously allocated in the government's published plans. The spending round, completed each autumn, is 'raw politics', characterised by tough bilateral meetings between the chief secretary and each spending minister, and by leak and counter-leak in the press. Major successfully completed the round without recourse to the so-called Star Chamber in which a small group of senior ministers adjudicate on unresolved disputes between the chief secretary and departmental ministers. In October 1987, Tebbit became the first senior Tory to identify Major as a leadership prospect.

Any politician's rise to the position of leadership contender depends crucially on the demise of his potential rivals. Major was no exception. His success at the Treasury coincided with the eclipse of John Moore, who had entered the cabinet a year before Major and who was seen as a rising star of Thatcherism. Moore, like Major, was from a very ordinary background and first came to prominence at the Treasury, where, as financial secretary after the 1983 election, he supervised the development of privatisation as a central plank of government policy. When he was promoted to the cabinet in 1986 as transport secretary, he was quickly identified in the media and within the party as the right wing's most realistic prospect for the leadership. Moore misguidedly appeared to revel in his role as heir apparent, antagonising other ministers and Tory MPs whose own ambitions had been disappointed.

But Moore's appointment as health and social services secretary in 1987 proved his undoing. In the winter of 1987–8 he took the brunt of the fierce attacks on the government for its failure to provide sufficient funds for the NHS, followed in the spring of 1988 by equally bitter attacks over the reform of the social-security system. Moore's ill health was seen as the sign of a man who buckled under pressure and his leadership hopes were crushed. The right wing of the party now lacked any credible candidate for the succession to Thatcher. Major, the Treasury minister responsible for avoiding excessive spending, was ideally placed to establish his credentials with the Tory right. He was also a more skilful political operator than Moore, careful not to irritate his fellow ministers and MPs by active self-promotion and even turned down an opportunity to deliver the prestigious annual Conservative Political Centre lecture at the party conference.

Major's evident success at the Treasury endeared him to Thatcher, readily impressed by mastery of detail and good housekeeping. He was first clearly identified as her preferred successor by his shock promotion to foreign secretary in the July 1989 reshuffle. He was fortunate, however, that his spell at the Foreign Office was short-lived. Diplomats and fellow ministers thought him out of his depth and he endured a traumatic Commonwealth Conference at Kuala Lumpur when Thatcher overruled patient efforts to avoid Britain's isolation over sanctions against South Africa.

Just as good generals need luck, so do political leaders. Major's great stroke of good fortune occurred when Lawson resigned as chancellor in October 1989 and Major took command of the familiar terrain of the Treasury in the ensuing reshuffle. Although in time he might have mastered the Foreign Office brief, his relationship with Thatcher would have been sorely tested on Europe, the issue which wrecked the careers of several of Thatcher's ministers. Major was also assisted by the myth – sedulously fostered and developed by Thatcherite loyalists – that Lawson, who had previously been acclaimed as the architect of Thatcher's so-called 'economic miracle', was the guilty man who had single-handedly created spiralling inflation and high interest rates. Major was portrayed as struggling manfully with the Lawson legacy. It became common knowledge that one day Thatcher would like to see the Majors move into Number 10; not that she had any thought of its happening for some years ahead.

Major had clearly emerged as a potential Tory leader by the autumn of 1989 although nobody then expected the 46-year-old chancellor to be a serious contender in the immediate future. Hurd had also benefited in the reshuffle after Lawson's resignation, his appointment to the Foreign Office considerably enhancing his claim as a possible successor to Thatcher. He had become the 'Number 11 bus' candidate, the minister most likely to be drafted as prime minister in the event of Thatcher's sudden demise through some unforeseen event. At the age of fifty-nine, he seemed of the right generation to serve as the ideal 'unity' candidate who could block the ambitions of the 56-year-old Heseltine until members of the next generation, probably Major and Chris Patten, were ready to battle for the Tory crown.

Hurd's supporters in the Blue Chip dining club realised that Major's rapid rise might eventually put them in a dilemma, although they thought that it still lay beyond the horizon of the next election. Inclined in a jokey and informal way to distribute posts in future governments among themselves, they had initially identified from their generation in the 1979 intake Chris Patten and William Waldegrave as putative prime ministers. Major had joined the Blue Chip group only in 1983 at the suggestion of Garel-Jones, then a colleague in the government Whips' Office. But Major had achieved cabinet rank earlier than any other Blue Chip minister, and it was two years before he was joined at the cabinet table by Chris Patten on the latter's appointment as environment secretary. As a disappointed Waldegrave languished outside the cabinet, Major and Patten were increasingly talked about as possible premiers of the mid-1990s.

The Blue Chip members recognised that in time they would face the awkward problem of having to back either Major or Patten for the leadership. They did not want both to stand for fear of dividing their efforts and risking another candidate stealing the prize which they regarded as theirs for the taking. Major, however, had clearly established a clear edge over Patten, so much so that during 1990 he was beginning to emerge even as a potential rival to Hurd.

The possibility that the party might be tempted to 'jump a generation' in the event of Thatcher's sudden demise put the Blue Chip members in an increasingly difficult position, none more so than Patten. If Major was to win an early leadership contest, Patten's prospects of being leader would be ruled out for years, possibly for good. It was therefore in Patten's interest that Hurd should be the single 'unity' candidate. His backing for the foreign secretary was bound to raise suspicion of being motivated by personal calculation.

During 1990 Patten and Major had several informal conversations in which they discussed the leadership. Their talks can best be described as being of the 'what if' variety – what if Thatcher falls under the Number 11 bus sooner rather than later, what if the leadership becomes vacant during the next parliament, and so on. Patten had made a realistic assessment of his position and said that he would not be a candidate in the near future. Major would not rule himself out, and Patten acknowledged that if there were to be a candidate from their generation in any early leadership contest, Major was the only realistic contender. But Patten made it clear that he would not be able to support Major in such circumstances. Having served Hurd as a junior minister at the Northern Ireland Office and sharing his traditional Toryism, Patten argued with conviction that Hurd was by far the best person to become prime minister. Major was therefore left in no doubt that if he decided to stand for the leadership in the near future, his candidacy would be opposed by his leading colleague in the Blue Chip group and would split its members. Major also appreciated as clearly as any other cabinet minister the risk of division while Heseltine remained a strong challenger.

II

'Whichever one of us has a run of good form over the preceding four or five months will win,' a leadership contender had confided several years ago,[2] resorting in the pragmatic way of many Tories to the language of the racecourse. During the autumn, Hurd displayed his statesmanship in the tragic circumstances created by Saddam Hussein's invasion of Kuwait. But, had Major been able to plan the circumstances of late November 1990, he could not have timed his 'run of good form' any better. At the end of September his decision to take sterling into the European Exchange-Rate Mechanism settled the debilitating divisions within the government on stable exchange rates and Britain's commitment to Europe. It also demolished the suggestion that he was 'Mrs Thatcher's poodle'. His ERM initiative, the accompanying cut in interest rates and a well-received speech, about which he had been nervous beforehand, at October's party conference briefly buoyed the Tories, who had become desperate for some glimmer of hope.

When Howe's resignation catalysed Tory unrest and brought Thatcher's leadership into question, Hurd's name was highlighted in the media as the most likely cabinet 'unity' candidate to block Heseltine. Major, however, was also being mooted among Tory MPs as a possible contender in the event of Thatcher's defeat in any leadership contest. But the general assumption, shared by Hurd and Major, remained that there should be only one cabinet candidate for fear of splitting the potential vote and allowing Heseltine to win.

Both Hurd's and Major's closest supporters were seriously concerned that their preferred candidate would be the one who would step down. Hurd's backers feared that he would 'do the decent thing' and withdraw in favour of Major. Their anxiety had been increased during a television interview as speculation that there might be a leadership contest was building. Hurd was advised beforehand not to back Thatcher too strongly for fear of jeopardising his own leadership prospects, but when pressed about his ambitions replied that he was not interested in the premiership. It was not a politician's disingenuous disclaimer but reflected his true feelings.

Hurd's strongest advocates were frequently exasperated by his attitude. They were telling him not to rule himself out or to let the chance of the premiership slip by simply because he would not fight for it. But attempts to draw him into discussing his prospects were resisted. Friends would sometimes try to raise the leadership obliquely. To the suggestion that 'if all this comes to pieces, people may come knocking at your door,' Hurd retorted, 'So I hear.' He was told by one of his closest aides, 'The only bar on you getting the top job is your own reluctance.' There are shades of Austen Chamberlain, the only twentieth-century Tory leader in the Commons never to have become prime minister, who, in the lacerating phrase variously attributed to Churchill and Lord Birkenhead, 'always played the game and always lost it'.

Major's supporters, on the other hand, feared that he would be the victim of the 'Tory establishment'. Hurd had long been the favoured 'unity' candidate and was an archetypal Tory paternalist from the section of the party which had dominated the leadership for forty years before Thatcher became leader. Some right-wing MPs who saw Major as Thatcher's chosen heir and Tory populists like Tony Beaumont-Dark, who had known Major from their days as new MPs together and who saw his appeal to the voters, worried that Major would come under pressure to allow Douglas Hurd a clear run. 'Don't you dare give way to Douglas,' Beaumont-Dark admonished in an aside to Major in the Commons chamber. His comment evidently pleased the chancellor.

Assessments of the level of support for both Hurd and Major were already being made among Tory MPs even before Heseltine formally declared that he would challenge Thatcher in the first ballot. In large part, these assessments were based on the spontaneous talk in the tearoom and corridors of Westminster about the leadership. Tory MPs were talking about little else after Howe's resignation. But the soundings were conducted with great discretion since either 'unity' candidate would run only in the event of the defeat of the Prime Minister. MPs' opinions were generally gauged by ministers' PPSs as part of their normal duties as ministerial 'eyes and ears' at the Commons, but they were acting without the sanction of either the foreign secretary or the chancellor. Hurd's supporters frequently attest to his explicit instructions against any assessment of MPs' opinions. Major's supporters also repeatedly stress that he would have had nothing to do with anything which remotely resembled a leadership campaign. Both men were anxious not to be seen to undermine the Prime Minister. Similarly, their supporters knew that any hint of actively organising to seize the Tory crown would be the kiss of death for their favoured candidate.

The soundings were more contingency planning than conspiracy. Hurd's supporters generally observed their candidate's ban on approaching MPs or ministers, but did not discourage anybody who raised the issue with them. As a result of their discussions they felt confident that Hurd would enjoy considerable support. Major's allies wanted to ensure that in the event of Thatcher's resignation the chancellor was not overlooked through a general assumption that Hurd was the rightful candidate. Many MPs who were approached were known to want an outright Thatcher victory. Conversations with backbenchers were conducted 'very casually, informally' and the chancellor's case was not pressed 'too openly' for fear of undermining Thatcher. As a result of their soundings, Major's supporters were confirmed in their view that he would be 'a formidable candidate'. They believed that in the event of Thatcher being defeated, Major would be a stronger runner than Hurd and also that Heseltine would not be able to win such a contest.

Policy played only a part in determining which MPs would support either of the two would-be candidates and who would actively campaign for them. Hurd tended to be bracketed with Heseltine on the economy by many Thatcher loyalists, but this was to be expected since the Prime Minister was known to favour Major. Departmental ties exerted a strong pull in a party which puts the winning and holding of office before party loyalty. Hurd's supporters would include ministers who had worked with him at Northern Ireland (Chris Patten), the Home Office (John Patten) and Foreign Office (Waldegrave). Major's would include Treasury (Lamont, Maude) and other former departmental colleagues from the DHSS and the whips' office (Lyell, Lilley). Personal ambition, loyalty to the boss and mutual respect through working closely together created a powerful combination of motives. As the 1990 leadership contest progressed, a shrewd backbencher observed that the tussle was increasingly coming to resemble eighteenth-century politics, with factions grouped round particular individuals rather than neat ideological divisions.

During the weekend before the first ballot, conversations between the would-be candidates and their supporters about what might follow after the first ballot were only 'very general'. Hurd was low as a result of the reports that he was not giving Thatcher his full backing. Major was due to go into hospital in Huntingdon for his wisdom-tooth operation, which would necessitate between a week and ten days' convalescence. Despite suggestions that he ought to postpone the operation in order to be on hand for events at such a 'crucial and fluid time', Major adamantly refused. He had the Prime Minister's permission to miss meetings – what impression would it create if he suddenly changed his mind? He would 'look like a vulture hovering about'. Shortly before his operation, however, friends phoned him suggesting that Heseltine would do better than expected and urging him not to miss any opportunity which might arise.

The day after his operation, Sunday 18th, Major was thinking of returning to London for the first ballot on Tuesday 20th, earlier than originally planned. But friends who telephoned him thought he sounded 'woozy' and advised him against attempting an early return. They also volunteered conflicting advice on his best tactics. Some advised him to be on hand for events, others said that he would be better placed if he were to remain relatively inaccessible in Huntingdon. His health ruled out the former course. Jeffrey Archer, who visited him on Tuesday, found him feeling unwell but in no doubt that he would continue to second Thatcher's nomination.

Hurd and Major remained in close touch on the telephone over the next few days. After the declaration of the first ballot, Major was kept informed of the mood of the party at the Commons through regular phone conversations with his colleagues and supporters. Major reported his own agreement to continue to second Thatcher, although he would obviously not be required to sign Thatcher's nomination paper until her return from Paris. He also learned of the late-night gathering at Garel-Jones's house. He was a regular visitor himself to Catherine Place, so that would have come as no surprise.

One purpose of the late-night meeting was to discuss the problem of who should stand as the cabinet 'unity' candidate to block Heseltine. Chris Patten was the strongest advocate for Hurd and Lamont was the most enthusiastic champion of Major. More than twenty years earlier, Patten and Lamont had shared an office in the Conservative Research Department, where an earlier generation of Tory politicians, Enoch Powell, Reggie Maudling and Iain Macleod, had also cut their political teeth. Patten and Lamont were not only championing rival contenders, they would also have to stiffen their contenders' resolve.

There was no hard and fast deal between Hurd and Major, but they had both assumed that whoever had the strongest support should stand, with the backing of the other. But it was becoming clear that they wanted somebody else to reach an assessment of their support. The ministers gathered at Garel-Jones's felt that it would be possible to arrange an estimate of their respective support in the Commons.

This idea found general favour. There was a continuing fear among Hurd's supporters that in any discussion with the Chancellor to settle the issue their candidate would concede to Major, in the way that Lord Halifax conceded to Churchill in May 1940 after Neville Chamberlain's resignation as prime minister. Hurd viewed the leadership as a matter of duty and sensed that Major would be more likely to attract Thatcher's former supporters. But Major's supporters were never entirely confident of their candidate's resolve; fearing that any conversation might be a case of 'after you, Claude'. The line urged on the Chancellor in the event of such a discussion was 'I'm proposing to stand, what are you proposing to do?' The plan for an agreed assessment struck both sides as a 'shrewd and sensible idea', since they were confident that they could manipulate opinion in the tearoom as effectively as anybody else.

As Tuesday night wore on, however, and Thatcher loyalists digested the result of the first ballot, those who concluded that the Prime Minister would lose to Heseltine in a second ballot were already beginning to suggest Major as the best 'unity' candidate. This support for Major had been partly prompted by the earlier soundings, although many loyalists say that they were not aware of active lobbying and simply believed Major to be the man most likely to carry on Thatcher's policies, as Hurd had suspected that they would – after all, Major was regarded as her chosen successor. The numbers favouring Major grew during Wednesday morning and lunchtime, particularly among MPs and PPSs from the 1983 and 1987 intake, who stood to benefit most from a new broom in Downing Street. Other MPs feared that jumping a generation would bring their careers to a premature end, but there were also some older MPs who thought that by choosing Major the party would 'be doing the clever thing'.

But the plans for an assessment of support for Hurd and Major among Tory MPs had assumed that the Prime Minister would announce her decision not to fight on after her lunchtime meeting with the 'men in grey suits'. While Thatcher's future was being debated in the cabinet room, Hurd was joined for a sandwich lunch at the Foreign Office by Yeo, his PPS, and Patten. Yeo passed on the whips' estimates of the loss of support for Thatcher, but was dismayed to hear the foreign secretary say that he thought the Prime Minister might well continue to the second ballot. When the Prime Minister later declared that she would fight on, it became impossible for Hurd and Major to sanction the agreed assessment of their respective support – indeed, Thatcher's continued candidacy appeared to render any such exercise futile.

During Wednesday, as the implications of the result of the first ballot and the procedure for the second ballot were discussed, several MPs and ministers became convinced that more than one candidate should stand against Heseltine. Michael Jopling, the former chief whip, suggested the idea to Kenneth Clarke at lunchtime. Alan Clark was also arguing the case for extra candidates as the best guarantee of defeating Heseltine. It made political sense to allow the party a wider choice. If only one alternative candidate to Heseltine emerged in place of Thatcher, it was clear that some MPs would see it as 'an establishment carve-up'. There was a danger of opinion polarising in a second ballot which appeared to be 'the government versus the pretender'. Heseltine would need only a simple majority to win in the second ballot, and a straight fight with an 'establishment' candidate would therefore provide his best opportunity of winning the leadership.

Running more than one candidate in the second ballot would also be a more effective way of draining support away from Heseltine and denying him a simple majority. The likelihood was that if at least three candidates stood, no single contender would win an overall majority. As stipulated under the rules, the contest would go to a third ballot. Heseltine, who was strongly opposed by a sizeable minority of the party, would be most unlikely to win such a vote, which is decided by proportional represent-ation. One of the 'unity' candidates would then become leader with the support of most of the second preferences from his cabinet colleague.

These were the arguments that cabinet ministers thrashed out at the Commons during Wednesday afternoon and evening. The need to remove support from Heseltine prompted one minister to propose as candidates Tebbit, who would secure the support of the right, and Patten, who would win the 'goody-goody' or 'Guardian-reading' vote – in fact, Patten later heard that he would have won the endorsement of the *Economist* magazine. But Tebbit was no longer a serious contender, and Patten had no intention of standing when he believed that he would not stand a good chance of winning at that stage of his career. In the end, the view which prevailed among cabinet ministers was that Hurd and Major were the best contenders.

The problem would be persuading the Chancellor and Foreign Secretary that they should stand against one another. They were waiting for their friends to tell them who should stand aside, but nobody had been able to establish which of them had the stronger support. The PPSs and junior ministers had theories, but there was no reliable estimate available to cabinet ministers. Anyway, the procedures for leadership elections enabled both of them to stand in the second ballot – assuming that Thatcher finally withdrew. The issue of who had the stronger support would become clear in the process of their blocking Heseltine's hopes of victory.

Kenneth Clarke, who had earlier in the afternoon proposed to Thatcher that she should stand down to allow both Hurd and Major to counter Heseltine's challenge, was delegated by his cabinet colleagues to tell Hurd of their view that both he and Major should stand. Accompanied by Alastair Goodlad, the deputy chief whip, Clarke tracked down Hurd at the Commons, where he was due to speak at a dinner in one of the downstairs dining rooms. Clarke and Goodlad managed to catch a word with him in the corner of the room, and told him that he had to stand against Major in order to give the party the choice which it wanted. Hurd replied that he would do so if Major agreed.

Meanwhile, Major had been kept in touch during the evening with events by phone. While one minister was calling Major from the chancellor's room at the Commons, Lamont rushed in and took the phone, telling Major, 'You must run, you must run!' After seeing the foreign secretary, Clarke and Goodlad phoned Major and told him of Hurd's conditional agreement that they should both stand.

But the final decision would rest with Thatcher. Hurd had already signed Thatcher's second-ballot nomination paper and Jeffrey Archer's driver was taking it to Huntingdon for Major's signature. But how to ensure that Major's own nomination paper arrived in London before the noon deadline the next day? One option which Major considered was that Archer's driver could return with his nomination form in addition to

Thatcher's: all that he needed to do was to sign a piece of paper, expressing his consent to being nominated, leaving sufficient space for his proposers to sign. In the event, Major travelled to London the following morning in time to sign and submit his nomination form and declare himself a candidate for the Tory leadership. Assuming, of course, that the post became vacant.

The prospect that both Hurd and Major would stand in the second ballot presented an unexpected dilemma for ministers and MPs who were close colleagues or friends of both men. One junior minister with torn loyalties sat up till three o'clock on Wednesday morning debating with his wife whom he would support.

III

At around 10.30 am on Thursday 22nd, as Thatcher's resignation cabinet ended, ministers rushed from Downing Street to their offices round Whitehall and began to confer with colleagues and advisers about their next steps. The defence secretary, Tom King, had previously served Heseltine at Environment and wanted to see him back in the cabinet, but not as prime minister. He would support Hurd and, as a long-serving and centrist member of the cabinet, agreed to the suggestion that he should be one of the Foreign Secretary's proposers. Hurd had in fact tried to raise the issue with King when they were at cabinet that morning, but King had not seemed to understand what was being said to him.

Within moments of King's political adviser rushing from the room to take King's signature to Hurd at the Foreign Office, the phone rang. Heseltine, returned from his engagement at the zoo, came on the line. Would King support him? King explained his position, and that he had just proposed Hurd. Heseltine thanked him courteously and put down the phone. He had not been able to approach anybody in the cabinet while Thatcher was still in the running, and by the time he could do so there was little more than an hour left before nominations closed. His lack of support in the cabinet was a severe setback – his only declared supporter would be David Hunt, Peter Walker's successor as Welsh Secretary.

At the Foreign Office, Hurd and his predominantly left-of-centre supporters gathered in his room. Sir Giles Shaw, formerly one of Hurd's ministerial team at the Home Office and a member of the 1922 executive, was appointed campaign manager. John Patten, a long-standing Hurd supporter, would handle the media as campaign director. Garel-Jones, one of Hurd's Foreign Office ministers, deployed his whip's expertise to oversee a fifteen-strong team of canvassers, which included his PPS, Ann

Widdecombe, initially the most right-wing member of Hurd's team, and Andrew MacKay, King's PPS, from the centre-right of the party. Chris Patten and William Waldegrave would help draft Hurd's statements and press articles, and Tim Yeo, Hurd's loyal PPS all the way through the leadership crisis, would act as a link between Hurd and his team. Clarke, Rifkind and King would try to rally support.

Absent from the Foreign Office gathering was Alan Clark, who had been a supporter of Hurd's 'mothball fleet' back in 1989 and who had attended the discussion at Garel-Jones's house two nights earlier. Clark had told Garel-Jones that he wanted to consult his constituency party, and was seen on television that morning lambasting Heseltine for bringing about Thatcher's downfall. His purpose, and that of some other Tory MPs fulminating into the TV cameras on College Green, opposite the Palace of Westminster, was to stoke up anger and indignation in the party outside Westminster. Clark wanted to prevent Heseltine becoming leader and believed that he would best bring pressure to bear on his fellow MPs, particularly undeclared potential Heseltine supporters, by building up the opposition to Heseltine among local Tory party associations before the weekend. He was playing on activists' feelings of outrage at Thatcher's downfall and their sense that they had not been consulted before the first ballot and wanted to make sure their voice was heard before the second.

While Major was still on his way from Huntingdon, Lamont had sat in Thatcher's resignation cabinet drawing up a list of positions for Major's campaign team, identifying the need for people to handle the press, deal with media interviews, canvass MPs, and so on. But at that stage he did not put names against the various functions. At the end of the cabinet meeting Lamont 'rocketed' from Number 10 and appeared at the Treasury within moments, where his PPS, William Hague, had already arrived, having heard the news of Thatcher's resignation as he left the Commons gymnasium. They were quickly joined by Lamont's cabinet colleagues Howard and Lilley, and his fellow Treasury ministers Maude and Ryder – Maude had had no idea that Ryder was a supporter of Major's. At the Commons, Atkins and Major's PPS, Graham Bright, who had only recently been appointed, met in Major's room and found offers of help pouring from MPs. Atkins and Bright rushed across to the Treasury, and were soon followed by John Gummer, who had returned to consult colleagues at the Ministry of Agriculture. What followed suggests little pre-planning.

They initially met in the Chancellor's room but were advised that they had no right to be there in Major's absence. The debate on who should propose and second Major was unduly prolonged. At first it was thought that the proposer and seconder ought to be senior backbenchers, but it was recognised that cabinet ministers' names would carry more weight with MPs. One suggestion was that Howard ought to propose and Lilley second. But both ministers were regarded as right-wing on economic policy and a more balanced ticket was needed. Gummer, who was seen as more left-wing on the economy and a strong pro-European, became Major's proposer. Tebbit's name was floated as a seconder but ruled out as too right-wing. The choice lay between Howard and Lilley. The discussion continued for some time after Major's arrival around eleven o'clock, although Lamont had been anxious to settle it quickly and move to the many other urgent decisions which had to be made. In the end, Major's proposers were Lamont and Gummer.

A convenient operating base for the campaign now had to be found, since Treasury offices could not be used for party purposes. Hague recalled that when he needed to be near the Commons overnight he sometimes stayed at the house of a friend from Oxford days and prospective parliamentary candidate, Alan Duncan, in Gayfere Street within minutes of Whitehall and Westminster. It was a propitious address, although whether Major's campaign team would entirely agree is a moot point. In 1965, the first time the party chose its leader under the election procedure used for the 1990 contest, the key organisers of Edward Heath's successful bid – Ian Gilmour, Charles Morrison (elder brother of Peter) and Peter Walker – had shared an office in Gayfere Street. Hence talk at the time of the 'Gayfere Street plot'. Not only was Duncan's house ideally located, but unusually it already had three phone lines, the capacity for an extra ten lines and a fax machine. Duncan was at his tailor's but Hague had a set of keys and left messages for Duncan, who eventually called back agreeing that his house could be used by Major's team. Duncan did not return unawares, as has been suggested, to discover his house overrun by ministers and MPs – although it is true that during the campaign they sometimes wondered who he was, not appreciating that they were his guests.

At midday, Cranley Onslow confirmed that he had received three valid nominations for the leadership of the Conservative Party, and shortly afterwards Hurd and Major issued a joint statement declaring that they were both running in order to provide the party with a choice. Over lunch at the Commons, Major discussed the need for a balanced ticket and co-opted Gillian Shephard, a junior social services minister, and Ian Lang from the Scottish Office on to his campaign team, since they would both help to broaden his appeal.

The chaos that surrounded the early stages of Major's campaign continued because of the candidate's reluctance to impose a clear line of command and his preference for decision-making by committee. At 2.30 pm Major chaired a further meeting to review the position and discuss strategy. Others continued to join as the meeting progressed, including David Mellor, the Putney MP and arts minister, leftish-inclined, and a pro-European and Andrew Tyrie, a former Treasury political adviser and a parliamentary candidate, who had been phoned by Major's office and Lamont's office within an hour of Thatcher's resignation and had dashed from Oxford, where he is a don at Nuffield College. One of their main concerns was how to play the issue of the poll tax, which was the single most important issue of the campaign. It was also Heseltine's great strength, his hard-core support being drawn from Tory poll-tax rebels.

Despite Major's wish to avoid a hierarchy in the campaign team, Lamont's emergence as *de facto* campaign manager was essential in order to create an effective organisation. The main functions were divided between Number 11, the political headquarters, and Gayfere Street, which served as the operations centre. At Gayfere Street, the basement dining-room or 'bunker', was devoted to the canvass of MPs, containing the team's master-list of voting intentions and files on individual MPs. Maude, the Treasury minister and a former government whip, oversaw the operation, but the acknowledged number-cruncher was Bob Hayward, the MP for Kingswood. The bunker team held three to four meetings a day to discuss numbers and where they should focus their efforts. Hague and other colleagues from the 1987 intake, David Davis, James Arbuthnot and Andrew Mitchell, were among Major's assiduous canvassers both at the Commons and in the bunker. The cabinet ministers Gummer, Howard and Lilley canvassed MPs by phone and at the Commons.

On the ground floor Ryder, a former journalist, dealt with the media, along with Michael Jack, who shares a secretary with Major at the Commons, and Angie Bray, who that morning resigned her job at Conservative Central Office in order to join the team – she subsequently returned to Tory headquarters. They supplied the broadcast news and current-affairs programmes with a flow of Major supporters and organised articles and interviews for the press. Atkins was based at the Commons on Thursday afternoon, briefing journalists in the lobby with information supplied by Ryder, and was joined by Tyrie, who would also help draft Major's press articles. Hague liaised between Gayfere Street and Number 11, using the canvass intelligence to determine which MPs Major should approach and to ensure that the Chancellor's time between interviews and press conferences was used to maximum effect among the electoral college.

With the entry of two new candidates, the spotlight was inevitably drawn away from Heseltine. Previously the challenger, he became the challenged. Heseltine's chief of staff, Mates, had calculated, the minute he heard that Thatcher would resign, that the net effect on the second ballot would result immediately in an increase of eight votes in Heseltine's support. But he had always feared the danger of more than one candidate entering the field, and on learning that both Major and Hurd were standing realised that it would be virtually impossible for Heseltine to win. Major's candidature provided a welcome haven for the vast majority of Thatcher loyalists, and Heseltine's team had always known that a number of their voters would desert to Hurd if Thatcher withdrew after the first ballot. Although Heseltine lost the services of two of his key allies, Mates and John Lee, for most of the second ballot campaign because they were away on a visit to the Gulf with the Commons Select Committee on Defence, he was able to field a team of around thirty MPs. In Mates's absence, Sir Neil Macfarlane took charge of their master list of MPs and organised team meetings.

By the time Thatcher arrived in the Commons for questions and the no-confidence debate, the lobbying for the second ballot was in full swing. Major's Young Turks among the 1983 and 1987 intakes were 'effectively rubbishing' Hurd. He was easily portrayed as a 'toff' and the 'Alec Douglas-Home candidate' whose only hope was to squeeze through as a compromise on a third ballot. The parallel was wounding, since it highlighted Hurd's own lack of experience in any economics department and his old-Etonian background.

This inverted snobbery among Tory MPs ruined Hurd's chances and was one of the most extraordinary aspects of the contest. In the end one of Hurd's canvassers was unable to resist asking MPs who said that they would not support Hurd because he was an old Etonian why they were putting their own children at a similar disadvantage by sending them to public schools. A fair point, but one which was unlikely to win converts in the electoral college. Hurd's canvassers attempted to hit back by arguing that their candidate was tried and tested in three of the most difficult departments, the Northern Ireland, Home and Foreign offices, whereas Major was unproven.

Thatcher's remarkable performance at the dispatch box during Thursday afternoon heightened what one Hurd supporter described as 'the mood of guilt and sympathy at what had been done to Thatcher'. The beneficiary was Major, whom MPs knew to be Thatcher's chosen heir. Moreover, the right wing 'had nowhere else to go' and Tebbit was also known to be backing Major, although both Hurd and Heseltine were to attract some Thatcher die-hards, such as Michael Fallon, who backed Hurd, and Edward Leigh, who opted for Heseltine.

By Thursday night, although they had not started their detailed canvassing, Major's team already had over 130 MPs pledging their support. This was the basis of their claim on Friday morning that Major could not now come third, a shrewdly judged statement which would help maintain their momentum. Garel-Jones reckoned that Hurd had around 60 supporters, of which up to 30 were drawn from Heseltine's votes on the first ballot, MPs who had seen Heseltine as their stalking horse. Garel-Jones realised that Heseltine would not win, but that Major's campaign had the momentum. That night he made his own private estimate of the second ballot: Major 180 votes, Heseltine 132, Hurd 60. He would not tell Hurd till much later in the campaign.

Thursday evening had also brought the first evidence of Major's appeal in the country at large. Alan Clark, still uncommitted, was among a throng of Tory MPs and television crews on College Green when Bob Worcester, head of the opinion-poll organisation MORI, emerged from the gloom beyond the television lights and told him of a poll which revealed that Major was catching Heseltine in terms of winning back voters for the Tories. Clark had told both the Hurd and Major teams that he wanted to consult his constituency party before making his final decision, but he realised that support for Major would be strengthened when MPs learned of his growing appeal in the polls. Tory MPs would be able to salve their consciences for their treatment of Thatcher by supporting her chosen successor and by voting for a winner.

Tory consciences were given no respite by Friday morning's papers. Banner headlines and scores of pages were devoted to Thatcher's downfall. Treachery was not only in the air, it screamed from the quotes carried by the press. 'The rats got at her,' a member of Thatcher's campaign team claimed. Tebbit was excoriating about the cabinet. 'If they had the balls, she would have won,' he reportedly told friends.

Major's team realised the importance of winning the early battle in the media. They ensured that the dramatic coverage of Thatcher's resignation was accompanied by reports of the surge in Major's support from the moment he had declared himself a contender. These reports would improve Major's position in the constituencies and among local Tory activists before MPs left Westminster for their weekend meetings. Most MPs would consult their local associations on Friday and Saturday, and would come under great pressure from party activists. They were angry at what had happened to Thatcher and wanted to have some say on the next ballot. Also, since Hurd and Major were both standing on the second ballot in order to give the party a wider choice, many MPs wanted to hear the thoughts of their local parties, and their constituents, before reaching a final decision.

The Friday-morning press conferences, aimed at Friday's television and radio and Saturday's papers, were also vital. Major's team gathered at eight o'clock in Gayfere Street, before going to Number 11 to meet the Chancellor half an hour later. Overnight, Major had received a briefing of one and a half pages prepared by Tyrie for his press-conference statement. Tyrie advised Major to emphasise his Brixton background as showing his social mobility. But it was Major who included the term 'classless society'. By nine o'clock the main thrust of his 'election address' was agreed, which Tyrie then drafted.

At Major's 10.30 am press conference, his opening comments were well-judged: he emphasised the extent of his support from all sections of the party and stressed that the economy would be the battleground at the next election, a line which played to his strongest suit, his experience at the Treasury. He then spoke of his belief that there should be more social mobility and that more must be done to increase the morale of teachers. On Europe, the issue where divisions in the government had triggered Howe's resignation and the leadership crisis, he struck a consensual note, believing that it would be possible to find unity, based on pragmatism, common sense and the protection of British interests. As regards the vexed issue of the poll tax, where he feared being outbid by Heseltine and even by Hurd, he held to the line that further changes could be made and that his record in government showed that he was not against making changes.

Whereas Major's campaign was now functioning to an agreed strategy, Hurd's lacked direction. As a Hurd campaigner later ruefully admitted, 'There had been no scientific analyses of what we were trying to do each day, or who our target groups were, or how the press were being used, and nor was there enough recognition of the need for a high profile early on.' It is a devastating catalogue of errors, but at least it disposes of any theory that his supporters had prepared carefully laid plans for Hurd's accession. At Hurd's 45-minute campaign meeting before his Friday press conference, Garel-Jones kept his gloomy prediction of the second ballot to himself but initial canvass returns estimated that Major had 92 firm pledges, Heseltine 69 and Hurd 52. The Hurd team's plan had to be to try to overhaul Heseltine, since, despite brave claims later that whoever was third might still win on the third ballot, it was clear that the candidate trailing last would be badly squeezed. But Hurd's team were seriously underestimating Heseltine's support.

Hurd's appeal at his press conference as the 'unity' and healing candidate was pitched at a party which threatened to become polarised as it was swept by anger and outrage. There were growing signs of a desire for retribution. He spoke with casual aplomb, adopting shirtsleeves in front of a riot of cameras and microphones, but he lacked any distinctive policy ideas and it was becoming clear that he would remain rooted in third place unless he took risks. In addition to the poll tax, on which he might have made a firmer pledge to relate it to ability to pay, education and health offered scope for adventurous proposals, and both secretaries of state, Clarke and Waldegrave, were members of his campaign team. But Hurd was concerned in a party leadership contest not to 'make policy on the hoof' and was fastidious about not floating ideas which had perhaps only partly been discussed by colleagues in government. He would consider suggesting policy ideas at the Monday press conference. By then, however, it would be too late.

Heseltine's team had watched the focus shift from their candidate. By Friday morning Heseltine was on the defensive, justifying his decision to challenge Thatcher and arguing that he was helping to unite the party. His supporters hoped that the weekend press and television interviews, and particularly the opinion polls showing Heseltine as a vote-winner, would revive his support. Some were deeply aggrieved at the alleged spiking of an opinion poll which had been due to appear in the London *Evening Standard* on Friday and which they believed would have reported a commanding Heseltine lead among the young and the skilled working class, the very groups that the Tories had to win back. In fact, the poll was not carried because of the appearance of another poll, by On-Line Telephone Surveys, a MORI subsidiary, which had appeared in *The Times* that morning. In any event Worcester, MORI's chief, had already told Alan Clark the previous evening of early polling evidence that Major was catching Heseltine as a potential vote-winner, a view which would be borne out by the polls published over the weekend.

IV

'Raw and strong' is how Nicholas Budgen, MP for Wolverhampton South West, described the anger at Mrs Thatcher's 'assassination' which confronted him and other Tory MPs as they returned to their constituencies on the weekend before the second ballot. At his constituency association's dinner Budgen said that he had supported Thatcher on the first ballot but admitted that the guest speaker, Tony Beaumont-Dark, MP for Birmingham Selly Oak, a more marginal seat, had voted against her.

The scene that night was a microcosm of the arguments and emotions raging throughout the party, flavoured by Midlands Toryism. Budgen represents the seat which Enoch Powell held for twenty-four years. The Powellite flame burns bright. Beaumont-Dark is more in the mould of 'Radical Joe' Chamberlain, whose influence still lives on among Birmingham Tories. According to Budgen, Beaumont-Dark's accent moved 'between Birmingham and Blenheim' as he defied the hostility of his audience and launched into a robust speech. If Budgen himself had tried to defend Heseltine to his activists, he reckoned that there would have been a riot.

Despite Budgen's Powellite commitment to monetarism and criticism of the European Community, he opted for Hurd. He saw no policy difference between Major and Hurd on the economy or Europe, and his association chairman informed him that although the activists were mainly for Major, they did not feel strongly against Hurd. By Sunday, Budgen thought that 'it sounded like civil war in the party followed by certain defeat'. His vote would go to Hurd – 'Age, Authority and Unity by Compromise'.[3] Beaumont-Dark, also finding that his activists favoured Major, nevertheless did not reveal his vote on the second ballot.

'Horrendous' was how one Heseltine campaigner characterised the constituency pressures over the weekend. Heseltine, not Howe, was now seen as Thatcher's assassin. Even MPs in constituencies where the activists had been split between Thatcher and Heseltine the previous weekend reported 'consternation at what had happened once the deed had been done'. Some MPs who had supported him, including Mates, Peter Temple-Morris, Emma Nicholson, Ivor Stanbrook, Cyril Townsend and Charles Wardle, were threatened with deselection. Other MPs found 'such viciousness' towards Heseltine among the activists that they did not see how he would ever overcome it as leader and reunite the party. At constituency dinners in the northwest, where Heseltine attracted some of his strongest support among MPs in marginal seats, activists were inclined to boo the mention of his name and to cheer Major.

'Let's have no bloody messing about here, it's about who's going to win us the next election,' was the down-to-earth attitude that prevailed in one typical northwestern marginal constituency. But even there, with the activists clearly thinking in terms of vote-winning ability as the criterion for becoming party leader and prime minister, the MP found that his local association were two to one in favour of Major as opposed to Heseltine, with Hurd trailing a poor third. Heseltine was 'divisive', someone who would never unite the party, whereas Major's 'personal qualities' shone through. Hurd was 'a great foreign secretary' but 'lacked electoral appeal'. By contrast, a Tory MP who went hunting with the Belvoir foxhounds in Leicestershire found that the Tories riding with him were 'pretty detached' about Thatcher's demise and were more in favour of Heseltine.

MPs told Heseltine's canvassers of their fears that, if Heseltine became leader, key members of their constituency associations would not pull their weight in an election campaign. One Home Counties Tory commented, 'Some of the stalwarts would simply have gone off and worked for something else, like the NSPCC or the local golf club.' Heseltine's team responded that their candidate was the most likely election winner and that party workers would first wait and see how a new leader performed – 'if the guy's a winner they'll rally, nothing unites the Tory Party like winning'. But drawing analogies with the party's triumphant recovery after Suez under Macmillan in 1959 meant little to MPs from the 1983 and 1987 intakes. In any case, they were not particularly inclined to reflect on historical parallels that weekend with their activists 'after them'.

During Friday and over the weekend all three campaign teams conducted detailed canvassing. Their varying methods of double- checking brought some complaints from MPs called more than once by the same team, but at least one MP contrived to convince all three teams that he was a 'firm pledge'. By Saturday lunchtime, Major's team had more than 50 MPs actively helping. They had to counter two specific concerns. A small number of Thatcher die-hards felt that Major's entry into the contest had been part of a conspiracy plotted by Treasury ministers, whereas at least Heseltine had had the courage to 'stab her in the front'. But Major's canvassers encountered a more serious concern on the left of the party. The vast bulk of his support was known to be coming from Thatcher loyalists, and he was, after all, her preferred candidate. Although Major had been concerned to ensure that his team was balanced, worries on the left were acute. As a result, campaign members like Robert Hughes, both Edward Heath's unofficial PPS in the Commons and a member of the Tory Reform Group and Nick Lyell, the Solicitor-General, and Gillian Shephard were featured in the Major team's photo calls. Strident right-wingers like Norman Tebbit were kept at a distance from the public campaign. Although Thatcher wanted to take an active role, her involvement was limited to trying to persuade former die-hards who were not firm Major supporters that he was the right candidate.

Major's greater ability than either Hurd or Heseltine to be all things to all men predated the leadership campaign. This can be illustrated by an incident after Major had spoken months before to the No Turning Back group. A member of this right-wing group met a member of the leftish Blue Chip group and commented of Major, 'He's one of us you know.' Back came the reply, 'Oh no, he's not, he's one of us.' Major's ability to avoid being categorised was reflected by his canvassers. Pro-European Tories were being reassured of Major's European credentials by the backing he was receiving from the likes of Gummer and Mellor, while an MP who took a sceptical view of the Community was told by Bruce Anderson, the journalist who campaigned for Major, that the Chancellor was more firmly against European integration than Hurd.

By the time the Sunday papers appeared and the lunchtime television interviews were broadcast, most MPs had made up their minds. Heseltine's backing by Carrington, the former foreign secretary and a patrician figure, and by Thatcher's ex-chancellors, Howe and Lawson, was welcome in view of his lack of support from all except one of the cabinet and it also dented, without completely demolishing, the notion that he lacked judgement. But it came too late to have any impact. The coverage of the opinion polls, suggesting that Major would be almost as strong a vote-winner as Heseltine, confirmed the impression which most Tory MPs had gained from their constituency parties. 'Major had achieved in four days what it had taken Heseltine four years to achieve,' commented one of Major's campaign team. On Sunday evening Garel-Jones warned Hurd of the likely result, although he did not tell him his detailed private estimates until the following day.

The strength of Major's support was confirmed by Maude, who applied a rigorous discount to their canvass returns. He adjusted 'firm pledges' downwards by 15 per cent – some said it should be by 20 per cent, but Maude had a sunnier disposition of human nature; 'probables' were adjusted downwards by 50 per cent; and 'possibles' downwards by 75 per cent. Even so, the confidence within the Major camp was such that one of Major's senior campaigners phoned a recent convert that evening 'from the office of the next prime minister'. Major was finally recovering from the after-effects of his operation, and his adrenalin was flowing.

On the final day of the campaign, Monday 26th, the focus shifted back to the Commons, where canvassers patrolled the corridors and tearoom, and the candidates met MPs throughout the day in private one-to-one meetings. But in accordance with the procedures laid down for leadership elections, all sections of the party have to be consulted and their views made known to the executive committee of the 1922 Committee on the Monday before the first and second ballot. The exercise revealed a remarkable degree of support for Major, again reflecting both the spontaneous response and the efforts by his team, notably Ryder and Atkins. By comparison, the Hurd and Heseltine teams had made little effort to 'win' the consultation exercise. Major won the support of 438 of the 490 or so constituency Conservative associations in England and Wales, against only 41 for Heseltine and 16 for Hurd. In Scotland, 37 associations backed Major, 24 Heseltine and 6 were for Hurd. All 10 Northern Ireland associations supported Major. The Young Conservatives and the women's organisation also favoured Major. Tory MEPs, who had backed Heseltine on the first ballot, felt that all three candidates had good European credentials, and only 'business' was reported to back Heseltine. Hurd scored his one success in the Lords. Among those Tory peers who registered their support, Hurd won the support of 45, Major 38 and Heseltine 17.

Tory MPs persisted in their obsession with class. Among the Heseltine team there was concern at yet more pictures over the weekend and in Monday's papers of Heseltine *en famille* at his country estate with 'the green wellies and great gates' while Major was in London in his blazer and flannels appearing as the 'ordinary guy'. Alan Clark, like Hurd an old Etonian, eventually decided to back Major after consulting his constituency party but was surprised to discover widespread unease about Hurd's background among his parliamentary colleagues. Jocularly falling in with the fashion for dissecting social origins, he told a Tory MP from a working-class background who was considering voting for Heseltine, 'I'm going to be a class traitor and vote for Major but you must be true to your class and not vote for a yuppie in green wellies.'

'We're down to the venals,' one Major campaigner told a counterpart on Hurd's team as they organised Monday's procession of MPs trooping to see the candidates for fifteen-minute chats, from morning till late at night. According to the campaign teams of all three candidates, a minority of the electoral college attempted some 'deeply pathetic' attempts to put a price on their votes, 'blathering on about the bypass which they'd always wanted'. One southeast Tory produced a list of eight demands, a Midland MP sought a new wing for a local hospital, another demanded the successful candidate's pledge to speak in his non marginal seat during the election, and a senior backbencher pompously declared, 'I hope if you become leader you will remember that there's a reservoir of talent on the backbenches.' For the most part the one-to-one chats were devoted to the waverers, the probables who needed firming up with a personal word from the candidate or needed to clarify one specific issue, and those who wanted to let their chosen contender know personally of their support.

A former Thatcher die-hard, genuinely undecided on the second ballot, saw all three contenders. He found that Hurd was 'charming, courteous', giving him the impression that 'Major would keep running the economy in the same way' and that the policy on Europe would be 'unchanged apart from the rhetoric'. Major's message was 'similar' but he was 'more aggressive' in his delivery, creating a feeling that the party would have a 'safe ride' but 'whether they were going to Euston or King's Cross wasn't clear'. Heseltine emphasised that he would create 'a government of all the talents' and was 'spilling over with ideas', notably on local government reform, which suggested a 'roller-coaster ride' not dissimilar to the party's experience under Thatcher's leadership.

The outgoing prime minister held a lunch at Number 10 on Monday, inviting what one Downing Street insider called 'her real friends'. Around thirty of her most loyal supporters attended this 'wonderful occasion', a high point in what one of her staff described as 'the awful days' between the announcement of her resignation the previous Thursday and her eventual departure. Guests at her farewell lunch included Lord Joseph, whose conversion to monetarism in 1974 had paved the way for Thatcher's ascent to power, Lord Thorneycroft (her first party chairman), Parkinson, Tebbit and, among members of the No Turning Back group, Brown, Forsyth, Leigh and Portillo. Thatcher took the opportunity to press everybody who had a vote to support Major, telling them that he was the best candidate to ensure that her policies continued.

Yet it seemed that other comments apparently made that day by Thatcher might undermine Major. Before her lunch at Number 10, she had visited Conservative Central Office to say her farewells to the party's staff. Commenting on the Gulf crisis and President Bush, she claimed that she would be a good 'back-seat driver'. But she was subsequently quoted with the implication that she would interfere more generally, an impression which would most damage Major as her preferred candidate. When the *Independent* ran the story as its front-page lead on Tuesday morning, the day of the second ballot, Major's team feared a last-minute loss of support from their start-of-day estimate of 165 votes.

During the previous day, both Major and Heseltine had attempted to squeeze Hurd's vote as the candidate who was trailing third. There had been some sharing of intelligence by the Hurd and Major camps, but there were never any formal pacts. Maude's final estimate of Major's vote was 175. Hurd's vote had oscillated between 55 and 65 votes during the campaign, and Major's team reckoned that in the event of a third ballot their candidate would probably receive between half and two-thirds of Hurd's second preferences.

Heseltine's team knew that Major was in the lead, but thought that by the end of the campaign the result might be too close to be decisive. If Major received around 160 votes and Heseltine took some of Hurd's support, he might secure 150–60 votes and have some hope of winning on the third round. But then Mates, who had returned from the Gulf on Tuesday, inspected the figures and immediately scaled down their estimated total vote. Even so, Heseltine was advised that he would be behind Major on the second ballot 'but not terminally', and he should be able to win most of Hurd's second preferences on the third ballot.

Meanwhile, more big guns were ready to enter on Major's side in the event of a closely run race. Shortly before the count on the second ballot, Wakeham, who had deliberately kept a low profile after Thatcher's withdrawal, consulted Viscount Whitelaw, the Tory elder who remains an astute operator behind his carefully cultivated bluff countenance. Whitelaw had publicly endorsed Hurd and said that Major was too young and untried to become party leader. Wakeham and Whitelaw agreed, however, that Major would win most votes, but it seemed likely that he would fail to win the necessary number, 187, to secure an overall majority. The third ballot would therefore be held, in accordance with the rules, two days later, on Thursday 29th. They discussed what they might do and, with Hurd standing no chance of winning, were both ready to announce their backing for Major soon after the second ballot declaration in order to try to ensure his victory and block Heseltine on the final ballot.

During the afternoon, as voting continued in Commons Committee Room 12, Major slept for a couple of hours in his flat above Number 11, then had a bath and sat around in his dressing gown for the final half-hour or so before preparing to join his supporters downstairs for the result. He was 'quietly confident, though he didn't really let on too much'. As the throng of supporters gathered in the main dining room, Major, now in his shirtsleeves, seemed the most relaxed. A portable television set had been brought into the room, but the reception on it was poor. Suddenly the result was about to come through. Atkins, who had first shared Major's thoughts about becoming party leader on a narrow boat four years earlier, could not bear to catch Major's eye and looked out of the window into the dark evening across Horse Guards Parade. Heseltine's 131 votes was greeted with a great cheer – he had fared worse than expected. Hurd's 56 indicated a very good result for Major, but before people could calculate precisely how good, Onslow declared that he had received 185 votes. Everybody was cheering, but almost immediately checked as they realised that he had missed the target of 187 for an outright win.

Within moments, however, Hurd phoned Major to concede defeat and say that, although he understood that there would have to be a third ballot, he would recommend his supporters to vote for Major. As they spoke, Heseltine appeared on the television screen, standing on the steps of his London home where he had first declared his challenge for the leadership thirteen days earlier. The instant Heseltine had heard the figures he asked Mates what he thought. Mates told him that the maths were hopeless. Heseltine's reaction appeared to be unprepared: he immediately headed down the stairs and out of his front door. Under the rules of the election contest there had to be a third ballot, but he announced that he would advise his supporters to vote for Major in the interests of party unity. Hurd's public announcement of what he had already told Major soon followed.

Thatcher and a few close friends, including Tim Bell, former mastermind of Tory advertising campaigns, Peter Morrison and Wakeham, who had been watching the result in Number 10, walked through the inside passage between numbers 10 and 11 to congratulate Major and join his celebrations. Major took it all very calmly, shaking people by the hand and then donning his jacket in order to go into Downing Street and make his victory statement. Thatcher was keen to accompany him but was dissuaded. Instead, she watched from the window, visible to the cameras below through the net curtains, which she pulled back a little.

The immediate disappointment that the second ballot had failed to produce an outright winner was soon forgotten as Cranley Onslow announced that the third ballot would be abandoned. Few Tories openly questioned his decision, although he was flouting the rules.[4] Constitutionally the Tories never completed the 1990 leadership contest; but traditionally the Tories have not bothered with written rules as far as the party and its leaders are concerned, and many Tory MPs, including Onslow, were plainly irritated by the whole election process. The prevailing mood seemed to be that in the second ballot the party had stumbled on a decision which would restore unity, and it was better to throw away the wretched rule book. In consequence, however, Major was denied the unanimous vote which, presumably, he would have won in the third ballot. Thatcherite die-hards remind anybody who will listen that whereas Major won 185 votes and became leader, Thatcher received 204 votes and yet was forced to resign.

The result was best summed up by Tony Marlow, the Tory MP for Northampton North: 'Michael had the passion, Douglas had the pedigree, but John had the party.' The two main losers were Thatcher and Heseltine, bitter rivals since the Westland affair five years earlier. The great majority of Major's 185 supporters were drawn from Thatcher's votes on the first ballot, and after the second ballot she was able to tell close friends, 'It was everything that I'd ever dreamed of.' Later at the Commons, however, Major's supporters were drinking champagne in the smoking room when in walked Heseltine. He was clapped and cheered.

There was much Tory self-congratulation on the outcome. It allowed Heseltine and Hurd to participate in the unifying process. Loyalty was transferred to the new leader, a process hastened among Tory activists because their choice had won. The week after his second ballot victory, Major was officially endorsed as party leader at the traditional formal gathering of Tory MPs, peers, candidates and representatives of the party in the country. Their queen was dead; long live the king.

The Tories had experienced a severe crisis. Just as doctrinaire Thatcherites and Heseltine's hard-core allies were left to ponder what might have been, other Tories were inclined to view the episode as one in which the party miraculously conjured triumph from near-disaster. Time will tell whether that remains their view. The cabinet's role at the height of the crisis is cited as proof that, in the last resort, the Tories reasserted constitutional propriety.

Portrayal of the contest as a feud between Thatcher and Heseltine is only part of the story. Though her leadership and his ambition were undeniably important ingredients, refuge in the notion of the Tory Party as a tribe, in which nobody quite knows what they are doing or why they are doing it, entertains without informing. November 1990 must be viewed in perspective. It was only the latest in a series of Tory leadership crises. The explanation is to be found in the unique role of the Conservative leader, a creation of Tory values and the party's experience.

4

Tory Democracy

'Government of the people, for the people, with, but not by, the people'.
Leo Amery, the former Tory statesman, on the Tory view of
democracy, 1953

I

As Tory leader, Major has an unrivalled opportunity among British politicians to achieve what he wants. Conservatives vest great authority in their leader. Formally the party is at his disposal. As Thatcher discovered, however, Tories are inclined to dispose of their leaders.

No other party leader is allowed such free rein to determine party policy and distribute party patronage. Party policy is Major's prerogative, as it has been that of every Conservative leader since Sir Robert Peel in the 1830s. The preparation and presentation of the general-election manifesto is the leader's domain. Policy groups are established solely on the leader's authority, their terms of reference and membership dependent on his approval. He is not obliged to accept the views of any policy committee or any resolutions of the annual party conference. In opposition, the subordination of his most senior colleagues is formalised: the Tory shadow cabinet's weekly meetings are properly meetings of the Leader's Consultative Committee.

The party machine is Major's personal office. He appoints the chairman of the Party Organisation and through him controls the party's professional apparatus, Conservative and Unionist Central Office, in Smith Square. The party treasurer, responsible for raising funds, is appointed by the leader. The party's voluntary organisation in the constituencies is coordinated by the National Union, which has traditionally existed to serve the party leadership's aim of winning power.

The corollary of Major's unique authority is that Conservatives hold their leader uniquely responsible. In practice, the exercise of a Tory leader's power is less autocratic than the formal position allows – even the most strong-willed leader has to take some account of opinion among front-bench colleagues, MPs and the party in the country. None the less, there is a parallel with English monarchs: medieval kings possessed more power than their modern counterparts but, as Ian Gilmour has observed, 'almost half of them were murdered, deposed or had to contend with serious revolts at one time or another'.[1]

Of Major's dozen predecessors as Tory leader in the twentieth century, Thatcher was the sixth to fall victim to her party in one way or another. The precise reasons for their going varied, but Balfour in 1911, Austen Chamberlain in 1922, Sir Alec Douglas-Home in 1965 and Edward Heath in 1975 resigned because they either had no alternative or judged that they should stand down as a result of party pressures. Balfour, Douglas-Home and Heath quit in opposition. Austen Chamberlain's resignation destroyed Lloyd George's coalition government. The fifth victim, Neville Chamberlain, resigned as prime minister following a revolt by Tory MPs in 1940, although he continued as party leader until ill health forced his retirement five months later. Thatcher was exceptional in that her resignation as prime minister flowed from her loss of authority as party leader and her presumed defeat in a leadership contest.

Age or ill health accounted for the remaining half a dozen twentieth-century Tory leaders, but three only narrowly escaped being brought down by their party. In the case of Sir Anthony Eden the distinction is very fine since he would almost certainly have been forced out during 1957 had he not resigned through ill health. Harold Macmillan quit in October 1963 for health reasons but his authority as leader had been undermined and he had been on the brink of quitting only days before he was struck down. Stanley Baldwin, who was eventually able to choose his own time of going in 1937, had barely survived the most bitter attacks on his leadership during the 1920s and early 1930s. The unfortunate Andrew Bonar Law was the victim of ill health twice, in 1921 and 1923. The Marquess of Salisbury retired in 1902, as did Sir Winston Churchill in 1955 after doggedly resisting several attempts to persuade him to make way for Eden.

Viewed in the context of their powers and their record of sudden dismissal, the provision for annual re-election of the Tory leader, which was introduced in 1975, appears less as a breath of democratic fresh air and more as an assertion that the leadership is held on leasehold, not freehold. The occupier's rights are undiminished but the leader's status is as tenant, not owner-occupier. This requirement was initially brought in to deal with the specific problem which faced the party in 1974–5, when the Tories had suffered two successive election defeats under Heath's leadership but lacked any mechanism whereby the leader was required to submit himself for re-election. Fifteen years later, the revision facilitated the demise of a leader who had led the party to an unprecedented hat-trick of election victories.

Following Thatcher's downfall, Cranley Onslow, chairman of the back-bench 1922 Committee, initiated a review of the procedure for Tory leadership elections. Some Tories favoured limiting annual leadership elections to periods when the party is in opposition. This rule change would bring the Tories into line with the Labour Party, which has had a formal procedure for annual leadership elections since Ramsay MacDonald, as chairman of the parliamentary party, first assumed the title in 1923, but which does not subject its leader to annual re-election in government even after its substantial rules revision in 1981.

In contrast with their Tory counterparts, Labour leaders are subject to more clearly defined limitations in determining policy and distributing patronage. Revolt has been endemic and there have been attempted coups and imagined plots but fewer Labour leaders have fallen at the hands of their party. Their tenure has been nearer freehold than leasehold. Of Neil Kinnock's eight predecessors since 1923, four resigned from the leadership largely of their own volition: Arthur Henderson, Clem Attlee, Harold Wilson and James Callaghan. Gaitskell died in office. Michael Foot resigned following Labour's shattering defeat in 1983 to make way for Kinnock, his protégé, effectively pre-empting pressures on him to go. MacDonald was stripped of the Labour leadership in 1931 when he continued in Number 10 as prime minister of the Tory-dominated National Government and George Lansbury resigned after the heavy defeat of a pacifist resolution, which he had defended, at the 1936 Labour Party conference.

It is sometimes argued that Thatcher's main legacy is the transformation of the Labour Party. The relative contributions of Thatcher, the defection of Labour's social-democratic wing in 1981, Labour's subsequent election defeats and the sheer force of social change can be analysed at length. The extent and nature of Labour's transformation in terms of presentation and policy is also open to debate. But it would be ironic if Thatcher's final bequest to Labour was a greater readiness to remove leaders who are seen as an electoral liability.

II

Why are Tory leaders granted such powers? The Conservative Party's values and historical experience accord with vesting political authority in its leader. Seventeenth- and eighteenth-century Tory antecedents preceded the first use of the term 'Conservative Party' in 1830. But whatever the date of origin, British government and the Tory Party have evolved together. Both incorporate assumptions and myths which have shaped and reflect the way Britain has been, and still is, governed.

The old Tory belief in a strong monarchy established the idea of a 'centralising, directing, energising body',[2] around which in future years the immense power of the modern cabinet and the prime minister would collect. It constituted a focus in politics as the prize for which factions competed in the eighteenth century and for which modern parties were subsequently to do battle. But its impact was not only organisational. It also acted as a myth, legitimising and shaping the Tory concept of political authority. Samuel Beer has written: 'Something of the older notions of both the monarch's independent authority and of his responsibility for the common good shaped the role of ministry and cabinet.'[3]

Major's advocacy of 'a classless society' as his principal aspiration during the Tory leadership contest was, in one sense, deeply ironic. For the eighteenth-century myth of a governing class has also underpinned the Tory concept of democracy and lies at the heart of the British parliamentary system. Its most eloquent and influential advocate was Edmund Burke. He legitimised the shift in political authority from the Crown to a 'balanced constitution' of Crown, Lords and Commons, dominated by the landed and the wealthy. He believed in a hierarchic body politic which would engender a 'habitual social discipline, in which the wiser, the more expert, and the more opulent conduct, and by conducting enlighten and protect, the weaker, the less knowing, and the less provided with the goods of fortune'.[4] When he spoke of the 'people' acting as a check on the royal prerogative, or praised the role of the House of Commons, Burke envisaged the people's views being expressed through a Commons controlled by great Whig families, whom he identified as society's natural leaders, 'the natural strength of the kingdom: the great peers, the leading landed gentlemen, the opulent merchants and manufacturers, the substantial yeomanry'.[5]

The governing class defended by Burke seems a far cry from the modern House of Commons or from a Tory Party in which its three leaders elected under the procedures adopted in 1965 have been the son of a craftsman carpenter, the daughter of a grocer and the son of a one-time circus artist. Yet Burke's guiding principle remains largely intact. Addressing his Bristol constituents in 1774, he argued; 'If government were a matter of will upon any side, yours, without question, ought to be superior. But government and legislation are matters of reason and judgement, and not of inclination.'[6]

His words are still quoted as the classic justification of parliamentary democracy. Members of Parliament effectively remain a governing class, elected to exercise their best judgement, not to carry out a mandate. In the age of mass democracy and party manifestos, there is inevitably tension between Burke's view of MPs as representatives and the notion of MPs as delegates of the people. Although the latter assumption has a pedigree dating back to Cromwellian times and is strongly, but not exclusively, echoed on the Labour left, Burke's view is predominant.

Burke's spirit makes guest appearances during Tory leadership contests. The Tories entrust the final decision to their MPs, unlike the case under Labour's leadership election rules, which were revised in 1981 to extend the electoral college to include trade unions and constituency Labour parties, and unlike the Liberal Democrats, whose leader is elected by the party membership. Although the Tory procedure requires that all sections of the party are consulted, their views are irrelevant to the result. In 1975, for example, Heath was endorsed by the party in the country and by Tory peers on the first ballot, but all that mattered was that most Tory MPs had voted for Thatcher.

The leadership selection procedure also specifically enjoins constituency associations 'represented by Conservative Members of Parliament, to inform the Member of their views regarding the candidates'. Tory MPs, however, are not bound by the views of their local party members. Any pressures to delegate Tory MPs are, in the main, stoutly resisted, and during the November 1990 contest, Burke's letter to his Bristol constituents was again cited in defence of MPs' duty to reach their own judgement. There were only odd cases, such as Dr Rhodes Boyson, the MP for Brent North, who agreed to vote in November 1990 according to the wishes of his local association's executive committee. If all Tory MPs had been mandated by their constituency activists on the first ballots in 1975 and 1990 when an incumbent leader was challenged, neither Thatcher nor Major would have been elected leader. In 1975, Heath received the support of up to 90 per cent of constituency associations before the first ballot, and in 1990 Thatcher was reported to have received the same level of support. The readiness with which the vast majority of party activists transferred their loyalty to the new leader is telling.

Burke's influence on the Conservative Party is pervasive, and goes much deeper than rationalising the present procedure for electing the party leader. Burke provides the philosophical underpinning for Tory paternalism and pragmatism. His riposte to radicals who championed the French Revolution was later taken as the basis for the party's claim to govern. Rejecting a narrowly reactionary approach, he argued that society was evolutionary. Revolutionary change would prove disastrous but some reforms were necessary from time to time if institutions were to

84

PAPA COBDEN TAKING MASTER ROBERT A FREE TRADE WALK.

PAPA COBDEN.— "Come along, MASTER ROBERT, do step out."
MASTER ROBERT.— "That's all very well, but you know I cannot go so fast as you do."

Richard Cobden, champion of free trade, drags an anxious Robert Peel, then Conservative prime minister, towards repeal of the protectionist Corn Laws.

survive the natural process of social change: 'A state without the means of some change is without the means of its conservation.' But what change? And when should change be made? This onerous duty falls to Burke's governing class. Their only guidance is that change should accord with the traditions of society. Judgement and wisdom are all.

Burke's pragmatic conservatism was echoed in 1834 by the new Conservative Party leader, Sir Robert Peel, whose 'Tamworth Manifesto' committed the party to modern reform. Conservatives had opposed the 1832 Reform Act but had to adjust or face political extinction. Peel acknowledged 'the challenge of his [Whig] opponents that a minister must accept the Reform Bill and act in its spirit'. If acting in the 'spirit' of the 1832 Act entailed 'abandoning altogether that great aid of government – more powerful than either law or reason – the respect for ancient rights and the deference to prescriptive authority', he maintained that the cost would be unacceptably high.

> But if the spirit of the Reform Bill implies merely a careful review of institutions, civil and ecclesiastical, undertaken in a friendly temper, combining with the firm maintenance of established rights the correction of proved abuses and the redress of real grievances – in that case I can for myself and my colleagues undertake to act in such a spirit and with such intentions.[7]

Peel had staked his party's claim to pragmatic conservatism and in 1841 led the Conservatives to their first outright election victory since the reform of the franchise. But the party remained the political home of many who were more concerned to protect 'established rights' than they were to see what their leader might regard as 'the correction of proved abuses and the redress of real grievances'. Such a conflict led to Peel's downfall in 1846 when he was unable to carry his own party with him on the repeal of the protectionist Corn Laws. Although he had become convinced that repeal was necessary and would remove one of the radicals' most emotive political targets, he was defeated by the majority of landed interests who dominated his party. The split shattered the party. The Conservatives were condemned to six successive election defeats and twenty-eight years in opposition, interrupted by brief interludes of minority government, until they eventually won an overall majority at the 1874 election. After Peel's defeat, who would assume the mantle of the Conservative Party? The party's name and resources became the inheritance of the anti-Peelites as Peelites diminished in number through death or, like Gladstone, joined forces with other groups and eventually formed the Liberal Party. Three years after the Conservative Party's split, Benjamin Disraeli emerged as the new Tory leader in the Commons, although the party leader was acknowledged to be the Earl of Derby until his retirement in 1868.

Disraeli had initially welcomed the 'Tamworth Manifesto', but, having been denied office in Peel's 1841 government, he wrote in his novel *Coningsby* that it 'was an attempt to construct a party without principles: its basis therefore was necessarily latitudinarianism; and its inevitable consequence has been Political Infidelity'.[8] Yet Disraeli's own pragmatism, not to say opportunism, as leader from 1868 until his death in 1881 was to prompt similar charges and worse. Claims to pragmatic conservatism and accusations of being unprincipled are two sides of the same coin. Every Conservative leader since Peel has led a party whose underlying rationale is the exercise of political authority but which provides scant guidance on the specific ends to which that authority should be directed.

Under Disraeli's leadership the Conservative Party adjusted to the significant extension of the franchise in 1867 and became a party of government as it had been under Peel after the more limited reform of 1832. Disraeli had long espoused the notion of 'natural leaders' in society and his restatement of the paternalist tradition created a legitimising myth which has been echoed by successive generations of progressive, reformist Conservative politicians from Lord Randolph Churchill in the 1880s to Peter Walker in the 1980s. The Disraelian concept of 'one nation' was taken as the title of the ginger group which was created by Tory MPs first elected in the 1950 Parliament and which included Iain Macleod, Enoch Powell, Edward Heath, Robert Carr and Angus Maude.

The power of the Disraelian myth is explicable through its moralistic appeal. The privileged had a duty not only to lead, but to lead with a sense of social responsibility. They could expect to retain the trust of the people only by acting in accordance with their responsibilities. The ethical element was coupled with self-interest: 'the palace is not safe, when the cottage is not happy'. The old Tory notion of strong political authority was emphasised – in order to fulfil their duty to others, political leaders had to be able to take strong action through the state.

Disraelian paternalism countered, as opposed to rejecting entirely, classical liberal *laissez-faire* beliefs. But as a result of the second Reform Act's extension of the franchise to urban householders – a reform which Disraeli's opportunism had helped to bring about – the 1868 election saw what Lord Blake has described as 'the beginning of a slow move of both the world of business and that of suburban villadom away from the Liberal party'.[9] These new supporters were not ideologues who would suffuse the Conservative Party with the pure doctrine of *laissez faire*, but their business and middle-class interests and values increasingly influenced the party over the next forty years. Their rise was symbolised in November 1911 when a middle-class Scottish businessman, Andrew Bonar Law, became party leader. Wealthy landowners who had previously backed the Liberals also shifted their allegiance to the Conservatives. This process received an impetus after 1885 when the Whigs were the main losers from the Redistribution of Seats Act, which drastically cut the number of two-member constituencies. Liberal seats had usually been represented by one Whig and one Radical member, but in the new single-member seats Radicals were preferred. In 1886 Gladstone's support for Home Rule split the Liberal Party, leading to the secession of the Liberal Unionists, who included the Radical Joseph Chamberlain, and the Whig Lord Hartington. The alliance between Conservatives and Unionists was the foundation on which Tories held office for most of the next twenty years.

The net effect of these changes was that the tradition of economic liberalism transferred to the Conservative benches, while the Liberal Party became more closely identified with radical liberalism. But the notion of a 'transfer' is misleading: 'restoration' would be a better term because Tories, since the days of Pitt the Younger in the 1780s, had espoused liberal economics and Peel's disciples had been founders of the Liberal Party. Paternalist and liberal strands have intertwined in Tory thinking for the past two centuries.

The enfranchisement of the working class between 1867 and 1928 presented a serious challenge to a party predominantly committed to defending the interests of the propertied and business classes. Disraeli's social reforms after 1874 were designed to persuade the new urban voters, his 'angels in marble', to support the Conservatives. Joseph Chamberlain, architect of 'gas and water' socialism as a Radical, developed the scheme of 'tariff reform' designed to consolidate the British Empire against American and German competition, thereby assisting the working-class voter through industrial protection and providing money for social reform. The clash with Tory free-traders threatened to split the party in the early 1900s and rumbled on as a recurring debate for decades.

Stanley Baldwin, Tory leader in the 1920s and 1930s, answered the challenge by seeking an accommodation with Labour instead of class strife. In the mid-1940s the free-market theories of Friedrich von Hayek inspired many Tories, including Thatcher, then a student at Oxford, but Butler and Macmillan developed a paternalism in tune with the postwar welfare-state consensus. Although the Tory bonfire of regulations after 1951 was rooted in events it owed more to liberalism than paternalism. After 1979 one of Thatcher's colleagues, Sir John Nott, commented that her government was really about 'nineteenth-century liberalism', yet public spending on the welfare state increased in real terms during Thatcher's premiership.[10]

Both liberal and paternalist strands have provided Tories with an extensive menu of arguments and myths around which to construct their appeal for winning and maintaining office. Of the thirty-one general elections since the 1867 Reform Act, the Conservatives have won sixteen, and have ruled either alone or in coalition for 78 of those 124 years. Over the 45 years since 1945, they have governed for 28. A large part of the Tories' success can be attributed to splits among their opponents, but by the same token it is a measure of the Tories' survival instinct that they have avoided a ruinous division since the mid-nineteenth century. Their unrivalled record of holding office underpins both their claim to competence and their belief that they are the natural party of government.

The Tory view of democracy remains true to the tradition of Burke. Leo Amery, a former Conservative cabinet minister, summed up modern Tory democracy in the words quoted at the head of this chapter.[11] It is not government 'by the people' because their role is largely limited to choosing between the competing alternatives presented by the leaders of the government and the opposition: 'alternative records, alternative promises, and especially alternative teams of leaders'. Authority is vested in political leaders, subject only to periodic review. It is a view that permeates the Tory Party.

III

During the nineteenth century the party leader was generally the politician who had last been commissioned by the monarch to form an administration, i.e. the prime minister or the last serving prime minister. This convention lies at the root of a Tory leader's power but has caused confusion about who was 'party leader'. In 1881, when the Conservatives were in opposition and the last serving Conservative prime minister, Lord Beaconsfield (Disraeli) died, there followed a period of dual leadership under Sir Stafford Northcote, the Conservative leader in the Commons, and Lord Salisbury, the leader in the Lords.

The reluctance to formalise the position exacerbated the leadership crises in government as recently as 1963, when the absence of an accepted and open selection procedure led to accusations that the Tory succession was decided by a 'magic circle'. The party finally adopted a formal selection procedure for its leader in 1965. The November 1990 leadership contest was the first occasion on which the resignation of a Tory prime minister was brought about by a formal vote of Tory MPs, although Lloyd George resigned in October 1922 following the vote by Tory MPs at the Carlton Club calling for an end to their coalition with the Liberals.

The Conservative Party's adjustment to successive extensions of the franchise has created tensions within the party. But it largely remains a 'top down' party, in which a parliamentary leadership has sought to mobilise support in the country, unlike Labour, which emerged as a political party from a mass movement. Tories reject the idea of the party outside Parliament playing anything more than a primarily supportive role. The parliamentary party is the driving force and the leader is at the steering wheel.

From the mid-1830s Conservative prime ministers, or putative prime ministers, became the focus of party organisation outside Parliament as a political adjunct to their constitutional role of being commissioned by the monarch to form an administration. Unless they were able to command sufficient support in the Commons, they would be unable to meet the monarch's commission. Electoral reform prompted the development of the rudimentary party organisation and the subsequent recognition of a voluntary party in the country. Their purpose was to deliver the requisite number of parliamentary seats. The first use of the title 'Conservative Party' heralded neither a wholly new beginning nor something radically different from what had gone before. The title dates from the *Quarterly Review* of January 1830, and within a few years was being repeated as if it was a well-established expression.[12] But the continuity is more striking than any change. The party's title was invented before the debacle suffered by those who opposed the first Reform Act in 1832, and the replacement of the Duke of Wellington as leader by Peel in 1834 did not mark a clean break. Those to whom the new title applied were the Tories, including Peel, the political descendants of the Pittites, followers of the Younger Pitt.

Reform in the early 1830s prompted the Conservative Party's first organisational response to the process of democratic change. In an age when few constituency elections had been contested and the patronage of a relatively small number of families was the key to a career in Parliament, there had been little need for any party organisation apart from the whips' office. Clubs like Brook's (largely Whig), White's (with no clear political leaning) and Boodle's were the main informal meeting places for the party leaders outside Parliament. Rather more formal meetings were held at premises in Charles Street, off St James's Square. It was at this house, as the reform agitation increased, that it was decided to establish a political club for Conservatives. After an abortive attempt in 1831, the club subsequently known as the Carlton (its first premises were 2 Carlton House Terrace) was established in March 1832.

The Carlton Club was soon being referred to as 'the headquarters of the party organisation'. Its initially amateurish bureaucracy coordinated party activity and was primarily concerned with the parliamentary side. It also helped fill the gap which had existed between local associations and Westminster – the importance of the registration clauses in the 1832 Reform Act led to the growth of local associations, whose principal task was to get electors on or off the register. During elections, party officials in the Carlton scrutinised the electoral rolls, and between elections they encouraged local parties to keep up with the vital work of electoral registration. The Carlton also provided a point of contact for the leading provincial party members and the parliamentary party.

During Peel's time as party leader, the party organisation consisted of three main elements: the chief whip; an election committee, which had been set up for the 1835 election to coordinate arrangements for registration and which continued thereafter; and F. R. Bonham, Peel's great party organiser, who had his desk at the Carlton and 'arranged for candidates, sought subscriptions, organised elections, and reported the gossip of the day to his master'. In 1841 his efforts helped the Conservatives win a 76-seat majority over all other parties, but this was to be their only outright victory during the thirty-five years between the 1832 and 1867 Reform Acts. The party's rudimentary organisation was thrown into chaos in 1846 by the split over the Corn Laws. The poor performance of the anti-Peelite Conservatives in the 1847 and 1852 elections prompted Disraeli, who had emerged as their leader in the Commons in 1849, to intervene in the party organisation. Bonham's post was revived, with responsibility for managing the party outside Parliament given to an agent, Philip Rose, Disraeli's solicitor, and later to a principal agent, Spofforth, who was a member of Rose's law firm. The 1867 Reform Act heralded a new age of mass democracy, doubling the size of the electorate to around 2 million. The Conservative Party's organisational response mirrored its response to the first Reform Act. The leadership was not shaken into action until after defeat in the 1868 election but the new party institutions created by Disraeli have survived to the present day, recognisable in their form and function.

The circumstances surrounding the formation of the National Union of Conservative and Constitutional Associations in 1867 and of Conservative Central Office three years later illustrated the nature of the relationship between the leadership and the party outside Parliament. The National Union received little initial support from the leadership: sixty-seven representatives from fifty-five cities attended the inaugural meeting, but there were no members of the government – the deferential tone of the occasion is illustrated by the fact that John Gorst, MP took the chair only in the absence of a peer. Not only was the leadership cool, so too were many local associations, who feared a loss of independence.

In 1870, however, Gorst was appointed principal agent of the party. The party bureaucracy moved into new offices in Parliament Street, which by the end of 1871 were generally known as Central Office. When Gorst also became secretary of the National Union in 1871 and transferred its headquarters to Central Office, the National Union 'became in practice what it had always really been in theory, the propaganda arm of the Conservative Central Office'.[13] Disraeli gave the National Union the seal of respectability by choosing it as the audience for his great Crystal Palace speech in 1872, and from that point on the National Union became 'an integral part of the Central Office organisation and was used by the party leaders as a mouthpiece and as an organisational front for popular demonstrations'.[14] The National Union had thus assumed its role as the main body through which the leadership could organise the party's voluntary workers.

The classic statement on the National Union's origins and role is that made by one of its founders, H. C. Raikes, MP, speaking at its 1873 annual conference: 'The Union has been organised rather as a handmaid to the party, than to usurp the functions of party leadership.' Yet ten years later, the role which the leadership had allotted to its voluntary workers, and which the National Union had accepted for itself, received the strongest challenge in the party's history.

The crisis was sparked off by the Conservative defeat in the 1880 election. The formation in 1877 of the National Liberal Federation suggested the Liberals had stolen a march on the Conservatives' organisation, despite all the criticism of 'caucus' politics which Joseph Chamberlain's new model of party democracy had attracted. There was growing criticism within the National Union, principally from the party bigwigs in the provinces and the influx of new middle-class supporters. Although there were no demands to interfere with policy, they complained that they were not being sufficiently consulted and not enough was being done to make the constituency associations effective. The death of the party leader, Lord Beaconsfield, in 1881 added to the confusion.

It was against this background that Lord Randolph Churchill attempted to democratise the party and transfer control of policy and finance to the National Union. Churchill's motivations are unclear – partly dissatisfaction with the performance of Sir Stafford Northcote as leader of the party in the Commons, and probably also his own ambition to be regarded as a senior party figure, or whatever. For all the rhetoric, after only a few years he lost interest in the National Union.

At the October 1883 annual conference, Churchill, a vice-president of the National Union, supported the call to secure for the National Union 'its legitimate influence in the party organisation'. He advocated that its council should control the party organisation and finances. He entered into protracted negotiations with the Marquess of Salisbury, party leader in the House of Lords, to secure these objectives, but 'throughout the negotiations Lord Salisbury never showed the slightest disposition to grant the National Union effective control over policy, finance or candidates'.[15] Churchill lost on every count, although he had established himself among the party hierarchy. Salisbury's reforms were limited. He scrapped the Central Committee, which Beaconsfield had originally set up to investigate the 1880 defeat and which had become the cause of much ill will among party workers. He also established a new provincial structure for the National Union and sought to meet the complaints from local associations about lack of consultation on organisational matters.

The Conservative Party leadership had come through its most serious brush with demands for party democracy unscathed. The vast majority of the party's own members had sought to challenge their leader's prerogative. The leader's relations, and those of the parliamentary party, with the party organisation were unaffected. In the words of Sir Winston Churchill, the National Union was 'peacefully laid to rest'. Although from 1885 the National Union was granted the right to pass resolutions dealing with current political issues, the leadership's control of the party was effected through a triumvirate consisting of the leader (Lord Salisbury), the chief whip (Akers-Douglas) and the principal agent ('Captain' Middleton).

The Tory party faithful have often appeared more docile than their counterparts in other parties, though never as markedly as during the Salisbury–Middleton years. The relative peace, however, has been punctuated by periodic explosions. Between 1903 and 1905 Joseph Chamberlain, founder of the Birmingham 'caucus' during his days as a Liberal, mounted a formidable challenge and sought to capture the National Union on the issues of tariff reform and greater party democracy. He succeeded, but Central Office remained loyal to the party leader, Arthur Balfour, who reputedly commented that 'he would as soon take advice from his valet as he would from a Conservative annual conference'. The main result of the party reforms introduced after the party's 1906 defeat was to give greater autonomy to the National Union.

The Conservative Party institutionalised its 'top down' bias. In the twentieth century the pressures associated with modern government and party politics have strengthened the power of the leader. The party in the country, however, is an indispensable source of support if the party is to win and maintain office. It is in this role, rather than in actively seeking to impose policy on the leadership, that Tory activists wield influence. It is a more indirect influence than in other parties, but it is real enough.

IV

Questions about the role and effectiveness of Tory Party organisation and the party in the country have invariably been prompted by heavy electoral defeat. In the wake of the 1945 debacle, the party's structure was modernised along lines which have largely continued to the present day. The reforms confirmed the party machine as being responsible to the leader, not to the parliamentary party or the party membership. The overhaul of Conservative Central Office created a professional organisation to service the party in the country. The Conservative Research Department developed an enhanced role and the Conservative Political Centre was created to organise political education. A review of the party in the country, chaired by David Maxwell-Fyfe (later Lord Kilmuir), recommended the abolition of unlimited contributions by candidates to their election expenses, thus reducing the purchase of parliamentary constituencies and improving the prospects for career politicians.

Major's power is exercised principally through his appointment of the party chairman, a post first created in 1911 when it had become clear, after successive election defeats, that the chief whip was unable any longer effectively to organise both the party in Parliament and the party outside. Of the six party chairmen who served Thatcher, Lord Thorneycroft (1975–81) was a member of the shadow cabinet but not the cabinet after 1979, and Gummer (1983–5) was outside the cabinet. But Parkinson (1981–3), Tebbit (1985–7), Brooke (1987–9) and Baker (1989–90) were cabinet ministers – Parkinson also served in the small war cabinet during the 1982 Falklands crisis, a remarkable appointment which reflected Thatcher's trust in him as a close political ally. Major's first appointment as chairman, Chris Patten, also holds cabinet rank.

The party chairman's formal title, which is chairman of the Party Organisation, properly defines his role as the head of Central Office and distinguishes it from that of a representative of the party in the country. Yet some Tory, notably the Charter group, have called for the election of the party chairman by party members. But Central Office remains the personal office of the Tory leader, a point spelled out by Baker, Thatcher's last party chairman, during the 1990 leadership contest. Although stating in his memorandum to Central Office staff that 'It is not appropriate for Conservative Central Office to seek to interfere in the parliamentary party exercising its responsibilities', he stressed that 'we are the office of the leader of the party and support her unreservedly'.[16]

Policy-making is entirely the leader's responsibility, since he appoints policy groups and approves their membership. He also appoints the chairman and deputy chairman of the Advisory Committee on Policy, which includes representatives of the National Union, but the committee reports to him and is merely a sounding board. The Conservative Research Department, which Thatcher brought under the control of the party chairman within Central Office, services the work of policy groups, provides briefings for the parliamentary party, and acts as a secretariat to back-bench committees of Tory MPs and also to the leader and the shadow cabinet when the party is in opposition.

Any Tory leader's policy-making prerogative is constrained because the process generally operates through consultation and discussion. The opinions of the cabinet or shadow cabinet, the parliamentary party and the wider party beyond, all have to be taken into account. None the less, the balance is more heavily tilted in the leader's favour than in other parties, and Tory leaders have exploited their prerogative to dictate party policy. Thatcher's comments on television rewrote immigration policy in 1978 and before the 1987 election her determination to press ahead with abolition of domestic rates was pushed through with little consultation.

The leader's other personal appointees in Central Office, the deputy and vice-chairmen, have the same executive responsibilities for key functions as in any modern mass party – including publicity, political education, youth and women's sections, links with ethnic groups, local government and industrial activity, party finance and parliamentary candidature. The party treasurer is directly responsible to the leader. He is assisted by a Central Board of Finance, which is responsible to the chairman. The failure to publish detailed accounts is symptomatic of a party which has never been democratised and in which the professional organisation still operates as the leader's personal office.

The leader looks to the party chairman for guidance on the views of the membership, but the National Union is technically independent of the professional staff in Central Office. Since 1871, however, when Gorst brought the National Union under the same roof as Central Office, the latter has kept a close eye on the activities of the party in the country. In the words of Maxwell-Fyfe, its role is to 'advise . . . to assist . . . to provide all possible help'. Party members belong to constituency associations, and the lack of a centralised membership hinders efforts by Central Office to reach all supporters with computerised direct mailings of party propaganda and financial appeals. The annual party conference is the National Union's conference and, as such, is chaired not by the chairman of the Party Organisation but by that year's elected chairman of the National Union, one of the party's senior voluntary workers.

The vice-chairman responsible for parliamentary candidates is assisted by the Standing Advisory Committee on Parliamentary Candidates, which is responsible for circulating a list of 'approved candidates' to the constituency associations. Tory associations jealously guard their independence over the choice of parliamentary candidates from the National Union and Central Office. In practice the vast majority of constituency party 'selectorates' do not seek to choose a candidate who would upset the leadership. Their prejudices generally inform but they can intrude, as happened in the winter of 1990–91 with the challenge, albeit ultimately unsuccessful, to the selection of John Taylor, the black candidate in Cheltenham. The Maxwell-Fyfe Report confirmed, perhaps more tellingly than the authors intended, the subordinate position of the party membership in the Conservative Party:

The functions of the National Union are primarily deliberative and advisory. Its various representatives in the Areas and at the Centre enable the collective opinion of the Party to find expression. Its views are conveyed to the Leader of the Party or the Chairman of the Party Organisation as may be necessary and convenient. The opinions of the Executive Committee are sought from time to time on matters of policy connected with organisation, political education and propaganda.[17]

In contrast to Major, Labour's Neil Kinnock and the Liberal Democrats' Paddy Ashdown have nothing like such a free rein in dealing with their party members. Labour and the Liberal Democrats embrace, to varying degrees, the concept of party democracy.

The Labour Party gives strongest endorsement to party democracy, reflecting the party's origins – as the Tories reflect theirs. Labour's origins created a 'bottom up' party, since it emerged from the extra-parliamentary labour movement and the parliamentary party was formed as an adjunct to secure representation in Parliament. Power is thus seen to lie with, and to flow from, the movement and the party in the country. In the purist view, as advocated most forcibly by Tony Benn, the parliamentary party and leader are delegates of the wider movement, responsible to the Labour Party annual conference, which is effectively the parliament of the labour movement and should therefore determine policy. Kinnock's great achievement during the 1980s was to establish his authority as Labour leader in the party outside Parliament, a process symbolised by his scathing criticism of the hard-left Militant Tendency and their supporters at the 1985 annual party conference.

The Liberal Democrats possess elements of 'top down' and 'bottom up', as did their founding partners, the long-established Liberal Party and the relatively infant Social Democratic Party. The annual Liberal Assembly periodically flexed its muscles, as for example when it voted against the Alliance's defence policy at Eastbourne in September 1986, a revolt which proved damaging to the Alliance's performance at the general election nine months later. The origins of the SDP, created by four senior politicians who quit the Labour Party, marked it as the ultimate 'top down' party, although its structures, if not always its leadership style, attempted to reflect the founding fathers' democratic objectives. The authority bestowed upon a Conservative or Labour leader through their position as prime minister or potential prime minister is denied Ashdown, as it has been denied every Liberal leader since Lloyd George.

The charge that the Conservative Party is 'undemocratic' is met with the argument that the leadership is influenced by party members through informal pressures, as opposed to the other parties' formal democratic procedures, and that there is a two-way flow of information in the party.

These claims have some validity. No leader would seek to antagonise or ignore completely the membership because if they are unenthusiastic prospects for mobilising the party's electoral support will be damaged.

Information flows in both directions between the party at the centre and constituency associations, the regional or 'area' bodies, various sections of the party and the National Union's annual Central Council meeting. The Conservative Political Centre, based in Central Office, circulates discussion briefs and arranges constituency-based meetings, seminars and conferences – although the pamphlets which it publishes carry the nervous disclaimer that the views expressed do not necessarily represent party policy. These regular opportunities for party members to express their views enable activists to exert some indirect influence on party policy despite their lack of formal power to enforce their wishes.

Until 1965 Conservative leaders did not attend the party conference but would descend on the day after the conference had officially ended to address a mass rally of the party faithful. Heath was the first leader to attend and listen to conference debates. The 3,000 or more party representatives (not delegates) attending their annual conference are less deferential than in the 1950s, although in those days 'empire loyalists' and 'hangers and floggers' gave Rab Butler a tough time. Most Tory conference representatives, however, patently regard the occasion 'primarily as a demonstration of party solidarity and of enthusiasm for its leaders'. This was never better demonstrated than at the 1986 conference, which was successfully orchestrated by the party chairman, Norman Tebbit, and his Central Office advisers as a launch pad for the next general election campaign. Their plan was to counter the impression which had developed since the Westland crisis at the start of the year that the government lacked any sense of direction. Their operation was one of the most explicit displays of the century-old relationship between Central Office and the National Union, in which the former is able to use the latter as a 'propaganda arm'. The conference slogan was 'The Next Move Forward'. The weekend before the conference, full-page advertisements were placed in the Sunday newspapers hailing the government's reputed success on inflation, strikes, income tax and economic growth. These advertisements were strategically placed round the main conference hotels, principally to reassure the party faithful – many representatives asked for copies to take back to their constituencies. Ministerial speeches were coordinated and drafted with the express aim of building up an image of a party bursting with new ideas and proposals. The conference helped revive Tory morale and appeared to reinforce the Tories' improved ratings in the opinion polls.

The great bulk of motions submitted for debate at the conference are laudatory of the leadership's efforts. Criticism tends to be reserved for presentation rather than the substance of policy. The bland motions chosen are generally representative of the vast majority which are submitted. These motions are almost invariably passed unanimously, or with overwhelming majorities, although since 1967 there has been provision for a ballot to be held if it was demanded by a substantial minority of the conference. Another innovation, the 'balloted motions', enables representatives at the conference to vote for debates on two areas not selected for debate on the formal agenda, and also to vote for the motions within their chosen areas.

The Tory conference has directly determined party policy on only one occasion, in 1950, during a housing debate. But the initiative stemmed from a small group of MPs, including Harmar Nicholls, whose proposal to the leadership that the party should promise at the next election to build 300,000 houses a year had previously been rebuffed. The MPs organised representatives to shout out '300,000' during the debate. When the platform failed to accept the target, the official report notes that there was 'uproar', but the party chairman, Lord Woolton, saw the electoral appeal of the 300,000 target and intervened to endorse it. At the mass rally on the day following the conference Churchill accepted the target as party policy. After the 1951 election victory, Macmillan was given the task of implementing it and, although he had hoped for a more senior cabinet post than housing, it launched him as a future contender for the leadership.

But the conference is not a policy-making body. Its influence is more indirect, and has more impact when the party is in opposition and the leadership needs to regain support. The conference acts as one factor among many which spur or constrain policy. In the late 1960s, the Tories' loss of office, Heath's launching of radical policy ideas, his own difficulty in establishing his authority as opposition leader and Powell's populist appeal after Heath sacked him from the shadow cabinet in April 1968, all combined to make the conference a more challenging occasion for Heath. His decision to attend the debates strengthened its legitimacy.

In the late 1970s and early 1980s a number of front-bench party spokesmen had a rough ride at the hands of the conference. In 1978 John Davies, then shadow foreign secretary, was harangued by representatives during his speech on Rhodesia. The same issue erupted at the following year's conference, when the new foreign secretary, Lord Carrington, had to bear the brunt of a strong attack from the right wing. Tackling the power of the trade unions also generated considerable heat when Jim (later Lord) Prior had to repulse strong criticism of his 'step-by-step' gradualist approach at the 1977, 1979 and 1980 conferences. Similarly, Willie (later Viscount) Whitelaw endured fierce attacks as home secretary in 1980 when he sought to defend government policy on law and order.

Critics of the party line during Thatcher's early years sensed that they were voicing their leader's sentiments more accurately than some of the party's official spokesmen. And not without reason, for in the law-and-order debate Thatcher had applauded a representative who demanded the return of capital punishment, provoking a furious private riposte from her home secretary after the debate. The most dramatic challenge to Thatcher came in 1981, not from the party faithful but from her predecessor, Edward Heath, who spoke from the floor during the main debate on economic policy.

The conference controversies of the late 1970s and early 1980s were a reflection of Thatcher's initial inability to establish her authority over her senior colleagues. But party activists felt that she shared their instincts on a range of issues, and, as the party chalked up successive election victories during the 1980s, her dominance became complete. What remains to be seen is how the conference responds to Major, whose social liberalism is not shared by a sizeable section of Tory activists. Much will depend on whether he proves an election winner.

As the annual Tory conference has become a media event, unofficial 'fringe' meetings have proliferated. In part, this reflects the debate and flow of ideas which has developed in the party over the past thirty years through the impact of Tory groups like the liberal-inclined Bow Group, the traditionalist Monday Club, the right-wing Selsdon Group and the left-wing Tory Reform Group. Yet the different strands of Toryism tend to remain relatively muffled and muted within the conference hall. Apart from a few star turns on the fringe, like Heseltine between 1986 and 1990, who attract great media interest, Tories with a contribution to make to party debate are marginalised – one notable example in 1990 being John Biffen, who delivered a little-reported but thoughtful speech on Europe. This problem points to a flaw at the heart of Tory democracy. The terms of debate in the party are severely constrained. Dependence on informal pressures and a 'hidden conference system' has its virtues, not least the impression created of a party united behind its leader. But the risks are considerable. Policy is not fully aired or openly debated. The leader can become out of touch.

V

The perils for a Tory leader who grows out of touch with the parliamentary party are severe, since Tory MPs determine his or her fate. The channels of communication between leader and MPs have evolved and reflect 'Tory democracy' in which the only formal constraint on the leader is periodic review of his or her tenure of office. The leader's main source of influence over Tory MPs are his power of patronage and his call on their loyalty. The former has become extensive during the twentieth century. The latter is often described in the words of Lord Kilmuir, the former Tory Lord Chancellor, who thirty years ago claimed that loyalty was the Tories' 'secret weapon'.[18] As Thatcher discovered, however, loyalty is a weapon which can be turned against the leader.

The curiously titled 1922 Committee is the principal mechanism through which collective Tory back-bench opinion is expressed and communicated to the leader. But it has also enabled the leader to influence and contain back-bench opinion, isolating the extremes, and rallying and maintaining the support of the majority of Tory MPs who want to see their leader and the party succeed. Any back-bench MP in receipt of the Conservative whip is able to attend its meetings, which are usually held every Thursday evening when the Commons is in session. Its meetings often last little more than a quarter of an hour, but longer when MPs are concerned about a particular issue.

The 1922 Committee is not, as is often stated, the direct descendant of the famous meetings of Conservative MPs held at the Carlton Club in October 1922, at which Austen Chamberlain was defeated and forced to resign as leader. This incorrect supposition, however, largely explains why the '22, as it is often called, is frequently referred to in awe-struck or conspiratorial tones, as though it is uniquely powerful and its principal *raison d'être* is to tell the party leader to resign. Reality is more prosaic.

Although the crisis of October 1922 persuaded some Tory MPs that the parliamentary party required more formal organisation, this was not the purpose of the original 1922 Committee.[19] It was not formed until after the November 1922 election, and did not hold its first meeting until April 1923. Initially it consisted exclusively of Conservative MPs who had first entered the Commons at that election and existed to provide the new intake with guidance on Parliament and party policy. But following the Conservatives' defeat in the December 1923 election, the '22 felt that as back-bench MPs they had been 'left too much in the dark regarding the purposes and policies of the Government'. They sought a meeting with the new leader, Stanley Baldwin, who had succeeded Bonar Law in May 1923, and pressed for 'regular party meetings under the chairmanship of the Leader or some deputy appointed by him'. Baldwin refused on the grounds that 'Party meetings would be a mistake, mainly because of the inevitable leakage to the press'. Following this rebuff, the format emerged over the next couple of years which still operates today. Membership of the 1922 Committee was extended to all Conservative MPs, and a whip began attending its meetings and reporting to the leader.

The chairman of the 1922 Committee has direct access to the party leader and is responsible for organising the annual leadership election.

The 1922 Committee chairman also faces annual re-election in the opening weeks of each new parliamentary session. In addition to electing the chairman of the '22 each year, the backbenchers also elect two vice-chairmen, two secretaries, a treasurer, and twelve others, who between them form the '22's Executive Committee.

The election of the chairman of the '22, like the annual leadership election, is often a formality, but in 1984 the chairman, Edward du Cann, was challenged by Cranley Onslow and defeated. Du Cann had chaired the '22 for twelve years, its longest-serving chairman, his recent predecessors having included so-called 'knights of the Shires' such as Sir Harry Legge-Bourke, Sir William Anstruther-Gray who proclaimed the Conservative Party's unique ability 'to push the ship of State uphill', and John Morrison, later Lord Margadale. Morrison's chairmanship co-incided with the leadership crises of 1957 and 1963. His sons Charles and Peter, who subsequently entered the Commons, played roles in later leadership contests.

The chairman of the '22 has sometimes been dubbed 'the Tory chief shop steward'. Meetings between the leader and the '22 Executive are held up to two or three times each year, at which the Executive can raise points which are concerning backbenchers. In Thatcher's day, however, the usefulness of these occasions was reduced by her tendency to hector and not to listen. It is also customary for the leader to address the '22 shortly before the House rises for the long summer recess. This is an opportunity for the leader to rally the troops and reassert the ties of loyalty. Only exceptionally has it been an occasion for any expression of back-bench opinion. The questions which were allowed at the end of Thatcher's speech in July 1986 were the first for more than twenty years since Macmillan's leadership.

The party leadership is able to gauge back-bench attitudes through the reports it receives from PPSs and Tory whips of the weekly meetings of the 1922 Committee and also from the network of back-bench party com-mittees and subcommittees. Formal liaison between the '22 and the various functional party committees is effected through the Business Committee, which consists of the '22 Executive and the chairmen of the other back-bench party committees. Meetings of the official, functional committees were first established in 1924 by the leadership to consider future party policy. They are open to all Conservative backbenchers and cover all the main policy areas, serving as sounding boards for the parliamentary party and enabling the leadership to influence and channel back-bench opinion. Major's PPS, Graham Bright, may also attend the more important committees and the '22. The late Ian Gow, Thatcher's PPS from 1979 to 1983, was such an assiduous attender and frequenter of the tearooms and corridors that he earned himself the nickname 'supergrass',

In government, ministers and junior ministers are not allowed to attend the '22 or other back-bench party committees. The '22 or a back-bench party committee, however, may invite a minister to address MPs and reply to questions. An invitation to address the '22 is rare and reflects deep concern within the party, as in February 1980 at the height of the national steel strike when the employment secretary, then Jim Prior, explained the government's policy on secondary picketing.

It is standard practice for a minister to be invited to attend the relevant functional committee, especially following a major policy initiative – the chancellor of the Exchequer traditionally addresses the Tory Finance Committee after delivering his budget speech. Ministers below cabinet rank have formed their own group and invite cabinet ministers, including the prime minister, to address them – they pride themselves on being leak-proof. Ministers' PPSs attend the '22 and relevant committees in order to inform their ministers of back-bench sentiment.

The chairmen and other officers of the functional committees, usually two vice-chairmen and two secretaries, are elected annually. The two main wings of the party compete for the various committee posts, privately preparing rival slates of candidates, although the designations of 'left', organised by the Lollards, and 'right', organised by the 92 Group, are very broad. In opposition, liaison between the leader and back-bench committees is assisted since front-bench spokesmen chair the functional committees – the shadow chancellor chairs the Conservative back-bench Finance Committee, the shadow foreign secretary chairs the party's Foreign Affairs Committee, and so on. The shadow cabinet and other opposition front-bench spokesmen can attend meetings of the '22 although they are not allowed to vote.

At the centre of the web of information connecting the Tory leader and Tory MPs is the chief whip. The party leader appoints the chief whip in government and in opposition, whereas Labour's chief whip in opposition is elected by the Parliamentary Labour Party. The Tory chief whip has always been a key figure in the party hierarchy, dating back to the legendary William Holmes in the early nineteenth century:

> For thirty years 'Billy' Holmes was the adroit and dexterous whip of the Tory Party, and his great knowledge of the tastes, wishes, idiosyncrasies, family connections of all members on the Tory side of the House made him a most skilful dispenser of patronage and party manager.[20]

The duties and skills required of Tory Whips have not changed.

It is through the fourteen-strong Whips' Office that the leader is kept most fully informed of opinion within the parliamentary party. Each whip is responsible for MPs in an area of the country and also covers the work of one or more government departments. Like his predecessors, Major's first chief whip, Ryder, attends cabinet meetings in order to report on parliamentary opinion but is not a cabinet minister. He has as his principal weapon in ensuring loyalty to a party policy the force of persuasion backed by the power of patronage – in government the chief whip is designated patronage secretary and serves as the parliamentary secretary to the Treasury. He largely determines which MPs are promoted by the leader to the 120-strong payroll vote of ministers and PPSs in government (there are fewer posts in opposition and they are unpaid). The chief whip is invariably on hand to advise the prime minister or leader during ministerial or front-bench reshuffles.

Patronage is seductive but it is not invincible. Few leaders are judged to have distributed political honours judiciously. Macmillan's distribution of peerages and knighthoods were thought to have been excessive. Heath failed to heed the advice of his chief whip, Francis Pym, that he should create more honours. Thatcher was in no danger of repeating Heath's error, but she rendered a knighthood *de rigueur* for any Tory MP who achieved a certain vintage except a few who remained irredeemably beyond the pale, such as the irreverent Julian Critchley. Heseltine's nomination for the leadership was proposed and seconded by two knights of Thatcher's creation, Sir Neil Macfarlane and Sir Peter Tapsell.

There is an apparent paradox in the increased rebelliousness of Tory MPs since the 1960s, because the past thirty years have seen the steady demise of the 'knights of the Shires' who entered Parliament with little thought of ministerial office and more through an old-style paternalistic sense of duty. By contrast, Tory MPs today tend to be career politicians, many having entered politics with the intention of exercising ministerial office, and they might therefore be thought to be more susceptible to patronage and appeals to party loyalty. The profusion of consultancies and directorships on the Tory back-benches might also be thought to increase the penalty of risking the loss of the party's endorsement at a future general election.

Yet over the past twenty to thirty years the occurrence and scale of back-bench Tory revolt has grown, not diminished. Various theories have been advanced to explain this, but Tory MPs have not become more ideological, as is sometimes claimed. A more convincing explanation is a less deferential attitude towards party policy, encouraged by MPs' participation in electing the party leader since 1965, and also the kind of leadership exercised by Heath (who, curiously, is the only former chief whip to become Tory leader) and Thatcher. Both were reformers and during their premierships came to display great insensitivity towards back-bench concerns and an impatience with cabinet discussion. They shared a belief in strong action by the government, whether the policies were deemed 'interventionist' or 'free-market'.

During Heath's premiership between 1970 and 1974, backbenchers rebelled on a range of issues, including British entry into the European Community, local-government reform and, following Heath's 'U-turn', the prices-and-incomes policy. When Thatcher was prime minister some rebel MPs – like the party faithful at the party conference – demonstrated a well-informed belief that they could help her to push her ministers into tougher action, as with the revolts on trade-union reform in 1980. But Tories also rebelled on a whole range of other issues during the 1980s, most notably registering their opposition to the government's refusal fully to index child benefit, objecting to the imposition of charges for dental checks and eye-tests, defeating the government on the second reading of its Sunday Trading Bill and mounting a large revolt against the poll tax.

Kilmuir's claim that loyalty is 'the Tories' secret weapon' rings hollow against recent events. But his own experience within a couple of years of having first coined the phrase gave him cause to ponder. In July 1962, he was one of the cabinet ministers unceremoniously purged by Macmillan in the 'night of the long knives'. The episode severely damaged Macmillan's authority, and Kilmuir later doubted that the party's loyalty had 'ever had to endure so severe a strain'.

Because the Tories vest unique authority in their leader, the party leader is the focus for loyalty to the party. Etched deep in the party's folk-memory is the shattering experience of the split over Peel's repeal of the Corn Laws in 1846. But there is also a lesson for Major. No leader can afford to take the loyalty of the cabinet or back-benches for granted. Peel's insensitive handling of the repeal of the Corn Laws contributed to the intensity of bitterness felt on his back-benches, and there have been instances since when a leader's handling of an issue has become as much a cause of Tory discontent as the issue itself.

Most Conservative MPs want to avoid challenging their leader's authority and thereby damaging the party. But by placing their leader 'almost on a pedestal', in the phrase of a former Conservative cabinet minister,[21] Tories heighten the risk that their leader will lose touch with the party. The fates of Tory leaders in the twentieth century demonstrate the danger, but toppling leaders from their pedestal invariably provokes a crisis.

5

Coups and Crises

'It is not a principle of the Conservative Party to stab its leaders in the back but I must confess that it often appears to be a practice.'
Arthur Balfour, former Tory prime minister, 1922

I

Persuading a political leader to step down is never easy. Choosing a successor is rarely straightforward. The Conservative Party finds both tasks exceptionally difficult. It has been prone to coups against its leaders and susceptible to crises when selecting replacements. Half of Major's predecessors as Tory leader since 1900 have fallen victim to their party. Equally striking is the turmoil into which the party has often been plunged at the prospect of choosing a successor.

The twentieth century is studded with Tory leadership crises. The nineteenth-century leaders, too, all experienced challenges and difficulties of one sort or another, and the party suffered its deepest ever split in 1846. Peel's reformist approach and ill-concealed contempt for Tory backwoodsmen, whom he regarded as 'the finest brute votes in Europe',[1] provoked discontent and revolt before the final split over the Corn Laws. In 1855, the Earl of Derby, who led the party from the House of Lords, infuriated Disraeli, leader in the Commons, by refusing the opportunity of office. In 1872, Disraeli survived a challenge as leader only because Derby (son of the former leader) refused to seek the leadership. After Disraeli's death, the dual leadership of the early 1880s by the Marquess of Salisbury in the Lords and Sir Stafford Northcote in the Commons faced the challenge mounted by Lord Randolph Churchill, who espoused progressive Toryism and founded the Primrose League to foster the Disraelian myth. Northcote's ineffectual leadership in the Commons had exacerbated the problem, and it was the traditionalist Salisbury who dealt with the threat.

But nineteenth-century politics was in other respects very different from its late-twentieth-century heir. The Tories were led from the House of Lords by Derby and Salisbury for a total of forty-three years. In both cases, their early years as Tory leaders in the Lords were spent as joint party leaders with their counterparts in the Commons. Each spell of dual leadership ended only when Queen Victoria commissioned the leaders in the Lords to form an administration – Derby in preference to the Commons leader, Disraeli, in 1852, and Salisbury instead of Sir Stafford Northcote in 1885. Sandwiched between the Derby and Salisbury years was Disraeli's thirteen-year spell as leader of the whole party, although for his final five years he led the Conservatives from the Lords as the Earl of Beaconsfield.

Derby led the party to five successive election defeats but survived as leader until his retirement through ill health in 1868. His performance would be unthinkable today. His leadership of the party was also more collective than in recent times. Cabinet ministers in his three minority administrations were virtually his equals. Salisbury, the longest-serving Conservative prime minister, never bothered to observe proceedings in the Commons after succeeding to his title in 1868 and failed to recognise many of his non-cabinet ministers. By 1887, he had disposed of both Churchill and Northcote and decamped to Hatfield House, the Cecils' family seat, where he was primarily concerned with his duties as foreign secretary. The use of the prime-ministerial offices at Number 10 and much of the burden of party and parliamentary management fell to the Conservative leader in the Commons, W. H. Smith, until his death in 1891 and thereafter to Salisbury's nephew, Arthur Balfour.

Before the introduction of a formal election procedure for the Tory leadership in 1965, the party's leaders were said to have 'evolved'. This curious concept dignified a great deal of back-stabbing and double-dealing which occurred beforehand. But if any leader can be said to have evolved, it was Balfour. Salisbury's appointment of his nephew as leader in the Commons accorded with the views of Tory MPs, who had been impressed by his performance since 1887 as chief secretary to Ireland. 'I shall have to lose life or reputation,' Balfour said on accepting the Irish post.[2] But he proved himself a tough administrator and dominated both Irish Nationalists and Home Rule Liberals in the Commons. His position in the Salisbury administrations of the 1890s as Leader of the House and First Lord of the Treasury, the title nominally associated with the office of prime minister, confirmed him as heir apparent.

By the late 1890s, Balfour was concerned at the ability of the ageing and ailing Salisbury to continue as both foreign secretary and prime minister. The impression that the real driving force in the government was Joseph Chamberlain, the Liberal Unionist who served as colonial secretary, was strengthened by Salisbury's leaked reference to the Boer War as 'Joe's war'. The September 1900 'khaki election', in which the Conservatives and Unionists secured another large majority, was largely Chamberlain's victory. Within two months of the election, Balfour led a ministerial conspiracy, with Queen Victoria's support, to remove Salisbury from the Foreign Office. But Salisbury was determined to remain prime minister until the war ended, and did not finally resign until 11 July 1902.

On Salisbury's retirement, Balfour was commissioned to form an administration by the new king, Edward VII. But Balfour first ensured that he had the support of the Liberal Unionists, visiting Chamberlain, who was incapacitated after a cab accident, and the Duke of Devonshire, nominally their leader. Only when they had given their backing did Balfour kiss hands as prime minister. The public announcement followed two days later. On 14 July Balfour summoned a joint meeting of Tory and Liberal Unionist MPs and peers at the Foreign Office to endorse his premiership. Devonshire pledged the loyalty of Liberal Unionists and Austen Chamberlain read out a message from his father to 'welcome Mr Balfour to the leadership'.[3] The succession was deceptively smooth in view of Balfour's fate as leader and the party's subsequent record of leadership crises.

II

Although circumstances differ, the questions raised about the Tory leadership during Balfour's day have echoed down the decades. Balfour's experiences as leader and the manner of his going reveal the same concerns that periodically preoccupy, and even transfix, the Conservative Party – questions about a leader's authority, whether or not too large a section of the party might withdraw its consent from the leadership, the potential conflict between loyalty to party and loyalty to leader, the risk of a divisive contest for the succession, and so on. These issues perturbed Balfour and his contemporaries just as they have troubled all subsequent Tory politicians, never more demonstrably than in 1990.

Balfour's leadership epitomised the inadequate response by much of Edwardian society to the tensions developing in a changing world. Reflective and relaxed, his languid style gave him the air of a dilettante. He seemed singularly ill-suited to dealing with the growing threat to the empire and the challenge of winning and holding office as the labour movement grew in strength. Protectionism, or tariff reform, brought both issues together, since its advocates envisaged it as a means to help industry and to finance social reform. But Balfour was unable to cope with the divisions created in the party.

Within months of his becoming prime minister, the cabinet was divided over the continuation of the corn duty. There was disagreement over what the cabinet had decided during their meetings in October and November 1902, a problem exacerbated by the absence in those days of any formal minute. The cabinet had endorsed the continuation of the corn duty, but whereas Joe Chamberlain, the advocate of protection, believed that the decision was lasting, free-traders like the chancellor, C. T. Ritchie, considered it subject to review. The failure was Balfour's as prime minister in allowing the issue to remain unresolved. By the following spring, Ritchie was planning to repeal the corn duty. His announcement in his 1903 budget was accompanied by a ringing free-

HISTORY REVERSES ITSELF ;

OR, PAPA JOSEPH TAKING MASTER ARTHUR A PROTECTION WALK.

PAPA JOSEPH. "COME ALONG, MASTER ARTHUR, *DO* STEP OUT!"
MASTER ARTHUR. "THAT'S ALL VERY WELL, BUT YOU KNOW I CANNOT GO AS FAST AS YOU DO."

Fewer than sixty years after Peel's conversion to free trade had split the Tory Party, Joe Chamberlain drags an anxious Arthur Balfour in the opposite direction towards protectionism.

trade declaration against the taxation of food. Within weeks, Chamberlain's speech in his political stronghold of Birmingham supporting imperial preference triggered a mass campaign for 'tariff reform'.

The Conservatives and their political allies, the Liberal Unionists, were split three ways between tariff reformers, free-traders and a centre group led by Balfour, the prime minister. If anything, Balfour moved closer to Chamberlain's plans, but on the eve of the crucial cabinet meeting in September 1903 Chamberlain resigned to campaign openly for a protectionist empire. Balfour plotted to remove the free-trade cabinet ministers, but he failed and eventually lost five of his cabinet. Chamberlain's son, Austen, was appointed chancellor, his promotion being balanced by that of the free-trader, the Earl of Derby (grandson of the former party leader).

Politically Balfour was in a hopeless position. The majority of his MPs and Tory activists backed tariff reform, and he encouraged them to believe that they had his broad support. But he suspected that the policy would prove an electoral albatross because of fears of 'dear bread', and sought to reassure voters that his party was unlikely ever to introduce such a scheme. He got the worst of both worlds.[4]

The crisis deepened. Some free-traders, including Winston Churchill, crossed the floor and joined the Liberals. In November 1905, Joe Chamberlain directly attacked Balfour's leadership. Tariff reformers won the day at the annual party conference, which also demanded greater democracy in the party. With the government under attack from all sides, Balfour resigned on 4 December 1905. The Liberal leader, Sir Henry Campbell-Bannerman, formed a minority administration before being granted a dissolution in the new year. At the 1906 election, the Tories suffered an unprecedented rout, losing 245 seats, including Balfour's Manchester, and were reduced to only 156 MPs in all.

Disaster on such a momentous scale had wider causes than the row over tariffs. Outside the party, Non-conformist opinion had been angered by Balfour's educational and licensing reforms. He had blundered in turning a blind eye to the slavery of Chinese workers in South Africa. His handling of disputes in India and Ireland had been indecisive. At home, he had done nothing to restrain employers' attacks on the unions, despite Chamberlain's warnings not to antagonise the labour movement.

The party's crushing defeat in 1906 inevitably raised questions about Balfour's leadership. Yet such was the magnitude of the debacle that there were no effective rivals. Tory leaders have generally been less vulnerable after heavy defeats than after narrow ones. The most forceful figure on the front bench, Joe Chamberlain, realised that the Tories would not hand over the leadership of their party to a Nonconformist and radical Liberal Unionist. As he admitted, 'the Conservatives who agreed with him would not follow him, because their party loyalty would be too strong'.[5]

Although Chamberlain was reconciled to not becoming Tory Party leader, his challenge to Balfour's leadership was real. He was determined to force Balfour unequivocally to accept tariff reform as party policy and to create a new democratic party organisation including both Conservatives and Unionists. The two men met on 2 February, by which time Balfour had found a new seat in the City of London. Balfour's anxiety to avoid forcing the remaining free-traders, like Derby and the Marquess of Salisbury (son of the former prime minister), from the party led to deadlock in their talks.

Chamberlain suggested that a party meeting of MPs should be held. Balfour, as party leader, was reluctant to accede to the request but replied surprisingly: 'If you desire it, a Party Meeting must be held.' He was puzzled, however, as to what would happen:

> There is no case in history, as far as I am aware, in which a Party Meeting has been summoned except to give emphasis and authority to a decision at which the Party have informally already arrived; still less is there an example to be found of a vote being taken at such a Meeting.[6]

Chamberlain reassured Balfour that 'there will be no question whatever as to the leadership.' He proposed, however, that their conflicting positions should be put to the vote, although 'it will be clearly understood that the decision is not binding on the leaders, or any of them, but is merely taken for information'. Balfour argued against allowing any vote but conceded that 'the members of the Party must have an opportunity of "blowing off steam".'[7] Chamberlain retreated over the vote.

Immediately before the meeting was held, the policy dispute was settled in two days of negotiations involving Austen Chamberlain, Acland-Hood, the Tory chief whip, and Akers-Douglas, a former chief whip. In the 'Valentine Compact', endorsed at the party meeting on 15 February 1906, Balfour accepted the principle of tariff reform and Chamberlain pledged his full loyalty to the leadership. Balfour had resisted any real change in policy, but the Valentine Compact firmly pinned him to a position in which he had little confidence. He was able to spin out the ensuing discussions on party reorganisation and reassert the leader's control of Central Office.[8]

Joe Chamberlain's ascendancy over Balfour's leadership lasted only a matter of months. In July 1906, after celebrations in Birmingham to mark his seventieth birthday and thirty years as an MP for the city, he suffered a crippling stroke. He remained at Highbury, his Birmingham home, until his death in July 1914, just days after the assassination of Archduke Franz Ferdinand at Sarajevo. Chamberlain's removal from active politics so soon after the party's heavy losses six months earlier left Balfour in control.

III

Balfour was an uninspiring leader of the opposition who led the Tory Party into one of the greatest constitutional conflicts of the twentieth century. His ineffectiveness in opposition was a matter of temperament and also of habit. The Tories had held office for most of the previous twenty years. Their sense of being the natural party of government had fostered an arrogant assumption that they had an inalienable right to rule.

After his own defeat in Manchester in 1906, Balfour had spoken of the duty to ensure that 'the great Unionist party should still control, whether in power or whether in opposition, the destinies of this great Empire'.[9] The party's majority in the House of Lords offered a ready means to realise Balfour's end. Tory peers harried the government of Campbell-Bannerman until his death in 1908 and Asquith's government thereafter.

The constitutional issue of the Lords' powers was brought to a head in 1909 by Lloyd George's 'People's Budget' and its proposed land tax. As the debate raged over these proposals during the summer of 1909, any scope for compromise disappeared. Balfour made it known that he would resign as leader if Tory peers did not reject the bill. On 30 November the Lords defeated the budget by 350 votes to 75.

In the election which followed in January 1910, the Conservatives and Unionists revived, gaining 116 seats. But the Liberals narrowly remained the largest single party and were able to retain office with the support of Irish Nationalist and Labour MPs. Deadlock over the constitutional role of the House of Lords continued, talks between the parties eventually collapsing in November 1910 and precipitating a second election within the year.

Balfour, however, again stumbled over tariff reform. He sought to free the party from the hook on which it had become impaled but ended up by creating deeper division. He announced that a future Conservative Government would submit its proposals for tariff reform directly to the people if the Liberals would do the same with Irish Home Rule. But tariff reformers openly rejected a referendum. The party was in disarray. Frustration increased when the Tories won the same number of seats as the Liberals but Asquith's government stayed in office on the promise of Home Rule to the Irish Nationalists.

Three successive election defeats had fatally undermined Balfour's authority. Most Conservatives and Unionists were in no mood to accept a reduction in the powers of the House of Lords, particularly since it would remove the last obstacle to Irish Home Rule. But reform of the Lords had become inevitable. The party was split between die-hards who wanted to fight to the last, and moderates who believed that it was better to accept reform while trying to retain some powers for the Lords. Balfour had fondly hoped that the new king, George V, would prove an ally, but the King had already indicated to Asquith that he would act according to convention and if necessary create the requisite number of peers to allow parliamentary reform to be passed by the Lords.

In July 1911, the Tory shadow cabinet was split down the middle. At the crucial meeting on the 21st, eight of the twenty-two present took a die-hard line, pushing for continued resistance. Balfour argued for accepting the inevitable, and a majority of thirteen others agreed. But his remaining authority was severely tested and the die-hards gave no assurance that they would accept the decision.

Balfour's resignation as leader was finally triggered by the rebuffs inflicted on him by his party. He declined to call a party meeting to try and secure a vote of confidence, as some friends suggested. But in response to demands for clarification of the shadow cabinet's line, Balfour drafted a minute setting out the position. Several colleagues, however, felt that he was taking a tougher line than most had wanted, and he reluctantly suppressed his draft.

The second rebuff was delivered, more predictably, by the die-hards. In a letter to *The Times* on 26 July, Balfour backed the call by the Marquess of Lansdowne, leader in the Lords, that the party's peers should no longer stand in the way of reform. The letter drew a bitter private reply from Austen Chamberlain, who took a die-hard line along with other shadow-cabinet members, like Carson and F. E. Smith. Chamberlain deeply resented Balfour's accusing colleagues of disloyalty in public print. The die-hards organised a snub to Balfour, holding a dinner in honour of their 86-year-old leader in the Lords, the Earl of Halsbury, which was attended by several hundred peers and MPs.

Despite the depth of the crisis, Balfour left for a holiday in Germany before the key vote in the Lords on 10 August. The Tories in the Lords were split three ways: die-hards; the majority who abstained; and a minority, led by Lord Curzon, who voted with Liberal peers and bishops to ensure that the measure was passed. 'Was ever a party so badly led as ours was on this occasion?' Austen Chamberlain wondered.[10]

When Balfour returned from Germany in September, he informed Lord Balcarres, the chief whip, and Arthur Steel-Maitland, the new party chairman, privately of his intention to resign as leader. On 8 November 1911 Balfour announced his resignation. He pleaded his health, pointing to his twenty years' service as party leader in the Commons. At sixty-three, however, he was capable of continuing had he wished to do so, and was to enjoy an active political career for almost twenty years. Explaining his decision to his constituency association, he referred, with great understatement, to 'a certain feeling of unrest in the party'.[11] Austen Chamberlain wrote to his father Joe, in Birmingham, that 'the restlessness in the Party, particularly outside the House, has affected him'.[12] It was a significant statement, showing that despite the immense formal power of a Tory leader, he none the less needs to retain the consent of his followers in the Commons and in the country.

Balfour resigned because he had lost his authority in the party. He had previously commented to a colleague: 'I cannot be evicted from the leadership.'[13] But there can be no doubt that the party effectively forced him to stand down. The only alternative open to him by the autumn of 1911 was to mount a fierce campaign to reassert his authority, but it was not in his character and would have risked inflicting even further damage on the party. His motivation as leader had been to hold the party together, but he had failed. The party needed a new focus of loyalty. At least by resigning he spared the Tories the appalling choice between loyalty to the party and loyalty to a particular leader.

IV

With Balfour's resignation in November 1911 the Tory Party had entered uncharted waters. No Tory Party leader had ever stepped down in opposition. The nearest parallel was 1881, when Disraeli died in opposition and the post fell into abeyance. Balfour's resignation would entail the selection of a new leader of the Commons, not a Leader of the Party as a whole.[14] Lansdowne would continue as party leader in the Lords.

Balfour had hoped that Austen Chamberlain would succeed him. Balcarres, the chief whip, and Steel-Maitland, the party chairman, were also Chamberlain supporters and hoped that they would be able to smooth his succession. But Walter Long, the Tory squire, whom Balfour, a philosopher, disliked intensely, attracted strong support among country Tories. Bonar Law and Edward Carson were also possible runners at the outset, although Carson soon withdrew.

Since there was no established procedure for the election of a new leader in the Commons, Balcarres proposed that a party meeting be held as soon as possible. Long objected to the whips' calling a meeting, saying that the decision was a matter for the party's privy councillors, that is, its most senior figures in the Commons, mainly former ministers. But the announcement of Balfour's resignation had already prompted MPs to insist on an early party meeting.

Added urgency was given to the need to settle the succession quickly since the annual party conference was to be held the following week in Leeds. Conservative and Unionist MPs shared the fears of Austen Chamberlain, one of the main contenders for the leadership, who wrote privately of the risk that 'the Leeds Conference would take it out of their hands; there would be resolutions, speeches, every kind of lobbying and intrigue'.[15] The danger was averted in 1911 but his comments would prove prophetic over fifty years later, in the autumn of 1963.

Chamberlain was aware of his dual handicap as a leading tariff reformer, who was blamed by some MPs for having stirred up party disunity, and, more important, as a Liberal Unionist who 'had only joined the Carlton Club a little time before'.[16] The fact that Lansdowne, the leader in the Lords, was also a Liberal Unionist increased fears among Conservative MPs that if Chamberlain were to become leader the Liberal Unionists would take over their party.

Walter Long, the epitome of an English Tory from the shires, was campaigning aggressively for the leadership. Chamberlain, in contrast, refused to indulge in any canvassing of support or even to visit the Commons or gentlemen's clubs while MPs pondered the succession. As Chamberlain acknowledged, however, Long appeared in the party as 'a life-time Conservative' and a 'typical country gentleman'. Balcarres would later comment to Chamberlain: 'The squires wanted Long because he was a squire.'[17]

But it was clear that neither Chamberlain nor Long could win a decisive victory. There were conflicting estimates of who had the stronger support. Chamberlain regretted that no successor had emerged naturally in the way that Balfour had done, and, although he expected to win on a second ballot of MPs, he feared the disunity which would result from the 'indignity' of a vote of MPs.

The third candidate, Bonar Law, had never held cabinet rank and was little known outside the Commons, but had enhanced his reputation in the cut and thrust of debate. He considered withdrawing from the contest so as not to stand in Chamberlain's way – he was also a tariff reformer and had achieved his prime purpose of staking a claim as a future leader. But Bonar Law was dissuaded from standing aside by his close political ally, Max Aitken, later Lord Beaverbrook, the newspaper proprietor.[18]

Balcarres was disturbed at the news of Bonar Law's continued candidacy as he wanted to minimise the risk of division. A further problem which troubled the chief whip was the method of voting to be used at the forthcoming party meeting of MPs. Should it be by simple majority? Or should the last-placed candidate be eliminated and a second ballot held, as Chamberlain seemed to anticipate?

Chamberlain, however, now decided that he should step down. No leadership contender has ever behaved quite so selflessly. Chamberlain was not only uncertain about commanding sufficient support to win outright but was concerned that even if he won a contest he would not be able to gain the loyalty of the sizeable minority who strongly backed his main rival, Long. When Balcarres heard Chamberlain's qualms, the chief whip suggested that Chamberlain should acquiesce in Long's succession in the full expectation that the leadership would be his within six months – Long's unreliability, his limited intellect and failings as a debater would soon be exposed. Chamberlain demurred.[19]

Chamberlain then asked Balcarres to approach Long and suggest that they should both withdraw in favour of Bonar Law. Long accepted the idea, but the news prompted Bonar Law to urge Chamberlain to reconsider his withdrawal. Chamberlain declined, and again rejected any notion of allowing Long to succeed on the assumption that he would soon be called on to replace him.[20] Bonar Law was finally drafted as the compromise candidate who was not opposed by any sizeable group in the party.

No ballot of MPs was necessary at the meeting held at the Carlton Club on 13 November. Chamberlain expressed his relief that the party had avoided 'an angry fight leaving bitter memories and unappeased enmities behind it'.[21] But when he seconded Long's nomination of Bonar Law, he acknowledged that 'there has been a little feeling that the matter has been taken out of the hands of the Party, and too much settled for you before you came to this gathering'.[22] Those Tories in 1990 who persuaded both Hurd and Major to stand on the second ballot had been anxious to avoid similar criticisms of what was described as 'an establishment carve-up'.

In 1911, however, the risks of a contest had seemed greater to the party managers than the criticisms of having settled the issue behind closed doors. Subsequently, Conservative and Unionist MPs formally elected Bonar Law their leader in the Commons 'unanimously and by acclamation'. But despite the stage-managed show of public unity at the Carlton, the succession had provoked anger and unease which at times were barely concealed behind the scenes.

V

'I am their leader, I must follow them', is Bonar Law's oft-quoted remark about the Tory leadership.[23] Bonar Law's words were about as convincing as if they had been uttered by Margaret Thatcher, as they might well have been, for there are strong similarities between her style of leadership and that of Bonar Law. There was an element of make or break about both of them.

Both Bonar Law and Thatcher led from the front. Both seemed to regard their shadow cabinet as more of a hindrance than a help. Bonar Law summoned it with growing infrequency, an action which was easier in the days before the system of shadow ministers was formalised, whereas Thatcher was inclined to declare party policy unilaterally. In debate, both leaders were direct, even blunt, and indulged in rhetoric which appealed to their extreme supporters. They helped to rally the party when it had lost its way after two demoralising election defeats in the same year, as happened in 1910 and again in 1974.

Bonar Law echoed the die-hard opinions which had emerged over the previous few years, expressing the fiercest opposition to Irish Home Rule. But the Tories were plunged into crisis when, in late 1912, the dual leadership of Lansdowne and Bonar Law announced their abandonment of Balfour's compromise on tariff reform and committed the party to full-blown protection. Lord Derby mobilised opposition in Lancashire, the traditional home of the Tory free-traders.

As a means to break the impasse, Bonar Law and Lansdowne offered to resign at a party meeting. But Bonar Law's stepping down threatened to exacerbate all the old party divisions without any sign that they would be healed. Carson organised a 'memorial' expressing full confidence in Bonar Law and asking him to continue as leader with a revised tariff policy. It was signed by practically all MPs. Bonar Law acceded, but as a result had by early 1913 lost his main, positive plank of policy.[24]

The party's standing had revived by 1914 but the political scene was transformed by the First World War. Initially Bonar Law's position as leader was weakened, particularly after he led the party into coalition with Asquith in May 1915 and accepted the Colonial Office. He seemed more willing to support Asquith's caution than to support Tory demands for stronger action, including conscription.

Party unease was intensified in the summer of 1916 when Bonar Law and Carson backed Lloyd George's plan for Irish Home Rule for twenty-six counties, exempting the predominantly Protestant six northeastern counties. The leaders in Commons and Lords were divided. Lansdowne, a member of Ireland's landed Protestant ascendancy, delivered a scathing attack on the proposed partition. Walter Long was also opposed, and die-hard opinion prevailed at a party meeting at the Carlton Club. Bonar Law was forced to abandon the plan.

On the overriding question of the war, however, Lloyd George and Tory opinion were in greater agreement. In November 1916 a large revolt by Tory MPs demonstrated to Bonar Law that if he was to retain the leadership he would need to support a re-invigorated war effort. These events culminated in Asquith's resignation in December, and with Lloyd George's succession the Tories consolidated their domination of the coalition. As chancellor of the Exchequer and Leader of the House of Commons, Bonar Law was de facto deputy prime minister. He continued in that capacity after the 1918 election in which 335 coalition Tory MPs and 133 coalition Liberals were returned.

In March 1921, Bonar Law's failing health forced him to resign as party leader in the Commons. Austen Chamberlain, one of the unsuccessful contenders in 1911, had emerged as Bonar Law's successor. With Long's retirement from politics, Chamberlain was the last surviving contender from ten years earlier and had served in the war cabinet and succeeded Bonar Law as chancellor in 1919. The formal merger of the Conservatives and Liberal Unionists in 1912 also helped, although Tory squires never entirely forgave Chamberlain the fact that his roots were in his father's Birmingham Unionist machine.

As had been the case in 1911, the vacancy was for the party leadership in the Commons. At the time many of the Tories' biggest guns were peers. Birkenhead, formerly F. E. Smith, Curzon, who had succeeded Lansdowne as party leader in the upper House, and also Derby and Salisbury would each have been strong contenders, had Tory MPs been selecting a leader for the party as a whole. But the dual leadership which had commenced on Balfour's resignation ten years earlier would continue until another Conservative was commissioned to form an administration.

Despite lacking any serious rivals, Chamberlain confessed to the same feelings that he had experienced during the leadership crisis of 1911 – a 'great horror of anything that savours of intrigue or pushfulness on the part of a possible candidate' and felt that the 'only right thing to do was to keep quiet and leave members to make up their own minds without either courting their favour or shunning responsibility if their choice fell upon me'.[25] It was just as well for Chamberlain's sake that his selection was a foregone conclusion.

Chamberlain's smooth succession prompted the classic statement that Tory leaders 'evolved'. Conservative and Unionist MPs, meeting at the Carlton Club on 21 March 1921, extended a 'hearty invitation' to Chamberlain to assume the party leadership in the Commons. Proposing the resolution, the Right Honourable Captain Ernest Pretyman, MP for Chelmsford and a former minister, recalled the 1911 meeting which had elected Bonar Law and declared:

Great leaders of parties are not elected, they are evolved. Our leader [Bonar Law] who has just laid down his sword for the moment was never elected formally leader of the party at all; he was evolved, and I venture to hope it will not be necessary – and I think it will be a bad day for this or any other party to have solemnly to meet to elect a leader. The leader is there, and we all know it when he is there.[26]

Within eighteen months, however, Pretyman and the majority of his parliamentary colleagues would gather at the Carlton Club and seal the fate of the man who, like his father, was destined never to become prime minister.

VI

Pretyman and his colleagues at the Carlton Club in March 1921 would have been well advised to heed Austen Chamberlain's words in his acceptance speech as leader of the party in the Commons:

> There are moments when the insistence upon party is as unforgivable as insistence upon personal things, when the difficulties which the nation has to confront call for a wider outlook and a broader union than can be found even within the limits of a single party and when the traditions of more than one party need to be put into the common stock.[27]

There are shades of Peel in Chamberlain's unequivocal placing of country before party. In the 1970s Edward Heath expressed similar sentiments. Peel, Chamberlain and Heath were disinclined to share the ready Tory assumption that party interest and national interest are necessarily one and the same thing.

The crisis which rapidly engulfed Chamberlain's leadership was the most serious since the party's split over the Corn Laws in 1846. At the height of the crisis, Tory MPs were warned explicitly of risking a repetition of the events of seventy-six years earlier, which had resulted in the party spending almost three decades in the political wilderness. They had no intention of being sacrificial lambs to Chamberlain's Peel.

The prize which had eluded Chamberlain in 1911 had unexpectedly fallen to him, but he was ill-suited to deal with the exceptional challenge that faced the party in the early 1920s. He regarded the leadership as a call of duty which, as he once commented, he wished had not come. A man of palpable honour who lacked political guile, he needed to display less of the former and develop more of the latter. His Liberal Unionist roots, although no longer a bar to the leadership, remained a severe handicap since he lacked an instinctive feel for the mood of Tory backbenchers and grass roots. It was this failing that would ultimately prove to be his downfall.

Sir Robert Peel (*above*) led the
Conservatives to their first election
victory since the 1832 reform act but
in 1846 split his party over Corn Law
repeal. The Tories eventually revived
under the leadership of Benjamin
Disraeli (*right*), shown perusing a
document with leading Tories of the
late 1870s. Lord Salisbury (*below, left
of picture*), the longest-serving
Conservative Prime Minister, leans
forward to listen during a 1901
Cabinet. Arthur Balfour and Joseph
Chamberlain are to his left. Walter
Long, a leadership contender in 1911,
sits opposite, writing.

Arthur Balfour (*above right*), who in 1902 succeeded his uncle, Lord Salisbury, had to contend with the campaign for tariff reform launched by his frontbench colleague, Joseph Chamberlain (*above left*). Chamberlain had resigned from Gladstone's Liberal Cabinet in 1886 over Home Rule, ushering in twenty years dominated by his new Tory allies. In 1903 he resigned from Balfour's Cabinet. The Tories lost the 1906 election and were out of office for a decade. Andrew Bonar Law (*right, wearing top hat*) leaves the Carlton Club in October 1922 following the historic meeting at which Tory MPs voted to end their coalition with the Liberals. Lloyd George immediately resigned as Prime Minister.

Austen Chamberlain (*above*), Tory leader during 1921–22, never became Prime Minister. Stanley Baldwin (*right*), during the 1931 St. George's Westminster by-election. The Tory victory helped him to remain leader. Neville Chamberlain (*below*), in St. James's Park before resigning as Prime Minister in May 1940 following a Tory backbench revolt

The 80-year-old Winston Churchill handed over to Anthony Eden in April 1955 (*above*). When Eden resigned in January 1957 Macmillan (*far right*) triumphed over Rab Butler. Six years later, Butler was front-runner (*below*) until the Earl of Home (*below left*) became his rival. Iain Macleod (*below right*) later vilified the selection process as the 'Magic Circle'.

Macmillan's announcement of his
resignation in October 1963
transformed the party conference into
an American-style presidential
convention. Hailsham (*above right*)
threw his hat into the ring, declaring
that he would renounce his peerage
under legislation which had just come
into effect. Enoch Powell (*below left*)
hosted a late-night meeting of
ministers who supported Butler (*foot
of page, left*), but their efforts were in
vain. The 'Magic Circle' opted for
Home (*below right*), who agreed to
disclaim his peerage and form an
administration. Only Macleod and
Powell refused to serve.

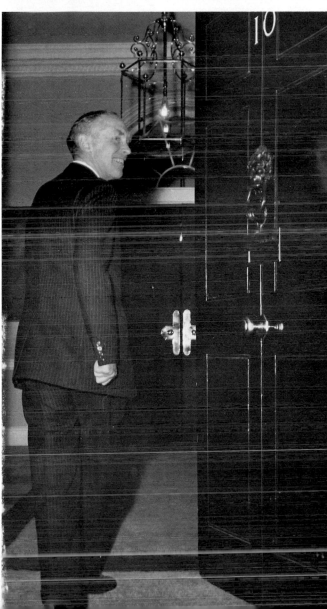

Following the Tories' defeat at the 1964 election, Sir Alec Douglas-Home (*centre*) finally bowed to pressure on him to resign as leader in July 1965. The criticism of his own selection led Douglas-Home to accept demands that the party leader should be elected by Tory MPs in a secret ballot. In the first election under the new procedure in July 1965, Edward Heath (*right*) defeated his main challenger, Reginald Maudling (*left*), on the first ballot, with Powell in third place. Although Heath fell short of the required majority, Maudling withdrew.

Margaret Thatcher, the first woman leader of a major British party, as Leader of the Opposition before 1979 election chairing the Tory Shadow Cabinet or 'Leader's Consultative Committee'. When in Februa 1975 she defeated Heath she was seen as an 'outsider', espousing free-market and monetarist policies w had become unfashionable in the Tory Party, and was unable to dominate her Shadow Cabinet. She is shown talking with two of Heath's closest former colleagues, Willie Whitelaw, who had run against he the second ballot in 1975, and Lord Carrington. Her ideological mentor, Keith Joseph, sits alongside he

The 1990 leadership crisis was a story of changing relationships between Thatcher and her senior colleagues. Thatcher and Howe had worked closely together during his days as her Chancellor – they are seen (*right*) in 1981 – but relations had since become soured during his period as Foreign Secretary and then Deputy Prime Minister. It was not his resignation, however, but his 'devastating' resignation speech which triggered the challenge to Thatcher's leadership.

The challenge was taken up by Michael Heseltine, who earned Thatcher's plaudits at the 1983 party conference (*above*) but who became a deadly rival after his resignation over the Westland affair in 1986. When the leadership crisis broke, Douglas Hurd, Thatcher's Foreign Secretary, remained loyal to his Prime Minister but was seen as a 'unity' candidate to be drafted against Heseltine in the event of Thatcher's defeat.

'I'm enjoying this,' declared Thatcher (*left*) as she delivered her 'bravura' performance in the Commons 'No confidence' debate on 22 November 1990. Earlier that day she had announced that she would resign and not contest the second ballot of the Tory leadership election. With her on the Government frontbench are John Wakeham (*left*), her close Cabinet confidant, and Kenneth Baker (*right*), her Party Chairman.

The 'Magic Circle' becomes the manic circle as John Major (*above*) addresses a press conference during his campaign in November 1990 for the Tory leadership. After the leadership battle the new Prime Minister and his main adversary (*right*) attempt to heal the wounds and restore party unity. Heseltine returned to the Cabinet after walking out almost five years earlier but he had inadvertently served as Major's 'stalking horse'.

Chamberlain had become leader of the party in the Commons in the midterm of a parliament, invariably a difficult time for any government. But the Tories' difficulties in 1921 were compounded by their continuing commitment to the coalition headed by Lloyd George. They dominated the government numerically but increasingly felt themselves to be at the mercy of a dominant prime minister, who showed scant regard for cabinet or parliamentary government, and whose sale of honours scandalised the political establishment.

The Tories' new leader was less capable than Bonar Law of keeping Lloyd George in check. Unemployment was mounting. There was considerable industrial unrest. The Labour Party was performing well in by-elections at the expense of coalition candidates. The deep Tory unease which surfaced in reaction to the Irish Treaty in 1921 and the Chanak crisis in the autumn of 1922, when Britain almost went to war against Turkey, were the tip of an iceberg of discontent which Chamberlain never seemed to recognise.

The question of the coalition's future became more pressing as the next election loomed closer – Parliament would have to be dissolved at the very latest by the end of 1923. This raised the deeper question of the party's future. Tories and Liberals faced a growing threat from Labour, which had fielded 388 candidates and won 2.4 million votes (more than 22 per cent of the national vote) in 1918, the first election at which all men and the majority of women were enfranchised. How could the other parties prevent Labour from winning office?

The debate became a battle for the soul of the Tory Party. At stake was its identity and very existence as an independent party. Most of Chamberlain's colleagues in the cabinet agreed with his desire to see the coalition continue. They believed that the combined appeal of Lloyd George and Chamberlain, on the lines of a centre party, offered the best means to check Labour's advance and build a new natural party of government. Chamberlain increasingly visualised the coalition in these terms. He told Tory representatives gathered at Liverpool for their annual party conference in November 1921; 'I do not hesitate to say that out of this Coalition, formed in the midst of war, at a time of national necessity, cemented by common action in years of difficulty and danger, will come a new party, constitutional, democratic, national.'[28]

But the majority of Tories were restive of coalition and deeply hostile to any suggestion of merger with Lloyd George's Liberals. They yearned for a return to their political independence, and saw the prospect beckoning of lengthy rule over an opposition divided between the fragmented Liberal Party and the emergent Labour Party. Most of these party loyalists were on the back benches or in junior positions in government, many of them frustrated at the lack of opportunity for promotion. In the cabinet, where the party loyalists were in a small minority, their strongest representative was Stanley Baldwin, who had only achieved cabinet rank in April 1921 on his appointment as president of the Board of Trade and was already in his mid-fifties.

By the new year of 1922 Lloyd George was considering the possibilities for an election. The principal agent at Conservative Central Office, Malcolm Fraser, had warned Chamberlain that in the event of an early election the party would be split, the coalition would lose 100 seats and Labour would make substantial gains. Fraser's estimate prompted the party chairman, Sir George Younger, publicly to denounce the idea of an early election fought on the basis of coalition.

Pressure mounted on Chamberlain to declare his intentions for the next election – should the party go to the country as a partner in the coalition, or should Tories fight as an independent party and once more seek office in their own right? Chamberlain's answer on 22 January was that a pact with the Coalition Liberals at the next election was essential. Far from settling the matter, his statement prompted Younger to call for a 'bill of divorcement' to end the coalition. Such public disagreement between leader and party chairman is unparalleled. When Chamberlain gave a subsequent reassurance that the coalition parties would fight on separate manifestos at the next election, it seemed that he might at last have begun to sense the force of party feeling.

Tory criticism of the coalition intensified. At the end of February 1922, in an attempt to quell Tory unease, Lloyd George offered to resign as prime minister in favour of Chamberlain.[29] There was no guarantee that the King would commission Chamberlain to form an administration and Lloyd George was suggesting that Chamberlain should head a Tory government, to which he and his Liberals would give their 'independent support'. His offer was therefore a setback to Chamberlain's hopes for merger and a new party.

Despite the problems with Lloyd George's offer, it is astonishing that Chamberlain declined. Although his party was deeply divided, he could have wished for no better means to seize the political initiative than by becoming prime minister. Instead he remained certain that Lloyd George was the best man for Number 10 and persuaded him to continue. It is difficult to imagine any other senior Tory politician failing to be tempted.

Within days of spurning the premiership, Chamberlain was telling the Oxford Carlton Club in March 1922 that 'when we go to the country, we go as a Government'.[30] He subsequently denied that this contradicted his pledge of separate manifestos. His words were of little comfort to Tories who suspected that he still planned a merger. Seeking to reassure a senior Tory activist, he tactlessly wrote: 'I regard Unionists [Tories] and

National [Lloyd George] Liberals as, under present circumstances, two wings of one great constitutional and progressive party.'[31]

During his Oxford speech Chamberlain had acknowledged that 'no leader is indispensable, and no leader would or could desire to remain leader unless he could continue to receive the confidence of his Party in such a measure that in any great questions of this kind they would listen to his advice'.[32] Eleven days later, 200 Tory MPs met at the Commons and discussed the idea of a new centre party. It won little support, and the meeting was seen by many Tories as a vote of no confidence in the coalition and Chamberlain's leadership.

Chamberlain claimed that there was more support for the coalition in the Midlands and north than in the south, but during the summer die-hard opposition to a merger strengthened. In July, Salisbury was elected 'Leader of the Conservative and Unionist Movement', which he proclaimed as standing for 'the spirit of Conservatism and against the spirit of the Coalition'. In August, Birkenhead, a cabinet supporter of coalition, harangued junior ministers who were opposed to the coalitionists, but his outburst was of no help to his leader.

The cabinet responded to the mounting pressure by agreeing to call an early election. At the key meeting at Chequers on 17 September only Baldwin resisted the decision to fight the election as a coalition. Before the meeting Chamberlain was warned by Younger, the Tory Party chairman, of the heavy losses the party would incur in an election fought as a coalition partner. Younger had argued that Lloyd George should hand over the premiership immediately.[33] But Chamberlain failed to convey his party's unease about the prime minister. He seemed to have no idea what else he could do but back Lloyd George and stick to the coalitionist line.

Tory Party opinion was outraged. In early October 1922 the National Union called for the coalition to be ended before the next election. Their call was echoed on 10 October by Baldwin and Leslie Wilson, the chief whip, during a meeting with Chamberlain of Tory members of the coalition. Wilson subsequently warned his leader that he could no longer remain publicly loyal. Chamberlain was about to achieve the unique distinction for a Tory leader of facing open opposition from both his party chairman and his chief whip.

Chamberlain was pinning his hopes on the outcome of the Newport by-election, in which an anti-coalitionist Conservative had entered the field. He expected this intervention to allow the Labour candidate to win, thereby proving his point that the most effective means of defeating Labour was for the coalition to remain united. Chamberlain was planning to call a meeting of Tory MPs at the Commons on the day after the by-election, Thursday 19th, to secure a vote of confidence in his leadership. But at dinner at Winston Churchill's house on Sunday 15 October, attended by Tory coalitionist ministers and Wilson, Chamberlain offered a compromise. He would summon all Tory MPs to the Carlton on the morning of the 19th, where he would argue the case for the coalition.[34]

Peers in the coalition government were also allowed to attend the Carlton Club meeting, but they were not allowed to vote. Limiting the meeting to MPs and peers in the government annoyed other peers and members of the National Union. But Chamberlain was leader of the party only in the Commons and the restrictions on voting were therefore correct, although the presence of coalitionist government peers indicates a clear attempt to sway the meeting in his favour.

Baldwin made it clear beforehand that he would argue for Lloyd George's resignation. Unrest in the party was mounting by the day. The National Union Executive, feeling slighted, unanimously agreed to a call for an emergency conference to debate the coalition's future, and then

THE SCAPEGOAT THAT TURNED.

["If I am driven alone into the Wilderness . . . ." — *Mr. LLOYD GEORGE at Manchester.*
"My husband thoroughly enjoys a fight." — *Mrs. LLOYD GEORGE at East Ham.*]

The revolt by Tory MPs in October 1922 consigned Lloyd George, known as 'the Goat', to the political wilderness.

adjourned for twenty-four hours – their purpose had been to make clear their unhappiness to Tory MPs before the Carlton Club meeting. Chamberlain was shocked to receive a list of seventy MPs who wanted an end to the coalition. In the hectic toing and froing, Balfour and Lord Birkenhead persuaded Chamberlain to reject a compromise put forward by Leo Amery on behalf of junior ministers.[35] Under their scheme the election would be fought as a coalition, but a party meeting afterwards would settle the party's future.

Crucially, the former leader, Bonar Law, decided to return to the fray. He had stepped down eighteen months earlier because of ill health, but his seeming recovery would provide Tory MPs with an alternative as leader. Bonar Law, however, did not finally make up his mind on the question of the coalition's future until the evening before the Carlton Club meeting.

As MPs and government peers arrived at the Carlton Club on the morning of Thursday 19th, the news came through that against all expectations the anti-coalition Conservative candidate had won the Newport by-election. It was a shattering blow for Chamberlain, demonstrating that the Tories were in no need of Lloyd George's coalition. Yet Chamberlain continued to argue in his speech that the coalition under the leadership of Lloyd George was necessary to fend off the threat of socialism.

Chamberlain's domineering performance confirmed his party's worst suspicions. Instead of rallying his troops with a political speech, he delivered a lecture. He held out little hope for the Tories and his claim that there were no policy differences between the two wings of the coalition was met with cries of dissent. Chamberlain's stiff-necked attitude and rejection of a suggested adjournment to allow the leadership to find a solution confirmed him as the extremist and his opponents as the moderates.

It was to the deepest Tory Party instincts, survival and unity, that Chamberlain's opponents addressed their remarks. Baldwin warned that to continue in coalition with Lloyd George, 'that dynamic force', would inevitably result in political disaster. The Liberal Party had already been 'smashed to pieces', and the 'old Conservative Party' would follow, 'smashed to atoms and lost in ruins'. Lloyd George was splitting Chamberlain and Baldwin, and was doing the same to the whole party:

The result of this dynamic force is that we stand here today, he [Chamberlain] prepared to go into the wilderness if he should be compelled to forsake the Prime Minister, and I prepared to go into the wilderness if I should be compelled to stay with him. If that is the effect of that tremendous personality on two men occupying the position that we do . . . that process must go on throughout the party.[36]

Pretyman, the centrist Tory MP and one of the delegation who had delivered the list of seventy anti-coalitionist MPs to Chamberlain the day before, moved a prearranged resolution that the Tories should fight the election 'as an independent Party, with its own leader and its own programme'.[37] After the resolution was seconded, the debate ran on for a short while before the most telling contribution was made.

Bonar's Law's intervention was finely judged. He dealt with the leadership issue, reminding MPs:

> This is a question in regard to which our system (and a good system it has been) has hitherto gone on this principle: that the party elects a leader, and the leader chooses the policy and if the party does not like it they have to get another leader.[38]

Bonar Law argued that on this occasion he would have preferred it to be otherwise, and would have liked to see the question of whether the party should continue in the coalition put to the party for its decision. But it was too late, and the party faced an inevitable split.

Bonar Law's message delivered the final blow to Chamberlain's leadership. 'If we follow Austen Chamberlain's advice our Party will be broken and a new Party will be formed,' he warned. Casting Chamberlain in the role of Peel, he added: 'It will be a repetition of what happened after Peel passed the Corn Bill. The body that is cast off will slowly become the Conservative Party, but it will take a generation before it gets back to the influence which the Party ought to have.'[39]

In a last attempt to rally support for Chamberlain, another former leader, Balfour, spoke in his favour. But like Chamberlain, he misjudged the mood of the meeting. Balfour sought to appeal to the parliamentary party's obligation to remain loyal to its leader: 'I understood that by a unanimous vote he was made our leader, and the only legitimate way in which you can make a leader is to treat him as a leader.'[40] But this argument cut no ice. Tory leaders cannot simply take their party's loyalty for granted, despite the great trust which the party places in them. It was a lesson that Balfour should have learned from his own experience in 1911.

After a few remaining speeches, Tory MPs voted on Pretyman's resolution. It was carried overwhelmingly, the result at the time declared as 187 to 87 votes. J. C. C. Davidson, Bonar Law's PPS, reported the figures as 185 to 88, with one abstention. Chamberlain recorded it as 186 to 85, with three abstentions.[41] The resolution did not rule out co-operation with the coalitionist Liberals in the immediate future, but Chamberlain had insisted on the resolution being put to MPs and regarded the result as a vote of censure. He left himself no alternative but to resign.

Predictably, Chamberlain conducted himself with dignity but he resented Bonar Law for having 'behaved badly to a man who, after all, had made him leader.'[42] Chamberlain was furious with his chief whip's open disloyalty at the Carlton and wrote to Wilson protesting that he had thought it necessary to 'work and speak against his leader at such a gathering. I hope you will find yourself in sufficient agreement with Bonar Law to make it unnecessary for you to repeat so unfortunate a precedent.'[43] Chamberlain's withering attack was justified. J. C. C. Davidson, Bonar Law's PPS, felt that Wilson had 'played rather a double game with Austen, not keeping him properly informed about the movements inside the Party'.[44]

Chamberlain had forced his MPs to choose between loyalty to their leader and loyalty to their party. Like Balfour in 1911, Chamberlain was affronted when the party rejected his policy as leader and he therefore resigned. Bonar Law had wished in his speech at the Carlton Club that there had been some means whereby the party could have settled its future without the issue becoming a challenge to the leadership. The crisis of 1922 revealed the poor communication between Tory MPs and their leader, and there was no formal machinery to bridge the gulf apart from relying on the party whips.

Although the formation of the 1922 Tory back-bench committee did not arise directly from the October meeting, its development in later years reflected a desire to establish a better flow of information between backbenchers and the leadership. Yet the Tory Party's view of the leadership has remained close to Bonar Law's pithy description that 'the party elects a leader, and the leader chooses the policy, and if the party does not like it they have to get another leader'.

VII

As soon as Lloyd George received the result of the vote at the Carlton Club on 19 October 1922, he went to Buckingham Palace and tendered his resignation as prime minister. Until Margaret Thatcher's resignation in November 1990, he remained the last prime minister to have resigned not as a result of a defeat in the House of Commons or at a general election, but after a private party vote. Unlike Thatcher, however, Lloyd George was turned out as a result of a revolt in another party.

Bonar Law was the clear choice as Chamberlain's successor as leader of the party in the Commons. He had no obvious rivals there. Immediately after Lloyd George's resignation, Bonar Law was summoned to the Palace by George V, but he realised that forming an administration would require some astute political management.

The bulk of the coalition cabinet, including Balfour, Birkenhead and the chancellor, Sir Robert Horne, remained loyal to Chamberlain. They would not oppose Bonar Law's becoming leader but had signalled their unwillingness to serve him. And as Tory peers like Curzon, Derby and Salisbury might also have expected to become prime minister, Bonar Law took the precaution of consulting his colleagues.

A precedent was also set. Because of the unusual circumstances in which Bonar Law had been invited to become prime minister, he insisted that he should be formally elected leader of the whole party *before* accepting the King's commission to form an administration. His 'election' was in fact a formality, because it was known that Bonar Law had seen the King four days earlier, but it signified a break with convention. Previously, a serving prime minister had automatically been regarded as leader of the party as a whole. Bonar Law called a party meeting at the Hotel Cecil on 23 October 1922, attended by MPs, Tory peers and parliamentary candidates, and chaired by the leader in the Lords, Curzon. He was unanimously elected leader of the Conservative and Unionist Party, and it was only afterwards that he kissed hands as prime minister.

Yet Bonar Law would remain the only Tory leader until Edward Heath in 1965 to be elected leader of the party as a whole before becoming prime minister. The next six Conservative leaders after Bonar Law were all appointed by the monarch to serve as prime minister without any formal party vote or meeting beforehand. Bonar Law had arranged the party meeting as a means of confirming his position and binding the party's wounds, not as a genuine experiment in party democracy.

This confirming and healing practice of the formal party meeting has been maintained. Every leader since Bonar Law has been officially endorsed at a similar Tory gathering – after having been either appointed prime minister or elected as leader under the rules first adopted in 1965, and in John Major's case in 1990 after both his election as leader and his appointment as prime minister. The precise composition of the formal party gathering has only slightly varied. In December 1990 Major was officially endorsed as leader at the Queen Elizabeth II Conference Centre in Westminster, where the meeting was presided over by Lord Whitelaw and attended by MEPs, MPs, peers, Tory candidates and the National Union executive committee.

But the monarch's role would, in certain circumstances, remain crucial. When throat cancer forced Bonar Law's resignation, the choice of successor in May 1923 lay between Lord Curzon, the Tory leader in the Lords and foreign secretary, an experienced but grand and arrogant figure, or Stanley Baldwin, who less than a year earlier had been a relatively junior member of the coalition cabinet. Although Baldwin had helped to demolish Chamberlain's leadership at the Carlton Club the previous October, he had only been appointed chancellor of the Exchequer in Bonar Law's cabinet – caricatured by Churchill as 'a Government of the second eleven' – after the former Liberal chancellor, Reginald McKenna, had declined the post.

As was the convention, the King's private secretary, Lord Stamford-ham, set about 'taking soundings'. The outgoing prime minister was reluctant to choose between Baldwin and Curzon, partly because he was in no fit condition and partly because he entertained doubts about both men. There were allegations of a Baldwinite conspiracy after the submission of a minute prepared by Bonar Law's PPS, J. C. C. Davidson, which amounted to a strong recommendation for Baldwin, but which Bonar Law's secretary presented to Stamfordham as an accurate summary of the former prime minister's views.[45]

Salisbury argued strongly for Curzon, but Balfour, who personally disliked Curzon, quite properly argued that, since the Parliament Act of 1911 and the decline in the power of the Lords, the prime minister needed to be a member of the Commons. Balfour's own leadership of the party in the Commons had been difficult during his uncle's premiership, but now it would be impossible. There were already six peers in the cabinet, including Curzon, but the official opposition, Labour, was completely unrepresented in the Lords. Balfour's argument proved decisive. Baldwin was more in tune with Bonar Law's approach than the rather superior Curzon, and Davidson's note had reflected party opinion.

Stamfordham, however, had done nothing to warn Curzon of his likely disappointment. The grandee travelled to London in almost triumphal procession from his Somerset estate, fully expecting to become the next prime minister. When the King's secretary finally broke the news, Curzon broke down.[46] But he had the consolation of great wealth through his second wife, Grace. As Blake has revealed, Curzon's disappointment prompted Balfour to observe that 'even if he has lost the hope of glory he still possesses the means of Grace'.[47]

In his initial shock, Curzon complained of Baldwin's 'utmost insignificance'.[48] But he recovered his dignity. Six days after Baldwin's appointment as prime minister on 22 May 1923, Curzon chaired the party meeting of MPs and peers at which the new prime minister was officially endorsed as leader of the Conservative and Unionist Party.

VIII

The Tory leadership had passed from a Glaswegian iron merchant to a Worcestershire iron master. It seemed a far cry from the days of the fourteenth Earl of Derby and the third Marquess of Salisbury. Baldwin developed a style of leadership which contrasted with that of his three immediate predecessors. Unlike the detached Balfour or the haughty Austen Chamberlain, Baldwin appealed to Tories as somebody who had risen from the party ranks and with whom they could identify. And whereas Bonar Law began his leadership as a crusader, Baldwin was always a conciliator – a change in character between leaders which the Tories would repeat in 1990 when Thatcher was succeeded by Major.

Baldwin saw leadership primarily as reflecting, but not leading, public sentiment. In cabinet he acted as a chairman, not an autocrat, and as a delegator, not a meddler. He recognised the Tories' need to adopt social reform and to develop a more professional organisation if they were to win and maintain office. His acceptance of the labour movement's rise at home and of Indian nationalism's emergence abroad antagonised Tory die-hards and romantic imperialists. But his mastery of communication, his cultivation of an image as the bluff English countryman and his skilful use of his powers as leader were indispensable assets in his periodic battles to retain the Tory leadership.

Baldwin inherited a solid Commons majority of more than 70 seats which the Tories had won in the November 1922 election. They appeared to be in a commanding position. The Liberals were split between Lloyd George and Asquith, and Labour was the next largest party and official opposition with only 142 seats against the Tories' 345. But within months of becoming prime minister, Baldwin restored the issue of tariff reform to the top of the Tory agenda. The electoral consequences would once more prove disastrous.

High unemployment and agricultural depression prompted Baldwin to seek a major new initiative. In October, at the Imperial Economic Conference, the colonies again demanded a policy of imperial preference. When the new prime minister told his cabinet of his intention to introduce tariffs, only Lord Robert Cecil voiced objections.[49] It seemed that the issue would no longer wreak the disruption which the Tories had experienced twenty years earlier. But the compromise on tariff reform which had preserved party unity prevented Baldwin taking immediate action. The Tories were still bound by Bonar Law's pledge that there would be no introduction of tariffs until after a second election.

Baldwin's plan was to announce the government's change of policy but not to be rushed into an early election. Accordingly, in late October 1923, he told representatives at the Tory conference that the 'only way of fighting' unemployment was 'by protecting the home market'.[50] Although he made no reference to an early appeal to the country, people read that as being his intention.

Pressure for an election became irresistible although the government still had four years to run. Most ministers reluctantly came to accept that the reaction to Baldwin's statement left them no alternative. On 13 November 1923 the Prime Minister announced a December election. Tory MPs and party activists were angry and confused, and the government was soon on the defensive. When the results were declared, the Tories had suffered a net loss of 88 seats. They remained the largest single party in the Commons but no longer had an overall majority.

Birkenhead, who had refused to serve Baldwin and was passionately committed to a new centre party, immediately began plotting to replace Baldwin with Balfour at the head of a Liberal and Tory coalition.[51] But the Tory Party remained as reluctant to surrender its independence as it had been at the Carlton Club less than fifteen months earlier. The conspiracy quickly collapsed when Balfour, who had unsuccessfully defended the coalition at the Carlton Club, now backed Baldwin as leader.

Baldwin's handling of the crisis was astute. Despite the fears of many Tories that a Labour government would amount to Bolshevism, he resisted all entreaties to form an alliance with either Asquith or Lloyd George to keep Labour from power. He faced Parliament after the election, challenging the Liberals to remove his government. On 17 January 1924, Baldwin was defeated in the vote on a Labour amendment to the King's Speech. Baldwin resigned, Ramsay MacDonald was appointed prime minister, and Asquith was held responsible for having installed the first ever Labour government.

The Tory backlash against Baldwin's leadership was expended within a month. The anger was greatest in Lancashire, traditionally a free-trade stronghold, where Lord Derby, whose family seat was at Knowsley on Merseyside, headed the protest. By the time that Lancashire Tories met, however, Baldwin had already retreated on tariff reform. But Alderman Salvidge, political boss of the Tory machine in Liverpool, won unanimous support for his criticism of the leader's decision to call an election without consulting the party.[52]

Baldwin had skilfully consolidated his leadership before the Lancashire meeting by summoning his former cabinet ministers and also the coalitionists who had refused to serve him – Balfour, Birkenhead and Chamberlain – to his shadow cabinet on 7 February 1924. The coalitionists' hopes were patently dashed, and he was able to win them back into the fold. Churchill's return was only a matter of time.

Having restored unity at the highest level of the party, Baldwin confidently faced the special party meeting which he had volunteered on party policy and his leadership. He presided at the gathering of peers, MPs and defeated party candidates at the Hotel Cecil on 11 February 1924, delivering a well-judged review of the Tories' position, setting out party policy and calling for a new approach to combat the challenge from

Labour. His triumph over his critics was confirmed by the endorsement of two former leaders. Balfour spoke in support of Baldwin's opposition to coalition with the Liberals. Austen Chamberlain, whom Baldwin had defeated as leader only sixteen months earlier, delivered a classic defence of the Tory leader's prerogative, rejecting the demands by party activists for a greater say. 'Do not weaken the hand of the man whom you choose for your Leader,' Chamberlain proclaimed to cries of 'Hear, hear!' He added, 'Do not ask of him or any of us that we should remit executive decisions to be debated in public meetings.'[53]

The party's instinct for survival had guaranteed Baldwin's continuation as leader. As his biographer, G. M. Young, commented, 'the instinct of self-preservation alone compelled the body of the party to range themselves under the only leader who could restore them to office'.[54]

IX

Tory confidence in Baldwin appeared to have been fully vindicated in October 1924, after the fall of the minority Labour government, when he led them to Britain's largest election victory by a single party. The Tories won 419 seats against Labour's 151 MPs and only 40 Liberals. Many Conservatives and their supporters had indulged in shameless red-baiting, but Baldwin's landslide was based on positive policies and his promise of strong government after three general elections in two years.

Baldwin was more strongly committed than almost any other Conservative to avoiding class war. He was deeply concerned that the great extension of the vote in 1918 might threaten the stability of British politics, particularly at a time of economic depression. He saw good industrial relations as crucial, believing that neither political stability nor economic recovery would be possible without better collaboration between employers and unions.

But Baldwin had to battle against enormous pressures. Many Tories wanted to use their majority to turn back the clock on trade-union law. Relations between employers and unions were embittered by the decline in Britain's inefficient traditional industries like coal and steel. Industry's problems were intensified as Churchill, whom Baldwin had appointed chancellor, restored sterling to the gold standard at its prewar parity, with the result that exports became even more uncompetitive.

Baldwin faced demands from his atavistic supporters in early 1925 to take over a private member's bill to reform the method by which trade unionists contributed to Labour Party funds – instead of having to contract out of the political levy, union members would be required to contract in. The Prime Minister saw that the bill would be portrayed as a vindictive attack on Labour and would undermine moderates in the unions. He staked his leadership on the issue, persuading the cabinet not to take over the bill, and developing his call for 'peace in our time' in highly effective speeches. Baldwin won this battle, but his party was not to be denied.

The crisis in the coal industry deepened. Contraction and wage cuts at a time when the cost of living had fallen were seen as unavoidable. Matters were brought to a head in the summer of 1925 when the Treasury subsidy, which the industry had been receiving, was due to expire. But the miners won the backing of other unions and threatened to strike from Friday 30 July 1925. Baldwin, supported by Churchill and Neville Chamberlain, Joe's younger son and a reforming minister of health, persuaded the cabinet to continue the subsidy for a further nine months. 'Red Friday', as it became know, was seen by Tory die-hards as a humiliating climbdown and evidence of Baldwin's weak leadership.

In October 1925, the party conference snubbed Baldwin with a demand for abolition of the political levy, a call which was repeated at the National Union's Central Council the following spring. Baldwin, meanwhile, struggled to find a settlement in the coal industry. But when the Treasury subsidy finally expired at the end of April 1926 the miners went on strike, and the trade-union movement blundered into a general strike.

Faced with a confrontation between the government and the labour movement, the Tory Party closed ranks and rallied behind its leader. But many Tories wanted the struggle against the miners pursued to a final victory, followed by a swingeing attack on the legal protections which trade unions had won over the previous twenty years. Baldwin fought off the most extreme proposals but after the strike had to concede much of what the party had demanded. The Trades Disputes Bill, published in March 1927, made general and sympathetic strikes unlawful although it did not go as far as removing the protection granted to unions in 1906 after the Taff Vale judgement. The bill also tightened the law on picketing and introduced contracting in for trade unionists' contributions to Labour.

The myth about Baldwin's leadership is that he lost his way after the general strike and his government drifted into narrow minded reaction and internal division. Although the general strike produced irresistible pressures for draconian anti-union laws and took its toll of Baldwin, who sank into a malaise during the early part of 1927, talk of his political demise is exaggerated.[55] Narrow-minded reaction had been present all along in the person of Joynson-Hicks at the Home Office. Despite talk of disunity, Tories thought that other parties were more divided, and only one cabinet minister, Lord Robert Cecil, resigned during Baldwin's four and a half years in Number 10.

As the next election approached, Baldwin was able to point to a record of reform. At the Ministry of Health, Neville Chamberlain implemented twenty-one of the Tories' twenty-five manifesto pledges and was considering plans for slum clearance, maternity benefits and child welfare. Baldwin encouraged employer-union talks, and union moderates consolidated their position in the labour movement. Churchill's de-rating of industry and agriculture was developed as an employment policy with the election in mind. Neville Chamberlain feared that the plans might disrupt his ambition to reform the poor law, but Baldwin prevented his resignation. De-rating and poor-law reform were introduced in stages during 1928, providing assistance to industry, agriculture, the railways and the depressed areas.

But increased unemployment during 1928 renewed pressure for industrial protection and threatened to split the party. The Empire Industries Association, with the support of 200 Tory MPs and Leo Amery in the cabinet, demanded an immediate extension of 'safeguarding', or protection, to all industries. The Prime Minister, however, had sanctioned policy work in 1927 and was armed with a policy-committee recommendation to extend safeguarding. After rejecting immediate action, Baldwin announced that the government would extend safeguarding after the election. His compromise fell short of protectionist demands and the row rumbled on. But Baldwin had kept the protectionist Amery and the free-trader Churchill in the cabinet and prevented a split at the election.

Baldwin made his leadership the centrepiece of the party's election campaign in May 1929. Most Tories subscribed to the Baldwin legend, accepting his unique appeal to ordinary voters. His 'Safety First' campaign was an attempt to play to his strength and to meet the danger of the revived challenge by the Liberals. The threat of more three-cornered contests than in 1924, together with Lloyd George's radical employment programme published as *We Can Conquer Unemployment* in March 1929, prompted Baldwin to stress that the Tories were 'the party of performance', not promises. He would not try to outbid Lloyd George but would counterattack by inviting people to renew their trust in his leadership.[56]

But Baldwin's one-man show failed. Defeat had been unexpected and shook the party. High unemployment and the sizeable increase in the Liberal vote cost the Tories dear. Labour emerged as the largest single party with 288 seats, the Tories were reduced to 260 and Lloyd George's 59 Liberal MPs held the balance of power. Baldwin immediately resigned and MacDonald formed Labour's second minority administration.

Baldwin's leadership was bound to come under attack. But he was under permanent siege for two years because of the party's concern at the direction in which he had led it since 1923. Like Balfour, Baldwin was not cut out by temperament for opposition. The party's losses had been heaviest among moderate and left-wing MPs who were his supporters, and the perceptibly more die-hard and right-wing party which he led in the Commons increased his vulnerability.

The Tories' defeat led to criticism of party organisation. Attacks on any Tory Party chairman are usually thinly veiled attacks on the leader who appointed him. This was specially so in the case of J. C. C. Davidson, who had increasingly antagonised the National Union. Party activists felt that, while he readily carried out Baldwin's orders, he did not impress their worries upon the leader. By the spring of 1930, Davidson realised that his position was impossible and resigned.

Criticism of Baldwin focused on the two policies where the party was more deeply divided; India and tariff reform. The die-hards had long been suspicious of Baldwin and his support for the Viceroy's call for greater self-government for India through dominion status. Baldwin had not consulted his shadow cabinet and his position left him virtually isolated within the party. But his debating skills and his critics' blimpish ineptitude enabled him to survive. It was little more than survival, however, and his inability to settle the issue further undermined his leadership.

Baldwin had barely held the party together on tariff reform in government, but it proved impossible in opposition. During 1930 Baldwin had to face three party meetings and was forced steadily to give ground, beginning with a return to the idea of a referendum on tariff reform. He faced additional pressure from the vigorous campaign for protectionism, or 'Empire Free Trade', launched by the press lords, although the continued attacks in Beaverbrook's *Daily Express* and *Evening Standard* and Rothermere's *Daily Mail* were unsettling, the press barons served primarily as channels for the deep discontent among Tories.

Force of events, in the shape of world economic slump, settled the debate. By the time of the third party meeting, held at Caxton Hall on 30 October 1930, Baldwin had accepted the call by the Canadian prime minister, R. B. Bennett, for a 10 per cent tariff on all goods from outside the empire. After delivering a strong plea for loyalty to the party meeting, Baldwin was endorsed as leader by a majority of 462 votes to 116.[57] Two factors had helped save Baldwin. In addition to MPs, parliamentary candidates were invited to the meeting, and their more moderate views swelled Baldwin's vote. Polling was also taking place in the South Paddington by-election on the same day but, unlike Austen Chamberlain in 1922, whose hopes were dashed by bad news from a by-election, Baldwin's leadership was confirmed before the polls had closed. It was just as well. The seat, previously held by the Tories, fell to Beaverbrook's United Empire Party.

The final act in the two-year drama of Baldwin's leadership was played out during February and March 1931. Churchill's resignation from the shadow cabinet at the end of January signalled die-hard determination to fight to the bitter end over India. More generally, many Tories saw no hope of improvement for the party without a change of leader. Neville Chamberlain, who had succeeded Davidson as party chairman in May 1930, had emerged as a credible alternative. 'The question of leadership is again growing acute,' Chamberlain wrote in his diary on 23 February 1931. But he faced a dilemma. 'I cannot see a way out. I am the one person who might bring about S.B.'s retirement but I cannot act when my action might put me in his place.'[58]

Two days after Chamberlain's agonised reflection, Sir Robert Topping, principal agent, wrote his party chairman a note which appeared to have handed him the means to remove Baldwin. Topping claimed that there was disquiet in the party, stating that 'from practically all quarters one hears the view that it would be in the interests of the Party that the Leader should reconsider his position'.[59] Chamberlain consulted shadow-cabinet colleagues, who agreed with Topping's line. Viscount Hailsham, formerly Douglas Hogg, a possible leadership contender until he became Lord Chancellor in 1928, suggested that because Baldwin was preparing a major speech, Chamberlain should postpone showing him the note. But Austen Chamberlain had second thoughts and advised against delay. Neville duly sent his leader a copy of Topping's note on the morning of Sunday 1 March. That afternoon Baldwin told Chamberlain that he and his wife felt he should resign.[60]

During the evening, however, Baldwin changed his mind, principally through the efforts of Davidson and Viscount Bridgeman, the former MP for Shropshire, ex-minister and an old political friend of Baldwin's. Baldwin's decision to fight on was shrewdly judged. Any Tory leader can call on a fund of loyalty and the party's poor showing in the East Islington by-election on 19 February actually worked to his advantage. The intervention of Beaverbrook's United Empire Party further demonstrated the danger of division. And as the economic crisis rapidly worsened, the mood for unity strengthened.

The next morning, Chamberlain was summoned to see Baldwin, who told him that he intended 'to go down fighting'. When Baldwin added that he intended to resign his seat and stand as the Tory candidate in the Westminster St George's by-election, where the party was without an official candidate, Chamberlain objected. Baldwin asked why. 'Think of the effect on your successor,' Chamberlain replied. Baldwin was enraged at Chamberlain's self-interest. 'I don't give a damn about my successor,' he retorted.[61]

Baldwin remained resentful at Chamberlain, angry at Hailsham, whom he suspected of having plotted against him, and suspicious of others in his shadow cabinet. Matters were made worse when Austen Chamberlain insensitively suggested that his brother be moved from the party chairmanship to strengthen the front bench.[62] It seemed like further evidence of plans for a leadership coup.

A week before polling in the Westminster by-election, Baldwin restored his authority over the die-hards on India with an outstanding speech in the Commons. He had decided not to resign and fight the seat himself and, breaking with the convention that the leader did not intervene at by-elections, Baldwin spoke for the Tory candidate, Duff Cooper. He lambasted the press lords, Beaverbrook and Rothermere, accusing them of 'wanting power without responsibility – the prerogative of the harlot throughout the ages'.[63] Two days later, on 19 March 1931, Duff Cooper was elected MP for Westminster St George's.

The siege on Baldwin's leadership was lifted. He and Neville Chamberlain, who resigned as party chairman, settled their differences in a frank interview. Baldwin had survived one of the Tory Party's most prolonged leadership crises. He did so partly because there was little agreement on policy or overlap in support between die-hards and the tariff reformers. Their ineptitude and intransigence allowed Baldwin to portray his critics as irresponsible. As the economic crisis worsened he was able to call on the party's overriding desire for unity.

The sequel came in August 1931, when, as a result of the country's financial crisis, the Tories returned to office in the coalition National Government. Although MacDonald remained prime minister, the Labour Party disowned their leader and his few supporters. The Tories' domination became complete when they won 473 of the National Government's 554 seats at the October 1931 election. So began fourteen years of coalition government, in which the Tories remained in the ascendant. Baldwin's policy of appeasing the dictators would prove disastrous, but his skilful handling of the abdication crisis in 1936 enabled him to retire with his reputation enhanced.

X

Neville Chamberlain remained Baldwin's heir apparent for six years, but he was the real driving force in the National Government. From November 1931, he served as chancellor of the Exchequer under both MacDonald, who retired in 1935, and Baldwin, who eventually retired in May 1937. The irony was not lost on Neville that it was he, not his father, Joe, or his elder brother, Austen, who eventually attained the highest office. Yet his succession as Tory leader was the smoothest since Balfour's in 1902.

Chamberlain never regarded himself as a Conservative at all. 'I was brought up as a Liberal, and afterwards as a Liberal Unionist,' the new prime minister told Tory MPs, peers, candidates and members of the National Union executive committee when he accepted his formal nomination as leader of the Conservative and Unionist Party.[64] In fact, in 1931 he had privately hoped 'that we may presently develop into a National Party and get rid of that odious title of Conservative which has kept so many from joining us in the past'.[65]

The difference in style between Baldwin and Chamberlain was striking. Chamberlain was quite incapable of adopting Baldwin's emollient approach. Anthony Eden, then foreign secretary, prophesied the contrast in March 1937. His private secretary noted Eden's fear that when Chamberlain became prime minister 'affairs would go less smoothly in the country than with Baldwin – there would be better administration and more discipline in the Cabinet, but he would not be able to resist scoring off the Opposition'.[66]

Churchill appeared to share Eden's qualms when, as the senior Tory privy councillor in the Commons, he seconded Chamberlain's nomination as the new Tory leader. Stressing that the leadership had never been interpreted in a 'dictatorial or despotic sense', Churchill believed that Chamberlain would 'not resent the honest differences of opinion arising between those who mean the same thing, and that Party opinion will not be denied its subordinate but rightful place in his mind'.[67] But coming from the arch-critic of the National Government's policy of appeasing Nazi Germany, Churchill's comments were more of a veiled warning than a confident endorsement.

Of all Tory leaders, the one whose leadership style most closely resembled Neville Chamberlain's was Thatcher. 'I always gave him the impression when I spoke in the House of Commons,' Chamberlain wrote of Baldwin's advice to remember that his opponents were gentlemen, 'that I looked on the Labour Party as dirt.'[68] Chamberlain was by nature a doer, a politician who believed in getting on with the job rather than spending time cultivating support or smoothing the way with opponents. Once he was convinced that the right decision had been reached, he regarded further debate as a waste of time.

Chamberlain treated his ministers as administrators who should run their departments while he dealt with policy. Leslie Hore-Belisha, his secretary for war, commented that being a member of Chamberlain's cabinet was 'like being a Departmental Director in a private company in which the Chairman owns all the shares. You are expected to report intelligently on departmental matters but keep quiet on everything else.

It's your job to do as the Chairman tells you and keep your nose out of general policy.'[69]

The Foreign Office was regarded as highly suspect by Chamberlain. He increasingly bypassed his foreign secretary and relied on a small group of sympathetic ministers and the advice of Sir Horace Wilson, his trusted adviser in Number 10. His PPS, Lord Dunglass (later Lord Home), found that he regarded the views of Tory MPs as a distraction from the business of government. Chamberlain also attached much greater importance to the press and broadcasting than to the Commons. He has rightly been described as the 'first prime minister to employ news management on a large scale'.[70]

And like Thatcher, Chamberlain eventually came unstuck at the hands of back-bench Tory MPs. Hailed as a national hero on his return from signing the Munich Agreement with Hitler in September 1938, he had been unable to resist repeating to the crowds in Downing Street the words used by Disraeli sixty years earlier on his triumphant homecoming after signing the Treaty of Berlin – 'peace with honour'. He immediately realised that it had been a mistake.

The words were haunting him by the time that Parliament debated the Munich terms the following week. Between thirty and forty government backbenchers abstained at the end of the four-day debate. Chamberlain had retained the loyalty of the great bulk of MPs and the party, but had permanently alienated a hard core of rebels. Many of these critics were subjected to intense pressure and threats of deselection by local Tory activists. Churchill survived a vote of confidence in his Epping constituency by a margin of only three to two.

The division in the party persisted as Chamberlain's policy of appeasement collapsed during 1939. It speaks volumes for his tenacity that despite the shattering impact of leading his country into war, he continued as prime minister and was determined to see the war through. But he was patently not a war leader and was incapable of inspiring national unity. The ending of the 'phoney war' on 9 April 1940, when Hitler's troops invaded Norway, brought to a head the growing criticism of Chamberlain's handling of the war.

The climax came in the two-day debate on the Norway fiasco in the Commons on Tuesday 7 and Wednesday 8 May 1940. 'You have been here too long for any good you have been doing,' Leo Amery told his leader, repeating Cromwell's declaration. 'Depart, I say, and let us have done with you! In the name of God, go!' The Labour opposition forced a vote. 'Quislings!' Tory loyalists shouted at the rebels on their own benches as the House divided. 'Rats!' and 'Yes-men!' Chamberlain's critics yelled.[71]

More than 40 government supporters voted with the opposition, including Duff Cooper, Leo Amery and Harold Macmillan. A further 60 backbenchers abstained, many of them ostentatiously remaining in their seats. The government's majority was cut from over 200 to 81. 'The final scene in the House was very distasteful,' wrote one of Chamberlain's most loyal acolytes, Rab Butler, a Foreign Office minister. 'It reminded me of certain scenes in the history of Peel. The singing of "Rule Britannia" by Harold Macmillan was much resented by Neville who rose looking old and white-haired, as he has become, and marched out realising, as he did, that he could not go on.'[72]

Chamberlain tried various manoeuvres to retain the premiership. He was prepared to sacrifice some of his cabinet and tried to persuade Labour to enter a coalition. In the end, it was Labour who forced his resignation. On the afternoon of Thursday 9 May, Chamberlain saw Lord Halifax, the foreign secretary, and Churchill, the First Lord of the Admiralty, at Number 10, and told them that Labour must enter the government. The Labour leaders, Attlee and Greenwood, then joined the meeting. 'Mr Prime Minister, the fact is our Party won't come in under you,' Attlee told Chamberlain. 'Our Party won't have you and I think I am right in saying that the country won't have you either.'[73]

Attlee and Greenwood then departed to consult their party, which was in conference at Bournemouth. After they had left, Churchill kept quiet. Halifax then ruled himself out as Chamberlain's successor on the grounds that the country could not be led from the House of Lords in wartime. 'I thought Winston was a better choice,' Halifax later confessed to Sir Alexander Cadogan, his permanent secretary at the Foreign Office. 'Winston did *not* demur. Was very kind and polite but showed that he thought this was the right solution.'[74]

The next morning, Friday 10 May, Britain awoke to news of the German invasion of the Low Countries. The war cabinet met before eight o'clock that morning. It seemed that Chamberlain thought that the crisis would make it impossible for him to resign. But Attlee had been contacted at Bournemouth and over the telephone confirmed that Labour would not serve in his government.

Later in the day, Chamberlain resigned as prime minister and was succeeded by Churchill at the head of a new coalition. But Churchill appreciated that Chamberlain still enjoyed considerable support in the Conservative Party. He was careful to retain him in the war cabinet, and thought it important that he should continue as leader of the party to show that the government was truly a coalition in which no party was pre-eminent.

Yet even if Churchill had thought differently, there was not much he could have done about the party leadership. Chamberlain's first appearance in the Commons after he had lost the premiership prompted the most extraordinary reception. 'MPs lost their heads,' noted Chips Channon, the Tory MP and diarist, 'they shouted; they cheered; they waved their Order papers, and his reception was a regular ovation.'[75] By contrast, when Churchill first entered the chamber as prime minister his own benches greeted him in silence. For some months, the only spontaneous cheers for Churchill came from the Labour and Liberal benches.

Within months Chamberlain fell terminally ill. By the autumn of 1940 he had to resign as party leader. If he had been able to continue, the situation would have become very awkward. Churchill had by that time come to the view, urged on by Lord Beaverbrook, that he needed to become party leader to avoid the fate of Lloyd George, a wartime prime minister who ended up without the backing of a party.

On 9 October 1940, at what had become the customary party meeting of MPs, peers, candidates and members of the National Union executive committee, Churchill received the unanimous approval accorded to a new Conservative Party leader. The party had developed an effective means of displaying public unity and healing its wounds after a leadership crisis. But as the fate of subsequent leaders would demonstrate, the notion that Tory leaders 'evolved' would cause ructions for Churchill's successors.

6

The Magic Circle and After

'The loyalties which centre upon number one are enormous. If he trips, he must be sustained. If he makes mistakes, they must be covered. If he sleeps, he must not be wantonly disturbed. If he is no good, he must be *pole axed*.'

Winston Churchill, on the position of the Tory leader

I

By the end of 1940 Churchill had decided that in the event of his being incapacitated in the war, Anthony Eden, a critic of Chamberlain and a member of the wartime coalition, should succeed him as prime minister. But Eden was to remain heir apparent for almost fifteen years. Rarely has a leader played such a game of cat and mouse with his party and his presumed heir, or given such a clear demonstration of a prime minister's ability to hold on to power.

After Labour's landslide election victory in July 1945, Eden held the official title of deputy leader of the opposition. When the Tories returned to office in 1951, he was de facto deputy prime minister, a position which Eden wanted formalised to block other rivals, like Rab Butler, the chancellor. But King George VI resisted the idea since it would remove the monarch's choice of prime minister.[1] In the end Eden did succeed Churchill, and the transition went smoothly, but during the years beforehand ministers repeatedly tried to persuade Churchill to resign and Eden was virtually driven to distraction.

The Tories, however, staged a remarkable recovery under Churchill's leadership after the war. This was largely due to the efforts of shadow ministers like Butler, Macmillan, Woolton, the party chairman, and Oliver Stanley, a younger son of the seventeenth Earl of Derby who might well have become a future Tory leader had he not died at the age of fifty-four in 1950. They realised that the Tories had no future if voters continued to associate them with the uncaring attitude to slump and unemployment of the 1930s.

Churchill helped set the tone and provide the vision. 'You have never been a real Tory,' George Bernard Shaw wrote to him in August 1946.[2] Churchill's commitment to the welfare state as a minister in the reforming Liberal government of 1905–16 and his continued reformist sympathies reinforced the postwar Tory image. He allowed his front-bench team to get on with their work in opposition and government – if anything, probably too much.

From the late 1940s, senior Tories became increasingly frustrated at Churchill's seeming indifference to them and to the party. At times he was badly out of touch. Churchill's wife, Clementine, had wanted him to retire in 1945 when he was already seventy years old.[3] But he hoped to lead the Tories to victory in a general election, which he had never done. When he finally achieved that objective, at the age of almost seventy-seven, he intended to serve as prime minister for only a year. But he dreaded the thought of not being at the centre of things and kept finding excuses for staying on.

Ill health might have forced Churchill to go sooner. In January 1946 he intimated his readiness to retire after suffering dizziness during a visit to America. But Eden was not keen to succeed as leader in opposition, partly because it would entail resigning his directorships and taking a cut in salary.[4] In June 1953, when Churchill suffered a stroke, his deputy was in the United States recovering from a third abdominal operation. The seriousness of the Prime Minister's stroke was hushed up and his recovery was remarkable.

As early as the summer of 1947, several shadow-cabinet ministers, including Rab Butler, Harry Crookshank, Lords Salisbury, Stanley and Woolton, had agreed that Churchill should resign. They tried to recruit James Stuart, the Tory chief whip, as their cat's-paw. 'None of the others present at our private meeting,' Stuart recalled, 'repeated to him the news which they had so kindly asked me to convey.'[5] If the Tories had lost heavily in the February 1950 election Churchill would have retired, but Labour's majority was reduced to five seats. In October 1951 the Tories won a majority of seventeen seats and the stage was set for Churchill to make a dignified retirement after a year or so.

The King's death in February 1952 caused Churchill's first postponement on the grounds that he could not step down before the Queen's coronation. In June, Crookshank, Salisbury and Stuart deputed Patrick Buchan-Hepburn, the new chief whip, to tell Churchill that he should go. Churchill refused. Before Christmas Eden pressed Churchill for a decision.[6] The foreign secretary was frustrated at the continuing delay but in the spring of 1953 he fell ill and was kept out of action for six months. After Stalin's death in March 1953 Churchill became preoccupied with the task of reconciling the United States and the Soviet Union.

As the next election approached, Churchill told Eden in March 1954 that he would resign by the end of the summer.[7] But as the deadline approached he said that he would not go until September. Macmillan wrote urging him to retire before the summer recess, but was rebuffed.[8] In July, the cabinet were outraged that Churchill had sent a telegram to Molotov, the Soviet foreign minister, proposing a meeting without consulting them. Macmillan was deputed by Butler, Salisbury and Buchan-Hepburn to see Lady Churchill and persuade her to tell her husband that he should go.[9] Churchill was furious and summoned Macmillan, who then did not raise the issue. More efforts were made to persuade Churchill to step down. But Churchill exploited his powers as prime minister and 'played off one against the other and has come off triumphant', as Macmillan observed.[10]

In the autumn of 1954, as Churchill approached his eightieth birthday, he thought of carrying on to the next election. But the Tories were trailing Labour in the opinion polls and the prospect worried the party faithful, as Christopher Soames, Churchill's son-in-law, discovered at the October party conference.[11] Churchill's tiredness and deafness were beginning to inhibit his ability to run the cabinet, and at one point the microphones installed to assist his hearing transmitted cabinet discussions to taxi drivers in Whitehall.[12]

Shortly before Christmas, Eden, Salisbury, Woolton, Butler, Crookshank, Stuart and Macmillan called on Churchill to tell him to go. Eden was in despair when Churchill said that he would carry on till the next summer.[13] But early in 1955, Churchill informed Eden and other ministers that he would resign around April. Then, in March, President Eisenhower suggested that he would be willing to visit Europe in early May to celebrate the tenth anniversary of V-E Day, as a pretext to encourage talks on easing the Cold War. Churchill told Eden that this meant postponing the handover. At a cabinet meeting on 14 March, Eden asked whether the 'arrangements' they had made still stood.[14] The meeting was adjourned after Churchill retorted that it was his business when he retired, and anybody who disliked it could resign. Ministers were alarmed that the delay would ruin plans for a May election immediately after Eden's appointment as prime minister.

Churchill soon learned that Eisenhower would not personally take part in the proposed East–West talks, and there seemed no further reason for him to stay on. By late March, however, the dock and newspaper strikes and a new Soviet offer of talks briefly provided fresh excuses. 'He could not possibly go at such a moment just to satisfy Anthony's pesonal hunger for power,' Jock Colville, Churchill's private secretary, recorded him as saying. 'If necessary he would call a party meeting and let the party decide.'[15]

But the game was up, as Churchill really knew. The party was geared for Eden's succession and an early election. On 5 April 1955 Churchill resigned. Eden had sought to restore their friendship, which smoothed the succession, but Churchill doubted that his heir was up to the job.

II

Having waited for so long to become leader, Eden lasted only one year and nine months in the job. He had acquired unrivalled ministerial experience of foreign policy but had never served in a ministry dealing with economic or social issues. Yet his great failure came on foreign policy. He fell in the aftermath of one of Britain's most serious political crises, which brought dishonour on him, his government and his party. The events surrounding the appointment of his successor are still disputed. The so-called 'customary processes', the methods by which the Tories sought to advise the monarch on her choice of prime minister, caused disquiet in the party. Six years later they would be utterly discredited.

Anthony Eden was appointed prime minister on 6 April 1955, the day after Churchill's resignation, not on the same day, so as to respect the Queen's prerogative in choosing her first minister. He was formally elected Conservative leader on 21 April at the usual party meeting. A month later, Eden led the Tories to victory at the general election, increasing the government's Commons majority to 53 seats, the first time since 1900 that a government had been returned to office with an increased majority.

Eden's premiership confirmed the paternalists' postwar grip on the leadership. As a young MP on the left of the party in the 1920s, Eden had been a protégé of Baldwin's. He had advocated a 'property-owning democracy' as early as 1929 and always shared his mentor's passion for better industrial relations. But his dealings with his cabinet were never easy. He was a meddler, phoning ministers at all hours and interfering in their work. Former colleagues speak of a Jekyll and Hyde character, charming and considerate one moment, petty and ill-tempered the next. His botched gall-bladder operation in 1953 meant that he relied on drugs and was susceptible to fevers.

His authority as prime minister was dented within a year. He had missed his opportunity for reshuffling the cabinet either on his appoint-

" HONESTLY SIR! NONE OF US EVER EVEN THOUGHT OF
DROPPING YOU !"

Eden returned from his convalescence in Jamaica after the Suez
debacle to an unconvincing welcome from Tory colleagues.

ment or after the election, and when his changes came in December he
moved Macmillan, one of his few earlier appointments, from the Foreign
Office to replace Butler at the Treasury. Macmillan was annoyed at what
he saw as demotion, and Butler, who became Leader of the House and
Lord Privy Seal, regretted the loss of a departmental base.

By January 1956, Eden was being subjected to fierce attacks in the
press. In March he gave a poor speech in a Commons debate on the
Middle East. 'If the year goes on as it has begun,' wrote Ian Waller,
political correspondent of the *Daily Telegraph*, 'it will not be Sir Anthony
Eden but Mr Harold Macmillan who reigns in Downing Street in 1957.'[16]

Without Suez, Eden would, even so, almost certainly have survived as
prime minister. The sequence of events of the crisis have been well
chronicled: the announcement in July 1956 ending Anglo-American
funding for the Aswan Dam; Nasser's response by nationalising the Suez
Canal; negotiations for a diplomatic settlement during September and
October; the Israeli attack on Egypt on 29 October; the Anglo-French
ultimatum to Nasser the next day; the Anglo-French invasion of Egypt on

5 November; the decision to stop on the 6th; and the agreement by the end of November for an unconditional withdrawal of Anglo-French troops. It is now clear that Eden colluded with the French and Israelis and sought to destroy evidence of the conspiracy. On 20 December 1956, he lied about his knowledge of Israeli plans to the House of Commons.

What is at issue is why Eden resigned as prime minister in January 1957, and why he was succeeded by Macmillan, not Butler. By mid-November, Eden was on the point of physical breakdown and was advised by his doctor to take a holiday. The Prime Minister spent three weeks in Jamaica and was virtually out of touch with London while Butler and Macmillan took the key decisions. When Eden returned on 14 December his authority was lost. He was even overruled by his ministers on the wording of his press statement on arrival at Heathrow. Butler, Salisbury and Selwyn Lloyd had rejected his draft and the Prime Minister reluctantly recited their anodyne words.[17]

The day after Eden's return, Macmillan warned Butler that several younger members of the cabinet did not think Eden could continue. Butler, however, agreed with the chief whip and party chairman that Eden should at least be able to survive until the summer recess.[18] But the Prime Minister's reception when he first returned to the Commons was excruciating. One Tory, Godfrey Lagden, the MP for Hornchurch, rose to cheer and wave his order paper, but he found himself alone. Other backbenchers and Eden's ministers sat in awkward silence. 'It was a grim and revealing moment,' Lord Kilmuir, the Tory Lord Chancellor observed.[19] Eden's days as leader were numbered.

At a meeting of the cabinet on 17 December, Buchan-Hepburn, the former chief whip, urged Eden not to resign on the grounds that the unity of the party would not survive it and it would signify that Suez 'had been a tragic mistake'. But when Buchan-Hepburn then wrote to Eden, his welcome support was qualified by his holding out the possibility of a later resignation.[20] The most likely scenario appeared to be that Eden would step down later in the year when the Government had recovered from the immediate aftermath of Suez, giving a new leader time to revive the party before the next election.

On 27 December, Eden met a small group of ministers at Chequers on official business. Afterwards he spoke privately with Kilmuir, asking him whether he should stay on as prime minister. Although 'the principal factor was his health' and Kilmuir advised him to continue, his confidant left 'with the feeling that he [Eden] was consumed with grave apprehensions about his personal position'.[21]

But the final decision was taken out of politicians' hands. On 7 January, Eden was told by his doctor that he could not expect to live long if he continued as prime minister or even as an MP. Eden fought against the medical advice, asking Lord Salisbury, leader of the party in the Lords, and the Earl of Scarborough (formerly Roger Lumley, a Tory MP and ally of Eden's) to question his doctor, but they confirmed the prognosis. Salisbury judged that Eden would not survive the strain of trying to stay on.[22]

Like Bonar Law in 1923, Eden was in no fit state to advise on his successor. He suggested to Sir Michael Adeane, the Queen's private secretary, that a senior cabinet minister who was not a contender in the succession should take soundings of the cabinet, and mentioned Salisbury.[23] On 9 January, Eden told Butler, Macmillan and Salisbury that he would resign and would be informing the cabinet that afternoon. Before the cabinet met, Salisbury saw Kilmuir, who advised him that the Queen was entitled to seek advice from anybody about who would command the support of a majority in the House of Commons. 'I took the view very strongly', Kilmuir later recalled, 'that she need and ought not to wait for a party meeting. To do so would be to abandon the most important part of her prerogative, whose maintenance might be of immeasurable value to the country in the later years of her reign should a political crisis develop.'[24]

This approach set the Tories apart from Labour, who promptly declared that in similar circumstances they would choose a new leader, and therefore the next prime minister, by a vote of the party. This was precisely what the Tories would do in November 1990, and even in 1957 there had been the precedent of Bonar Law's insistence in 1922 that he should be elected as party leader before he kissed hands as prime minister. But as Kilmuir appreciated, Bonar Law's election had been a formality. The difficulty in 1957 was that there were now two strong contenders. In 1940 Halifax had ruled himself out before the King had to make a choice. The nearest parallel was with 1923, when the choice had been between Baldwin and Curzon. The question was how the monarch should be advised. Kilmuir and Salisbury decided to consult all cabinet ministers one by one, which was unusual. Following the precedent of 1955, the successor to Eden was due to be appointed the following day. There was no time to organise any formal soundings of party opinion either in the Commons, which was in recess, or in the country, but this did not deter Kilmuir and Salisbury from taking informal soundings.

Eden's news that he was resigning on medical grounds came as a shock to the cabinet, as it had to Macmillan and Butler. Immediately after cabinet the two contenders left Number 10. Salisbury and Kilmuir asked all other cabinet ministers to see them one by one in Salisbury's office in the Privy Council Offices, which could be reached without leaving the building. 'Well, which is it to be, Wab or Hawold?' each minister was asked by 'Bobbety' Salisbury.[25] The overwhelming majority preferred

Macmillan. Kilmuir later told Robert Rhodes James that only Buchan-Hepburn had said Butler,[26] although Butler believed that Monckton, the paymaster-general, and Stuart, the Scottish secretary, had backed him.[27]

Salisbury and Kilmuir consulted the party chairman and the chief whip. They echoed the cabinet's choice. Heath had received a number of letters from MPs opposing Butler.[28] He strongly recommended Macmillan, demonstrating the importance attached by the Tories to avoiding a leader who is firmly opposed by a section of the party. The chairman of the 1922 Committee, John Morrison, undeterred by being on the Isle of Islay off the Scottish west coast, felt able to assess back-bench opinion and also recommended Macmillan.[29]

On the morning of 10 January, Salisbury was summoned to the Palace and reported his findings. The Queen also consulted Churchill, who advised that she choose 'the older man', namely Macmillan, on the grounds that he was more decisive.[30] There were echoes in his judgement of the bitter split over appeasement in the late 1930s, when Butler had been one of the most enthusiastic appeasers. Churchill and Macmillan had sat on the backbenches while Butler stood at the dispatch box as the senior Foreign Office minister in the Commons (Halifax, the foreign secretary, sat in the Lords), coolly defending Chamberlain.

Macmillan was appointed prime minister on the afternoon of 10 January 1957. He was confirmed as party leader twelve days later. Macmillan's appointment surprised most people, if not his cabinet. Butler had, after all, deputised as prime minister when Churchill and Eden were ill in 1953, and again when Eden left the country to recuperate after Suez. Eden, who was not consulted, had expected Butler to succeed. Most of the press had predicted Butler, reflecting the views of Tory supporters contacted immediately after Eden's resignation. Only Randolph Churchill, acting on a tip-off by Beaverbrook, predicted Macmillan.

Butler was bitter at his rejection. He later privately blamed 'the "ambience" and connections of the present incumbent of the post at Number 10' for his defeat, and regarded his treatment as 'definitely unfair'.[31] Was Butler the victim of a conspiracy by Macmillan? From mid-November Macmillan was certainly more aware that Eden might step down and that he should seize any opportunity that came his way. Butler, on the other hand, seemed to assume that he need not do anything more to secure the succession.

No better demonstration of the contrasting personae of Butler and Macmillan occurred than when they both addressed the 1922 Committee on 22 November 1956. Their agreed purpose was to hold together a party that was at breaking point as Tory MPs faced the humiliating prospect of an Anglo-French climbdown. The meeting was held on the eve of Eden's departure for Jamaica. Macmillan was convinced that Eden could never return and remain prime minister for long.[32] At the '22, Butler was subdued, but Macmillan unashamedly launched into a great peroration. It was nothing less than a bid for the leadership.

Butler later confessed his suspicions that Macmillan and his allies were preparing for an early change of leader and regretted that he had not seen how quickly things would move.[33] Butler's problem was that he had been ambivalent about Suez all the way through, was on occasion indiscreet about his views, and during Eden's absence had to carry the responsibility for the humiliating unconditional withdrawal of the Anglo-French troops. Macmillan had been the most hawkish minister at the outset, but then became the strongest dove: 'first in, first out,' as Harold Wilson alleged. But at least he seemed decisive, and his sang-froid reassured Tory MPs.

Macmillan's role led to allegations that he worked to topple Eden, and has also prompted claims that Eden's fall was the result of an Anglo-American conspiracy.[34] Macmillan's gearing up to challenge for the leadership in the event of Eden's going does not amount to proof that he was actively plotting the leader's downfall, as Brendan Bracken had suggested to Beaverbrook in early December 1956.[35] Nor is the argument compelling that a condition for the restoration of normal relations between the United States and Britain was a change of prime minister.

The Tory dilemma in November 1956 was caused by the conflict between its Middle East policy and its exchange-rate policy. Macmillan must bear a large part of the responsibility. He had warned Eden in the spring of 1956 that inflation and an import boom, caused by Butler's 1955 pre-election budget, would force devaluation by the autumn unless he was allowed to raise taxes or cut spending.[36] He was not allowed to do either. Yet by August, when Macmillan knew that Britain's financial position was weak, he was urging military action against Nasser while taking no steps to arrange financial aid from the United States or the IMF to shore up Britain's reserves. In fact, aid was not sought until 7 November, *after* the cease-fire. It was only then that the extent of American intransigence was discovered.

During November Macmillan came to realise that no loan would be forthcoming unless the government abandoned its Middle East policy. Either the troops would have to be withdrawn unconditionally or the government would have to devalue. The former would humiliate Eden; the latter would be unacceptable to Macmillan.

Eden's retreat to Jamaica enabled Macmillan to win the argument, with Butler as his accomplice. The unavoidable U-turn was made on foreign policy, not economic policy. Macmillan had helped create the dilemma in the first place. But in resolving it, he had constructed his springboard to the leadership.

III

Harold Macmillan's success in restoring the Tory Party after the debacle of Suez was such that the Conservatives appeared to be establishing a permanent political ascendancy. At the October 1959 election, the Tories were returned with an overall majority of 100 seats, almost double the majority won by Eden in 1955. They had revived their claim to be the natural party of government. Yet the Macmillan era would end in confusion and recrimination for the Tories as they experienced the most extraordinary leadership contest in their long history.

'Supermac', the image created by the cartoonist Vicky, captured Macmillan's personal dominance of politics during the first five years of his premiership. He was the consummate performer, developing a mastery of the new political medium of television. It is difficult to imagine any other Tory leader displaying quite the same aplomb as Macmillan when he dismissed the resignation of his chancellor and two Treasury ministers in January 1958 as 'little local difficulties'. He preferred to read the novels of Jane Austen rather than constantly meddle in his ministers' detailed work. But ministers had to keep their wits about them. Macmillan's relaxed façade could never entirely disguise the ruthless politician who lurked behind.

Although Butler had effectively been vetoed as leader by the Tory right wing, Macmillan was just as strongly on the left of the party as his rival and arguably more so. His views on the economy had been shaped by the mass unemployment of the 1920s and 1930s which he witnessed at first hand as MP for the northern industrial seat of Stockton-on-Tees. Many of the men in the dole queues had fought alongside Macmillan in the trenches in the First World War. It was a spectre which would never leave him.

Macmillan's interventionism was remarkably successful by comparison with the record of later governments, achieving simultaneously low levels of inflation and unemployment. But his much quoted comment in July 1957 that people 'have never had it so good' was delivered in the course of a warning about the perils of inflation. Taken out of context, his words came to symbolise an era of mass affluence in which it seemed that too little was done to prepare the country for the future.

In fact Macmillan was forward-looking, speeding Britain's disengagement from empire and believing that the country's future lay in Europe. But his grand strategy was destroyed by the French president de Gaulle's veto of British membership of the Common Market in January 1963. From that moment on his leadership lacked direction. His authority had already been weakened, in the wake of the shock Tory defeat in the Orpington by-election in March 1962, by a botched reshuffle in July that year, just as Thatcher's authority never fully recovered from her mishandling of ministerial changes in the summer of 1989. Macmillan's sacking of a third of his cabinet in the 'night of the long knives' smacked of panic, not firm government. 'Greater love hath no man than he lay down his friends for his life,' was the damaging barb from Jeremy Thorpe, the Liberal MP.

With his government at a low ebb by the spring of 1963, Macmillan's leadership was already in question before the full drama of the Profumo scandal unfolded. In March, Jack Profumo, his war minister, made a dramatic late-night statement in the Commons denying the widespread rumours of his affair with Christine Keeler, a call girl. In April, Macmillan already felt the need to reassure a luncheon meeting of the 1922 Committee that he intended to stay on as leader and fight the next election. But in early June, Profumo resigned, confessing that he had lied to the Commons.

Macmillan's handling of the Profumo scandal showed him to be out of touch. He found the Commons debate on the security aspects on 17 June 1963 deeply wounding. His arch critic, Nigel Birch, one of the Treasury ministers whose resignation Macmillan had treated so lightly five years earlier, told the Prime Minister he should make way for a younger man. Birch referred to Cromwell's words, which Leo Amery had quoted against Neville Chamberlain in May 1940, but instead chose to quote Browning's poem 'The Lost Leader', closing with the line 'Never glad confident morning again'.

In the vote at the end of the Profumo debate, 27 Tory MPs abstained, reducing the government majority to 57. Martin Redmayne, the chief whip, had warned Macmillan it might fall as low as 40. The whips minimised the revolt by hinting to Tory MPs that a large-scale revolt would prompt the Prime Minister's resignation, which might lead to an early election. With the party trailing Labour by 10–15 points in the opinion polls, it was not a prospect which any Tory would relish.

Macmillan was indeed contemplating resignation, although he did not want to step down immediately, since it would have made the crisis even worse. Butler later recalled that Morrison, chairman of the 1922 committee, was talking about a new government.[37] Macmillan's PPS, Knox Cunningham, warned him of disloyalty 'at the highest level'.[38] The Prime Minister seemed older and more tired, which Alistair Horne, his biographer, attributes to the onset of prostate trouble.[39] Macmillan's 'grouse-moor' image was mercilessly lampooned by cartoonists and satirists, and reinforced the sense of decline and drift which now characterised his government.

In that summer of crisis and gossip, there occurred in mid-July a seemingly minor but, as it would turn out, highly significant demonstration of the power of the House of Lords to amend legislation. The point at issue was contained in the Government's bill to enable hereditary peers and their successors to disclaim their titles. This was a reform for which the Labour politician, Tony Benn, had campaigned since the death of his father, Viscount Stansgate, in November 1960, had debarred him from membership of the Commons. Quintin Hogg, when he succeeded his father as the second Viscount Hailsham in 1950, had sought to have the law changed but his plea had been rejected by Attlee.

Butler, who was Leader of the House when Benn began his campaign, was unsupportive.[40] Whatever the motivation for his illiberal stance, it angered his natural supporters among younger Tory MPs and he finally agreed to the setting-up of a joint committee of Lords and Commons on the issue. The committee reported in December 1962, but the Government was still not prepared to give reform priority. That suddenly changed in the spring of 1963, which happened to be the period when Macmillan's leadership was under threat. On 9 May the government promised legislation. The bill was introduced on 30 May, received unopposed second readings in both Houses and was law three months later.

Initially, however, the bill granted the right of immediate disclaimer only to the successors of hereditary peers, whereas peers then sitting in the Lords would have to wait till the dissolution of Parliament, that is, the next general election, if they wished to disclaim. Benn, who had not taken his title, would be free to disclaim it straight away. Tory peers thought this unfair, and on 16 July, the Lords passed an amendment to allow sitting peers to disclaim as soon as the bill became law, a one-off right which they were granted for a limited period of twelve months. The amendment was accepted by the Government – a significant decision in view of the precarious state of Macmillan's leadership by the summer.

The Peerage Act received royal assent on 31 July 1963. Curzon in 1923 and Halifax in 1940 had been ruled out as prime ministers primarily because they were in the Lords. But the way was now open for hereditary peers to seek the highest office, provided that they renounced their peerages and won election to the Commons. But if this was to apply to peers sitting at the time, like Hailsham, leader of the government in the Lords, or the Earl of Home, they would have to disclaim within the twelve months' time limit and seek election to the Commons.

Hailsham has since discovered that Macmillan had been mentioning him as his possible successor since February 1963. In June 1963 he was tipped off by Lord Poole, the joint party chairman, to prepare himself to become the next Tory leader, although Hailsham himself continued to expect that Butler would be chosen. But Home and Hailsham did discuss disclaiming their peerages and agreed that it would be impossible for them to do so at the same time because of their roles as the party's leading spokesmen in the Lords.[41]

During the summer recess of 1963, Macmillan wavered about his future. He saw the need to announce a firm decision in his speech which he was due to deliver as leader on Saturday 12 October after the annual party conference in Blackpool. By mid-September he was resolved to stay on. By early October his doubts returned, and Hailsham, still his favoured successor, had proved his mettle that summer by negotiating the Test-Ban Treaty. Over the weekend of 5–6 October at his home, Birch Grove, in Sussex, Macmillan confided his renewed doubts about staying on to his son-in-law, Julian Amery, the minister for aviation, and his son, Maurice Macmillan, a Tory MP. They argued that he should continue and he even began to contemplate fighting the next election. Macmillan also saw Home, who still felt that he should resign in 1964.[42]

On Macmillan's return to Number 10 on Monday 7th, he was told that most of the cabinet would back his staying on. He saw Butler, Redmayne, the chief whip, Lord Dilhorne, formerly Reggie Manningham-Buller until his appointment as Lord Chancellor in 1962, and other ministers. Most would support him, but Poole thought he should stand down. In Horne's account, by Monday evening Macmillan had decided to fight on. Hailsham, however, recalls that when he saw Macmillan that day the Prime Minister told him that he expected to retire around Christmas and wanted him to succeed.[43]

Overnight Macmillan was taken ill. His prostate trouble had flared up. In obvious discomfort, he chaired Tuesday morning's cabinet. Before midday, he informed ministers of his intention to announce at Blackpool on Saturday that he would lead the party at the next election. He then left the room to allow discussion of his plan. Dilhorne told colleagues that in the event of the Prime Minister being unable to stay on, he would be available to help in any cabinet consultation on a successor. Home then intervened to say that since he was in no circumstances a candidate, he would also be ready to assist.[44] It appeared that Dilhorne and Home had cast themselves in the roles played by Kilmuir and Salisbury six years earlier. Redmayne later told Macmillan that the cabinet would back him if he decided to stay on, the only exception being Enoch Powell.[45] There had been little time for discussion as ministers had to leave for Blackpool.

But by the evening, Macmillan's medical advice convinced him that he was seriously ill, possibly with cancer. He would have to resign. He entered hospital that night. Unlike Bonar Law in 1923 and Eden in 1957, Macmillan was still determined to ensure that he would advise the monarch on her appointment of his successor. Ironically, if the outgoing prime minister had proffered his advice six years earlier, Butler would have stood a better chance of succeeding. But now, an outgoing prime minister's action would dash his hopes.

According to Iain Macleod's remarkable account of the ensuing struggle for the leadership, which he published in the *Spectator* in January 1964, Macmillan was determined to prevent Butler succeeding him.[46] He had hoped that one of the younger ministers – Edward Heath, deputy to the Earl of Home at the Foreign Office; Reggie Maudling, the chancellor; or Macleod himself, then leader of the House and joint party chairman – might emerge as his successor. But none of them had established their credentials sufficiently strongly by the autumn of 1963. Macmillan would have to look elsewhere.

On Wednesday 9 October, Macmillan was visited in hospital by Home, who later recalled that the patient mentioned the possibility of his becoming leader. Home demurred and Macmillan expressed his preference for Hailsham.[47] The next morning, Thursday 10th, Macmillan again raised the leadership question with Home, who was 'still reluctant but said if no one did emerge he would accept a draft'.[48] Butler's private impression remained that it was Home who persuaded Macmillan to resign and then extracted a resignation statement from him.[49]

Macmillan then prepared for his operation and Home left for Blackpool. As president of that year's conference, Home would deliver Macmillan's statement about his impending resignation. It was curious that the resignation of a prime minister should be announced to a party conference, and its timing would inevitably make the leadership the only issue in anybody's minds. But it suited Macmillan since it would help his favoured candidate, Hailsham, who was popular among the party faithful. And if Hailsham's bandwagon should become bogged down, entrusting the announcement to Home would help bring him forward as a possible contender.

Macmillan's statement, which Home read to the conference on the afternoon of Thursday 10 October, threw the party into turmoil. The conference came to resemble an American-style presidential convention. The Imperial Hotel, where ministers and party bigwigs stay and where journalists congregate, became the centre of canvassing, lobbying and intrigue for the next forty-eight hours. The front-runners were generally thought to be Butler, Hailsham and Reggie Maudling, the 46-year-old chancellor, with Iain Macleod as a long shot. Although Dilhorne and Redmayne would not be officially commissioned by Macmillan to take soundings of ministers and MPs until the following week, they both began doing so during the party conference. Both were actively supporting a fourth candidate, Home.

On the Thursday afternoon, Julian Amery and Maurice Macmillan arrived in Blackpool and sought out Hailsham. 'Their joint message was clear and was conveyed straight from Harold himself,' Hailsham recalled.[50] He was to act at once. He had already spoken with Home, reminding him of their earlier conversation about the impossibility of their simultaneously disclaiming their titles. Hailsham told Home that he (Home) did not have adequate experience of domestic issues to become prime minister and that afternoon told Butler of his plans to disclaim his title.[51] At the end of his scripted CPC lecture that evening, Hailsham did just that. His declaration caused pandemonium.

This episode reinforced doubts about Hailsham's suitability for the highest office, as did Randolph Churchill's distribution of 'Q' badges (Hailsham's christian name being Quintin). Hailsham was viewed as too much of a showman and unreliable, in much the same way as Heseltine was seen by some Tories in the 1990 contest. Heseltine's seizing of the mace and his walking out of the cabinet were always held against him. Likewise, Hailsham was never allowed to forget two incidents. In October 1957, at the close of the party conference, he had turned the humdrum ceremony of being presented with the chairman's bell into high drama, waving it wildly above his head and declaiming a modified version of John Donne's words to suggest that the bell was tolling for the Labour Party. In June 1963, when pressed about the Profumo scandal during a television interview, he had proclaimed: 'A great party is not to be brought down because of a squalid affair between a woman of easy virtue and a proven liar.'[52]

Most seriously for Hailsham's prospects, a section of the party strongly opposed his becoming leader. But his main rival, Butler, also had his strong opponents. Maudling was supported by younger MPs in the hope that the party would jump a generation and counter the challenge of the new Labour leader, Harold Wilson, who, like Maudling, was more than twenty years younger than Macmillan. But Maudling gave an uninspired speech. Iain Macleod, a brilliant orator, who had encouraged his friend beforehand, despaired at Maudling's inability to deliver a rousing peroration.

Butler seemed to be the favourite, as he had been in 1957. In Macmillan's absence he would deliver the leader's speech on Saturday afternoon after the end of the conference, although it was ominous that he should have had to insist on his right to do so. Late on Friday night, however, Macleod had got wind of Home's threatened emergence as a contender and tried to help Butler's cause. In the very early hours of Saturday morning he gave two of the most respected lobby journalists, David Wood of *The Times* and Harry Boyne of the *Daily Telegraph*, an off-the-record briefing in his room at the Imperial, confirming rumours that Home was a possible contender.[53] He was determined that the party should not disperse the next day without knowing what threatened. Butler would need a groundswell of support in the conference to promote his claim. Butler later revealed he and Macleod 'had a secret . . . he always said he hoped that I would be Prime Minister, and he wished himself to succeed me'.[54]

In Macleod's sensational article about the 1963 leadership crisis in the *Spectator*, he claimed that neither he nor Maudling had thought of Home as a contender, 'although for a brief moment his star seemed to have flared at Blackpool'. That night Macleod suddenly seemed to have spotted a possible supernova, although he then mistakenly assumed that it faded as quickly as it had 'flared'; he left Blackpool convinced that Home was not in the running.

At lunch on the Saturday, Home informed Butler that he was seeking his doctor's advice.[55] The implication was clear: Home was throwing his hat into the ring. He was being pressed to seek the leadership by a number of senior Tories in addition to Dilhorne and Redmayne, notably Selwyn Lloyd, the former chancellor and foreign secretary.[56] Another supporter was Heath, Home's deputy at the Foreign Office and former chief whip. Jim Prior, who served as Heath's PPS from 1965 to 1970, believes that Heath 'worked hard for Alec [Home] to be prime minister'.[57] Hailsham has little doubt that the leadership was discussed when Heath visited Morrison, chairman of the 1922 Committee, during his visit to the latter's retreat on the Isle of Islay during the summer of 1963.[58]

Home's revelation was shocking news for Butler as he was about to deliver the speech which might well determine whether he would become prime minister or again be overlooked. Like Maudling, Butler failed to make his speech rise to the occasion. One incident was particularly telling. Butler was heckled by an empire loyalist and paused to mop his brow. Home, as conference president, intervened to restore order.

The scene shifted to London, where Macmillan was told by his son, Maurice, and Lord Poole on Monday evening, 14 October, that the party in the country wanted Hailsham, MPs wanted Maudling or Butler, and the cabinet wanted Butler.[59] Macmillan then prepared his plans for detailed soundings of the party, which were announced by the hapless Butler – deputising yet again for an ill prime minister – to the cabinet the next day. Unlike 1957, when only the cabinet was formally consulted, Macmillan arranged to consult all sections of the party before presenting his advice to the Queen: the cabinet would be sounded out by Lord Dilhorne, the Lord Chancellor; Tory MPs by Redmayne, the chief whip; active Tory peers by Lord St Aldwyn, the whip in the Lords; and the party in the country by Lord Poole, the joint party chairman (not by the other joint chairman, Iain Macleod).

Macmillan, however, was determined to maintain control from his hospital bed. By Tuesday 15th, he had switched to supporting Home as 'he would be the best able to secure united support'.[60] A procession of contenders and ministers trooped through his sick-room. The reports of the key soundings which he received during Thursday 17th showed a first choice for Home, with the exception of the constituencies, which were split 60 per cent for Hailsham and 40 per cent for Butler but with strong opposition to both. Macmillan noted that Home had scarcely then emerged as a candidate but judged that 'everyone would rally around Home'.[61]

The Tory peers were two to one for Home, and Macmillan judged that Redmayne's soundings of MPs showed the largest group, 'not by much, but significant' for Home.[62] The controversy about Redmayne's conclusion has raged ever since among whips and MPs of the time. But some leading questioning of MPs, of the kind mentioned by Prior in his memoirs, in which Home's name was pushed by Redmayne, probably resulted in the chief whip's inflating the extent of support for Home.[63] Redmayne later admitted that his estimate was biased towards 'people on whose opinion one would more strongly rely than on others'.[64]

Even greater controversy surrounds Dilhorne's soundings of the cabinet. He reported that ministers' first choices were as follows: Home 10, Butler 3, Maudling 4 and Hailsham 2. Listed among Home's supporters is Macleod.[65] Yet Macleod subsequently refused to serve Home and nobody close to Macleod at the time considers for a moment that he would have backed Home. Macleod's brief but determined intervention against Home on the eve of Butler's speech is further evidence that Dilhorne was wrong. When Macleod later publicly challenged Dilhorne's conclusion that a majority of the cabinet backed Home, Dilhorne remained silent.

Macleod estimated that in his personal knowledge, eleven ministers were for candidates other than Home, Dilhorne's figures were 'simply impossible'. Seeking to 'explain the inexplicable', Macleod could only conclude that 'the expressions of genuine regard for him [Home] somehow became translated into second or even first preferences'.[66] Macleod's rejection of Dilhorne's estimates is supported by Dennis Walters, a back-bench supporter of Hailsham, and by Lady Butler, who has since published the list of eight ministers who telephoned her husband on the evening of the 17th and the morning of the 18th to say that they were supporting him.[67]

But it was Dilhorne's figures that mattered. Macleod only heard by chance on the morning of Thursday 17th that the succession was to be settled that afternoon. Maudling was also unaware that a decision was imminent. 'It is some measure of the tightness of the magic circle on this occasion,' Macleod wrote, 'that neither the Chancellor of the Exchequer nor the Leader of the House of Commons had any inkling of what was happening.'[68]

Butler had failed to arrange for a cabinet meeting to be held on the Thursday morning, which might have helped prevent what followed. He, too, learned that morning that a decision was imminent, but failed either to inform or organise his supporters even though he had reason to think that he would not be appointed.[69] In fact, before lunch Maudling sought to persuade Dilhorne to summon a meeting of ministers to discuss the leadership, or at least to review the procedures by which the Queen was to be advised, but the Lord Chancellor resisted both requests.[70]

During the afternoon Butler, Macleod and Maudling heard that Macmillan would advise the Queen to send for Home. There followed a series of meetings and telephone calls, interrupted by dinner engagements, which lasted late into the night. Butler played scarcely any part in these, other than taking calls from his agitated supporters. Macleod and Powell telephoned Home to tell him why they objected to his becoming leader. Powell's house in South Eaton Place became the location of the 'midnight' meeting attended by Powell, Macleod, Maudling, Lord Aldington, deputy chairman, and Frederick Erroll, president of the Board of Trade. Faced with the prospect of Home becoming leader, two of the other contenders, Maudling and Hailsham, who was in touch with the 'midnight' meeting by phone, said that they were opposed to Home but would agree to serve Butler. The chief whip was phoned, and he then called at Powell's house, trying to persuade the meeting to back Home. But he failed and agreed to convey the fact of the understanding which had developed between Butler, Hailsham and Maudling to the Prime Minister.[71]

On Friday morning, 18th October, Macmillan had heard of the overnight rebellion by 8.30 am. But instead of causing Macmillan to delay, this news only encouraged him to rush ahead as planned. Home had grown nervous about becoming leader if it would cause acrimony. Macmillan rallied him: 'Look, we can't change our view now. All the troops are on the starting line. Everything is arranged.'[72] Butler meanwhile telephoned Dilhorne to propose that Macmillan authorise a meeting of the three other contenders before a final decision was made for Home. No reply was made.[73] By the time the three other contenders met at midday, without Dilhorne, it was far too late. Macmillan tendered his resignation to the Queen at 9.30 am, she visited him at 11.15 am and he read out his memorandum of advice which incorporated the party soundings.

At 12.15 pm the Queen invited Home to form an administration and she did not formally appoint him prime minister until he had consulted his colleagues. Hailsham, Macleod, Maudling, Boyle and Powell refused to join. Butler reserved his position. But by the evening, Hailsham was indicating his readiness to serve: he had been warned earlier by Selwyn

*The manner of Home's triumph in 1963 utterly discredited the
customary processes 'by which Tory leaders revolved'.*

Lloyd, one of Home's strongest supporters, that his refusal would look
like sour grapes.[74] Butler caved in the next morning, believing he was
acting in the interests of party unity. Once their principal had agreed to
serve, Maudling and Boyle quickly followed. Only Macleod and Powell
refused office on grounds of 'personal moral integrity'.[75] Both had spent
the previous ten days or so arguing for Butler.

As in 1957, the Tory crown had been seized from Butler's hands
moments before his expected coronation. Yet, as Macleod said, his
supporters had 'put the golden ball in his lap, if he drops it now it's his
own fault'.[76] Powell spoke of having handed Butler 'a loaded revolver
and told him all he had to do was pull the trigger', but Butler hadn't
wanted to use it if it would make a noise or hurt anyone.[77]

Home was able to kiss hands as the new prime minister the following
day, Saturday 19 October. He duly disclaimed his peerage in order to
fight a by-election at Kinross and West Perthshire. For a period of three
weeks, Britain's prime minister was therefore not a member of either
House of Parliament. But he was duly elected to the Commons and on 11

November 1963, Sir Alec Douglas-Home, formerly the fourteenth Earl of Home, was officially endorsed as Tory leader.

It is argued that Douglas-Home was the right choice because he was the only candidate who could unite the party. But the other main contenders were prepared to support Butler, and there is little doubt that with their backing and with an election at the most a year away, the party would have united behind him. It is also said that Macmillan's system of consultation was democratic because all sections of the party were consulted. But that is to ignore the scope for bias and incompetence, which clearly were present, in the soundings of party opinion.

The manner of Douglas-Home's selection as leader had discredited the 'customary processes'. There was also a constitutional point: the Tories had claimed that their method upheld the royal prerogative, but the mishandling of the 1963 crisis raised questions about the role of the Palace in so readily acceding to Macmillan's plan.

Macleod's article in the *Spectator* in January 1964 delivered the *coup de grâce* to the 'magic circle'. Douglas-Home came to recognise that he owed it to his successor and to his party to try to prevent such chaos and rancour over the selection of its leader in the future.

IV

Macleod observed of Douglas-Home's leadership: 'The Tory Party for the first time since Bonar Law is now being led from the right of centre.'[78] But unlike Bonar Law or Thatcher, Douglas-Home was of the traditional right: the fourteenth earl lacked the cutting edge of either the Glasgow iron merchant or the Grantham grocer's daughter. 'There was a year in which we had nothing to do,' Home recalled of his 364-day premiership, 'because we had finished our programme and you couldn't do anything except await the election.'[79] His inheritance as prime minister was unenviable, but his approach to the task could scarcely be described as inspirational.

Douglas-Home dared not risk an early poll, as Eden had done in 1955, because of the certain knowledge that the Tories would be heavily defeated. He was advised by Conservative Central Office that an election in the spring of 1964 would result in an overall Labour majority of 30–60 seats, but that if he soldiered on till the end, in the autumn of 1964, there was a chance of victory.

But despite Douglas-Home's delaying the election for a year, the Tories were defeated. Labour returned to office although their majority had been held to only 4 seats. Under Douglas-Home's leadership, the Tories had made a significant recovery from their low point of 1963. Many Tories today attest to his achievement. Fewer were prepared to say as much in 1964. However much their position had improved, it was still not good enough. They had lost office.

Because the margin of defeat was so slender, there must have been a chance that with another leader the Tories would have won: Macleod and Powell would not have resigned. Butler would have been more popular with uncommitted voters; Hailsham would have inspired the party faithful; Maudling would have dealt far more effectively with Wilson's attacks on the Tories' economic record. Douglas-Home was plainly out of his depth on the economy; an earlier self-deprecating confession that he had to do economic calculations with the help of 'a box of matches' seemed all too evidently true. It made a pitiable contrast to Wilson's command of statistics and talk of 'the white heat of the technological revolution', and was not what people were looking for in an era of national planning and growth targets.

Moreover, the only significant reform of the Douglas-Home government, which stood out because of the absence of any other major measures, was the abolition of resale price maintenance. This enraged many Tory supporters who owned small shops. The policy was pushed through by Heath, then president of the Board of Trade and one of Home's strongest supporters, in October 1963. Although it made economic sense, it would have made more political sense to have delayed its introduction until after an election.

The Tory Party's damaging grouse-moor image was perpetuated with Douglas-Home as leader. The Tories were more easily portrayed as representing an outdated and self-selecting establishment which was increasingly seen to be making a poor job of running government, the city and industry. This sense that the Tories had identified themselves too closely with a narrowly based old-guard is what Macleod captured in his attack on 'the magic circle'. Identifying the senior Tories who had masterminded the soundings of the party and the selection of Douglas-Home in October 1963, Macleod wrote: 'Eight of the nine men mentioned in the last sentence went to Eton.'[80] Macleod had attended Fettes College, sometimes called 'Scotland's Eton', and was proud of his membership of White's, one of the most exclusive gentlemen's clubs in London. But he understood young people's aspirations and was sensitive to the changing national mood. He had hit a raw nerve in the party and was not thanked for it.

Immediately after the defeat of October 1964, Douglas-Home strengthened his team by appointing Macleod and Powell, the rebels of twelve months earlier, to his shadow cabinet. In February 1965, Heath became shadow chancellor and began organising detailed policy work. But although the front bench was revamped, Douglas-Home's authority was weakened. As Wilson continued to get the better of Douglas-Home in the Commons, an increasing number of Tory MPs wanted to see a leader who would give as good as he got. That was not Douglas-Home's style. As the criticisms grew, MPs began to group around the prospective successors, principally Heath and Maudling, who had become shadow foreign secretary.

The Tories faced a dilemma. Labour's wafer-thin majority made it impossible for Wilson to govern effectively for more than a year or two. He was therefore expected to seek an early election. Without a more dynamic leader, Tory MPs feared a heavy defeat, yet the prospect of an imminent election ruled out their making an immediate change in the leadership. Ironically, the Tory success in the May 1965 local elections triggered the sequence of events which led to Douglas-Home's downfall. It was clear that Wilson would not risk an immediate election. This provided the Tories with a window of opportunity during the summer to change their leader, although many MPs wanted to see Douglas-Home continue. On 26 June, Douglas-Home felt sufficiently confident to state that there would be no leadership election during 1965. But on the same day, Wilson announced that the Labour government would also soldier on into 1966.

The pressure against Douglas-Home rapidly began to build. On 1 July, there were calls for him to relinquish the leadership at the meeting of the 1922 executive committee. But he stuck to his guns, and it seemed by the middle of the month that he would reaffirm his determination to continue as leader when he addressed the 1922 Committee on 22 July. This occasion, the leader's customary address to backbenchers before the recess, would be the last opportunity for many months for any change in the leadership. On the Sunday before the meeting, the *Sunday Times* published an article by William Rees-Mogg entitled 'The Right Moment to Change'. Congratulating Douglas-Home on having played a 'captain's innings', Rees-Mogg none the less argued that it was 'hard to resist the widespread view' that the Tories 'will not win a general election while Sir Alec remains their leader'.

The article prompted a flood of messages to Central Office and the whips' office the following day called on Douglas-Home to stand down. Willie Whitelaw, the chief whip, and Edward du Cann, the party chairman, advised Douglas-Home that he should resign. But his strongest supporters, including Selwyn Lloyd, advised him to stay on.[81] Douglas-Home decided to sleep on it. In the end, he concluded that he should resign. What is said finally to have decided him were the findings of an opinion poll which showed that people thought Wilson had better qualities as a prime minister, including the view that Wilson was the more sincere.[82]

When the 1922 Committee gathered in Committee Room 14 at six o'clock on the evening of Thursday 22 July, Douglas-Home read a short statement declaring that he would resign as leader. Those present still recall the shocked silence, although more cynical observers noted that some of the strongest expressions of shock came from MPs who had been calling for Douglas-Home to go. Many MPs, however, were angry that a section of the party in the Commons had been determined to keep up the pressure on him until he stepped down. But this active campaign would not have been effective had Douglas-Home's authority as leader not already been fatally undermined.

In his appointment of Heath as shadow chancellor, Douglas-Home had created an obvious heir presumptive. By the summer of 1965 Heath was enjoying enormous success attacking Labour's finance bill, inflicting defeats on the government in early July. Tory MPs were delghted to see one of their spokesmen proving that Labour was far from invincible on the economy. Heath was the same age as Wilson and offered the dynamic, strong leadership which Douglas-Home would never provide but which the Tories wanted to see before the next election.

Douglas-Home's resignation meant that the Tory Party would be choosing a new leader in opposition for the first time for more than fifty years, since Arthur Balfour resigned in 1911. Douglas-Home's decision to stand down had about it shades of Balfour, another Tory leader of aristocratic background who had served as prime minister and who at the end of the day found the fight to remain leader of the opposition not worth the candle. Balfour's resignation had caused consternation at the possible 'indignity' of an election to settle who should lead the party in the Commons, and had created near panic in the whip's office as the chief whip hurriedly tried to decide on the election procedures. Douglas-Home had at least left his party better prepared.

The 1965 Tory succession signalled the first occasion on which the party leader would be elected by Tory MPs under the new, formal procedure which had been adopted to prevent any repetition of the crisis in October 1963. In the aftermath of that crisis, Humphry Berkeley, the Tory MP for Lancaster and an acolyte of Iain Macleod's, had started to campaign for the party leader to be selected by a new procedure. On 1 January 1964 he had written to Douglas-Home proposing that the leader should be democratically elected by Tory MPs in a secret ballot, possibly extending the franchise in some way to include the other sections of the party – Tory peers, the National Union and adopted parliamentary candidates. But Douglas-Home had deferred any review of the issue until the general election had been fought.

On 5 November 1964, Douglas-Home told the 1922 Committee that he would review the procedure for selecting the party leader. Berkeley submitted a memorandum proposing election by Tory MPs only. The committee set up and chaired by Douglas-Home included the chief whip, Redmayne (later replaced by Willie Whitelaw); the party chairman, Lord Blakenham (later replaced by Edward du Cann); the chairman of the 1922 Committee, Sir William Anstruther-Gray; the leader of the party in the Lords, Lord Carrington; and other senior members of the shadow cabinet, among them Butler, Hogg (formerly Hailsham), Macleod and Selwyn Lloyd. They spent a considerable amount of effort trying to devise a method of involving all sections of the party. It was agreed that the selection should be settled in a ballot, but who should vote?

Initially there was support for giving all sections of the party a vote, but the weight of argument increasingly favoured Berkeley's proposal of election by Tory MPs only. It was clear that the party leader held the position because he was leader in the Commons and had to have the authority of the party's MPs. The leader was bound to be an MP, and other MPs were better placed to judge leadership contenders than anybody else. There was also the need to avoid a situation in which the wishes of MPs were outweighed by other sections of the party. The committee finally opted for election of the leader by Tory MPs only. But the new procedure included a requirement for consultation of all sections of the party. As a member of the Douglas-Home committee once observed, however, the consultations are a 'complete nonsense, but they help to make the rest of the party feel better'.[83]

The question of whether the new selection procedure would apply when the party was next in government appears initially to have been left open. After all, Kilmuir had argued strongly that nothing should be done which appeared to remove the royal prerogative in choosing a new prime minister, and had criticised Labour's call for a leadership election in 1957 to choose a successor to Eden. It was only later, as a result of the amendment requiring annual leadership elections, that it became absolutely clear the new procedure would operate when the Tories were in office: Thatcher had to face re-election every year from 1979, whereas Heath had faced no such requirement.

The problem now resurfaced that had confronted the chief whip in November 1911: if the leader was to be elected by Tory MPs, what method should be used? It was clear that any new leader needed to enjoy the support of the majority of the party in the Commons, which ruled out simply operating a 'first past the post' system. Various methods of transferable voting were considered, but the system which was eventually agreed is basically the system which still operated in 1990.

The details were thrashed out in talks involving the 1922 executive, in which Peter Emery, then its joint honorary secretary, played a key role. The requirement that a winning candidate on the first ballot would need an overall majority and 15 per cent more of the votes cast than his nearest rival was designed to ensure that any outright winner enjoyed command-ing support. On the second ballot only an overall majority was required, but there was also provision for a third ballot in which MPs would list their preferences.

Douglas-Home had announced the new procedure to the 1922 Committee on 25 February 1965. Five months later, his resignation brought it into effect. The first ballot was held just five days later. Three nominations were received: from Heath, the shadow chancellor, Maudling, the former chancellor and unsuccessful contender in 1963, and Powell, who had been one of Butler's strongest supporters but who was regarded as the right-wing candidate. Macleod had considered beforehand whether or not to stand, but was told by close advisers that his support among MPs was still not strong enough after his refusal to serve Home in 1963 and his attack on 'the magic circle', and he therefore immediately said that he would not enter the contest.

From the outset, Heath and Maudling were the clear front-runners, with Powell entering the contest 'to leave my visiting card', as he commented.[84] There was little to choose between Heath and Maudling on policy, although Heath seemed more of a believer at that stage in competition and what would probably now be termed 'market forces'. What counted, however, was that Heath had run into the kind of good form over the preceding few months which is the prerequisite for winning the Tory leadership. He also ran an aggressive campaign, organised by Peter Walker from his house in Gayfere Street, the same street where Major's team were based in 1990. Maudling, whose team operated from Tory MP William Clark's house in nearby Barton Street, kept their canvassing low-key, hoping to benefit from a backlash against Heath's supporters for their part in Douglas-Home's downfall.

But the Tories were not in much mood to be gentle. As Butler commented at the time, the party could have an easier and gentler time with Maudling, or a more difficult and tougher time with Heath, but it would probably do the party good to have Heath. This appeared to be Macleod's judgement also. He switched his support from Maudling, his long-standing ally, and on one reckoning as many as 45 MPs followed suit.[85]

The result of the first ballot was declared at 2.15 pm on 28 July. Heath had won 150 votes, Maudling 133 and Powell 15. Heath had won an overall majority but had fallen short of the required 15 per cent margin of the votes cast. Maudling, however, saw that his position was hopeless and, like Powell, immediately withdrew. In marked contrast to October 1963, there was no doubt about the outcome and there were no recriminations afterwards. The new procedure had succeeded in its first test where the 'magic circle' had failed.

On 2 August 1965, Heath was endorsed as party leader at the traditional party meeting. The contrast between the old and the new could not have seemed more complete. After abandonment of the 'customary processes' and the resignation of the fourteenth earl from the Borders, the party had adopted a 'formal procedure' and elected the son of a carpenter and a housemaid from Broadstairs.

V

Despite Heath's very different background from those of his postwar predecessors as Tory leader – an earl (Home), the son-in-law of a duke (Macmillan), a baronet (Eden) and the grandson of a duke (Churchill) – he was not an outsider. By the time he became leader, he had been at the very heart of the Tory Party for a decade. In 1955, Eden appointed him chief whip, the most inside job available in politics; in 1957, Heath had endorsed Macmillan for the leadership, and on the night of Macmillan's appointment they celebrated together over champagne and oysters at the Turf Club; and in 1963, Heath had been a strong supporter of Home, his boss at the Foreign Office.

But Heath was determined to modernise Britain in a way which his mentors in the Tory governments of the 1950s and early 1960s had shied away from. Yet Macmillan had entrusted him with implementing the European part of his grand strategy, and Europe would remain Heath's overriding commitment – one which cut across party lines and reflected a vision of long-term national interest, not a commitment stemming from some partisan root. There are similarities between Heath and Peel as reformers-cum-strategists, almost seeming deliberately to seek a view of the national interest which challenges party loyalty, and making life even more difficult for themselves as leader by treating MPs in an unnecessarily offhand, brusque manner.

Heath was instinctively a paternalist Tory, but he was a reformer, even a radical, not a traditionalist. According to Jim Prior, Heath's PPS and then a member of Heath's 1970–74 cabinet, when Heath became leader he believed that 'the country was suffering from a malaise'. His prescription was a combination of state and free-market measures:

He was in favour of Government intervention to modernise the country's basic infrastructure; and [second,] he felt that he could release human motivation by freeing the country of controls, abolishing restrictive practices whether by the unions or management, reducing taxation and opening up new markets, particularly in Europe.[86]

Europe, in fact, became the means by which Heath would force Britain to modernise.

Heath was determined to develop detailed policies in opposition, ready for the day when he would head 'a great reforming administration'.[87] As Douglas-Home's shadow chancellor, he had set up the policy groups working from February 1965, but before the really grand schemes could be developed under his leadership, he had first to face an early election. Within nine months of his succeeding Douglas-Home, Parliament was dissolved and Labour sought their increased majority in March 1966. There was little that any Tory leader could have done to stem the tide, but it was none the less a bad defeat, the worst for the Tories since 1945. Labour's majority was 96. Heath faced a long, hard slog as leader of the opposition.

It is always more difficult for a leader to establish authority in opposition than in government, and especially for Tory leaders whose MPs expect to be restored to government as hastily as possible. Heath was not an orator; he did not have the timing and turn of phrase of a Macleod or the logic of a Powell. He could be forceful, but in a common-sense, matter-of-fact way, and he found it difficult at that stage to look relaxed or in command on television. From 1968, he had to contend with the fierce reaction in the party to his sacking of Powell over the latter's anti-immigration 'Rivers of Blood' speech, and also watched what had been a huge lead over Labour ebb away as the election drew nearer.

But in June 1970, against expectations, Heath led the Tories to victory at the general election, winning an overall majority of 30 seats. It was Heath's victory. It gave him new authority. Within a month, however, his chancellor, Iain Macleod, had died. It was a shattering blow from which Heath's Government never fully recovered. The Tories had lost their most effective communicator and shrewdest political brain. Perhaps most of all Heath had lost a minister who would have stood up to him. Certainly, Heath established a dominance of the cabinet which was not good for his ministers, or for him.

Heath had been elected on a manifesto markedly more radical than that on which Thatcher would be elected in 1979. What had promised to be a great reforming administration became overloaded. Heath's great achievement was to take Britain into the European Community, and that in itself was a major effort. In addition, his government had set itself the task of rewriting the whole of industrial relations law and reorganising local government. When the U-turn on economic policy led to the introduction of a statutory prices-and-incomes policy, overload threatened collapse: the government became overburdened with detail. Heath was relying increasingly on a few senior civil servants for advice on matters which the cabinet was better qualified to judge.

By the winter of 1973–4, Heath had become boxed in. Unable to seize an opportunity to settle the miners' dispute, he was torn between hawks and doves in his inner group of ministers on the issue of whether to call an early election with the slogan 'Who governs?' Hawks like Lord Carrington, the party chairman, and the Leader of the House, Prior, wanted a snap election. Doves like Whitelaw, the employment secretary, and Carr, the home secretary, were arguing against an election. Heath delayed briefly, then went to the country. In a campaign which rapidly widened from the 'Who governs?' issue, Labour narrowly emerged as the single largest party, winning four more seats than the Tories. Heath's last-ditch efforts to construct a coalition with the Liberals failed, and he was forced to leave Number 10.

With Wilson installed at the head of a minority Labour government, another election was imminent and any attempt to oust Heath was therefore postponed. But such was the decline in his authority after the February 1974 election that Sir Keith Joseph, a former cabinet colleague and member of Heath's shadow cabinet, launched a series of major speeches criticising the policies of postwar Conservative governments and advocating a switch to monetarism and economic liberalism. A further election followed in October 1974, as Labour consolidated their hold on office and established an overall majority. Heath fought a good campaign, preventing a repetition of the 1966 Labour landslide which many Tories had feared. But he had lost three elections out of four as leader, and his days were numbered.

Immediately after this second election defeat in a year, Heath was advised by Prior that his only chance of retaining the leadership was straight away to offer himself for re-election as leader. Even so, Prior did not give Heath much of a chance. Heath's response is revealing – he told Prior that he would try to stay on to prevent the right wing gaining control of the leadership. Yet, as Prior feared, this tactic was to play into the right wing's hands.[88] There was also considerable speculation that the economic crisis of the mid-1970s would prove too great for the Labour Government. Heath must have hoped that he would soon be leading the Tories back into office, possibly in coalition as Baldwin had in 1931.

The problem for the Tories was that the procedures for selecting the leader introduced in 1965 contained no provision for re-election. Douglas-Home had appeared to rely on the good sense of the leader to resign when he had lost the support of the parliamentary party, as he had done himself. But what was to happen if the leader had no intention of going quietly in the manner of a Balfour or a Douglas-Home?

Four days after the October 1974 election, the executive of the 1922 Committee met and advised Heath to offer himself for re-election. Heath refused to discuss the matter until the annual elections for the executive had been held the following month. This was a further miscalculation by Heath and showed how out of touch he had become with back-bench opinion. The existing 1922 executive was re-elected unanimously.[89] Eleven days later Heath agreed that a review of the rules for leadership elections should be undertaken by a committee chaired by his predecessor, Lord Home (the former Sir Alec Douglas-Home).

Home's review of the procedure produced three revisions: the leader would be subject to annual re-election (thus solving the problem of the leader who refused to resign); a stiffer hurdle was introduced to win on the first ballot, the winner needing an overall majority of 15 per cent of those entitled to vote and not only of those who voted; and the rules for consulting the rest of the party were modified and formalised.

The only problem was that those who wished to see an immediate challenge to Heath could not find a suitable candidate. Whitelaw made it clear that out of loyalty to his leader he would not put his name forward. Most Tory MPs had assumed that Joseph would be a candidate, but he withdrew for personal reasons, following a disastrous gaffe in which he seemed to advocate contraception according to people's class. Then the would-be kingmakers turned to du Cann, chairman of the 1922 Committee, and several meetings were held during November to try to establish his prospects. After Joseph's decision to withdraw, however, his closest ally, Thatcher, had said that she intended to stand. Du Cann and Thatcher discussed their position as likely contenders and agreed that one would not stand against the other for fear of splitting the vote. Over the 1974–5 Christmas recess, du Cann decided that he would not fight. By this stage, in mid-January 1975, about twenty-five MPs had been meeting as a group to back du Cann, among them Airey Neave, a former minister and senior backbencher who had long before fallen out with Heath. About fifteen of the du Cann group, including Neave, transferred immediately to the Thatcher campaign.[90]

There were less than three weeks to go before the date set for the first ballot. Neave discovered that although Thatcher had been a candidate since late November, she had not built up any campaign team. He immediately set to work, and, with Bill Shelton, a relatively junior backbencher, built up a team which eventually numbered around fifty MPs.[91] She lacked experience in government, but Heath had handed her a great asset, appointing her to lead the opposition team on the finance bill – the very position in which Heath had established his reputation in the months before he had won the first leadership election ten years earlier.

Heath's campaign was run by his PPS, Tim Kitson, and Kenneth Baker, who would play a central role in the 1990 contest as Thatcher's party chairman. Peter Walker, who had run Heath's campaign in 1965, also helped. But the Heath camp were deceived by the over-optimistic reports which they received of the likely level of his support – a problem for any incumbent leader – and some of his supporters made the mistake of being far too optimistic with other MPs. By contrast, Neave was cautious. 'Margaret is doing very well, but not quite well enough,' he would reply to enquiries about Thatcher's prospects, implying that she was worth support but would need more.[92] Some MPs voted for Thatcher on the grounds that she would receive sufficient support to oust Heath and they would then be able to vote for Whitelaw in the second ballot. Tebbit and John Nott persuaded Heseltine, who was a Whitelaw man, that unless he voted for Thatcher in the first ballot there would be no second ballot and no opportunity for Whitelaw to stand.[93] Also standing was the traditional right-winger, Hugh Fraser.

On 4 February 1975, voting took place on the first ballot in Committee Room 14 between 12 noon and 3.30 pm. At 4 pm du Cann announced the result: Thatcher 130; Heath 119; Hugh Fraser 16; abstentions or absent 11. Tory MPs were initially stunned. Neave's ploy had worked far better than he could have dared hope. Then pandemonium broke loose. 'She's won! She's won!' shouted Alan Clark, the maverick right-winger, as he ran from Westminster Hall.[94]

Tory MPs did to Heath what had been done previously to Austen Chamberlain in 1922, although their vote in 1922 had not been on the leadership: Chamberlain took it as such. Heath had lost because the parliamentary party regarded him as an electoral liability, but he was also not helped by his seeming aloofness, which backbenchers had cause to witness on more occasions than many others in the party. Indeed, had any other element in the party – the shadow cabinet, the peers, or the National Union and the local associations – had the decisive say on the leadership, Heath would have survived. But the electoral college was composed of his fellow MPs, and they were the least favourably disposed towards him.

Thatcher had not quite achieved the target figure of 139 votes, and there would therefore have to be a second ballot the following week. But she would now be the front-runner whom other contenders would need to defeat. Heath withdrew, and appointed Robert Carr as temporary leader of the opposition until the election procedure had been completed and a new leader had been elected.

Heath's deputy, Whitelaw, now entered the fray, but Thatcher's campaign had the momentum and Whitelaw never looked confident of victory. His morale was lowered by the entry of other candidates into the field, who he believed were more likely to take support away from him than from Thatcher. Prior and Sir Geoffrey Howe threw their hats into the ring, both intending to put down markers for the future – Prior as a future contender on the left, Howe able to attract right-wing support on the economy but socially liberal. The final candidate was John Peyton, the former transport minister and a Tory traditionalist, who had strongly backed Heath and entered the contest to gain a platform for his views.

The second ballot was held exactly a week after the first, on 11 February. That afternoon in Committee Room 14, du Cann again announced the results: Thatcher 146, Whitelaw 79, Prior 19, Howe 19 and Peyton 11. There would be no need for a third ballot since Thatcher had easily won an outright majority.

Thatcher's background was far closer to Heath's than to that of their predecessors as Tory leader, but she was patently far more of an outsider than Heath had been when he won in 1965. Her victory was more of a vote against Heath than an endorsement of her. Many Tory MPs had hoped to use her as the means to remove Heath: little did they realise what they had done.

But what has been her impact on the Tory Party?

7

Thatcher's Impact

'Mrs Thatcher was the great Tory radical of our times. She was determined to break away from the history of the past, and the consensus politics and the corporatism. And she was willing to tackle anything in that sense. There was no institution which was safe from her, none whatsoever.'

Norman Tebbit, MP, former cabinet minister, December 1990

I

By sheer dint of her length of rule as Tory leader and prime minister Thatcher's impact is considerable. Her spell of fifteen years and nine months as Conservative leader is unsurpassed in the twentieth century. Her nearest rivals are Churchill, who led the party for fourteen and a half years (1940–55) and Baldwin with fourteen years (1923–37). Only two Tory leaders have run the party for a longer period: the Earl of Derby (1846–68) and the Marquis of Salisbury (1881–1902), both of whom led the party for more than twenty-one years, although it was not until their appointment as prime minister (Derby in 1852 and Salisbury in 1885) that they were clearly established as party leader and not simply leader in the House of Lords. Disraeli was party leader for thirteen years (1868–81) but had been leader of the Conservatives in the Commons for the previous nineteen years, and Peel (1834–46) lasted as party leader for eleven and a half years.

The most striking feature of Thatcher's leadership is that she was prime minister for eleven and a half years. Her length of continuous rule is without comparison since Lord Liverpool's fifteen years more than a century and a half ago (1812–27). She far exceeded the previous twentieth-century record of eight years and seven months, for both continuous and total length of rule, which had been set by the Liberal Herbert Asquith (1908–16). Macmillan's six years and nine months (1957–63) was the previous record for continuous rule by a twentieth-century Conservative. Churchill's two stints (1940–45 and 1951–5) amounted to eight years and seven months – he failed to match Asquith's record total by only three days, raising the question of who miscalculated with the calendar in Number 10. In March 1987 Thatcher broke Harold Wilson's all-comer's postwar record total of seven years and ten months, achieved between 1964 and 1976. In the history of the Conservative Party, Thatcher's performance is exceeded only by that of Lord Salisbury, whose total of thirteen and a half years in office was achieved in three separate spells (one short and two longer periods) during a seventeen-year span between 1885 and 1902.

Timeserving, however, was never regarded by Thatcher as a sufficient means of shaping history, although she patently thrived on exercising power and even by the mid-term of her third parliament was plainly reluctant to quit. She had a mission. Her objective was to wrench her party in a different direction from the path on which it had been set since the 1940s and to hammer the contours of the British economy and society into a new configuration. Before she became prime minister she said that her priority of regenerating Britain's economy would take at least two parliaments. Purpose and office were inseparable.

Thatcher's mission was accompanied by a crusade to mobilise support by persuading the British people of the need for radical change, in effect to save them from themselves. The term 'Thatcherism' was first coined on the left to describe a supposedly new conservatism and came to be taken as a badge of honour by her supporters.[1] Thatcher was the first prime minister to have given her name to an ism, although Thatcherism was not the first ism to be coined in British politics. 'Butskellism' was derived from a composite of Butler, the Tory chancellor, and Gaitskell, Labour's shadow chancellor, and encapsulated the similarity of their parties' economic policies during the 1950s. 'Powellism' was coined to capture the populist blend of nationalism and right-wing economics developed by Enoch Powell in the late 1960s.

Whereas Thatcherism was held to represent a rejection of the consensus-style politics of Butskellism, it had much in common with Powellism. At its core lay a combination of *laissez-faire* liberalism and authoritarian populism. However, in one crucial respect Thatcherism inherited more from the former than from the latter. The prophet of Powellism found himself cast into the political wilderness. Thatcher would avoid his mistake. She was as determined as the alleged authors of Butskellism had been to win and retain office.

In the political acid test of winning general elections, Thatcher is unequalled. She won three out of three elections, a feat unprecedented in the history of the Conservative Party. The only previous Conservative hat-trick, in the 1951, 1955 and 1959 elections, had been achieved under three different leaders Churchill, Eden and Macmillan. No party leader had achieved an election hat-trick since Lord Palmerston between 1857 and 1865, but he died three months after his final triumph at the polls.

The only Conservative leader to have won even two successive election triumphs was Salisbury in 1895 and 1902, but the overall Tory majority in the Commons was reduced. By contrast, under Thatcher the party's majority increased in her second election victory from 43 seats in 1979 to 144 seats in 1983, the party's largest overall majority since the days of the Tory-dominated National Government in the 1930s. In Thatcher's third victory the majority fell but still remained in three figures, the majority of 100 in 1987 being the same as Macmillan's landslide win in 1959, which had been the Tories' previous best performance since the Second World War.

Yet the Tory election victories under Thatcher's leadership, however impressive they appear, were not synonymous with support for Thatcherism. The tension between Thatcher's desire to win and hold office and her sense of having a mission has been acute. It largely explains Tory politics during her leadership.

II

The notion that Thatcherism was a distinctive, new ideology was inadvertently assisted by Thatcher's critics within the Conservative Party. Thatcher, however, reflected strands of thought which had long existed within Conservative politics but had been marginalised by the party's leadership since the 1940s.

Thatcher combined a general sympathy for *laissez-faire* economics with traditionalist attitudes on issues like law and order. Her bias towards market forces and small businesses fused with a belief in discipline and strong government. During most of the postwar period, however, the party had been led by an alliance of the supporters of big business and socially compassionate paternalists under the leadership of Churchill, Eden, Macmillan and Heath, and the influence of Butler. They believed in strong government but its purposes were interventionist. Douglas-Home's leadership in the mid-1960s marked a brief turn towards the traditional right but was a short-lived aberration.

Thatcher's revolution was in part a reaction to Heath's legacy but it also represented a carrying forward of his radicalism. Following the defeat of the Heath government in the February 1974 election, Sir Keith, later Lord, Joseph began to develop a critique of successive postwar Conservative governments, and when he founded and became chairman of the Centre for Policy Studies, Thatcher was appointed its first president. Heath had approved the creation of the CPS on the condition that the aim was to study how private enterprise and social market policies worked in other countries, but the CPS became the base of the liberal economists' critique of party policy.

In a series of speeches during 1974 which were designed to begin the process of re-educating other Tories and the British public, Joseph advocated monetarism and free-market policies as the cure for Britain's relative economic decline. He berated Labour and Conservative governments alike for their readiness to boost the level of demand in the economy whenever unemployment increased, arguing that this policy had inevitably fuelled higher inflation and, in turn, created even higher unemployment. The solution to Britain's malaise would only follow when inflation had been eradicated, which could be achieved only by increased competition and tight control of the supply of money circulating in the economy.

Most significant was Joseph's identification of a 'ratchet effect' which had been at work in postwar politics, whereby no incoming Conservative Government had ever fully reversed the actions of its Labour predecessors. The net effect was that inexorably over the years and decades Britain had drifted towards a socialist economy. Joseph identified this as the Conservatives' major strategic blunder, and it was the basis for his extraordinary claim that although he had always thought himself a Conservative, he realised that he had never been one at all. Monetarism and market economics offered the only route by which the 'ratchet effect' would be reversed.

Joseph's fresh articulation of liberal economics, and his rationale of Britain's relative economic decline and the Conservative Party's traumatic loss of power in 1974 appealed to Thatcher's right-wing inclinations. As Joseph recognised, she appeared to understand instinctively the monetarist and market-orientated views which he came to adopt through an intellectual process. Whereas he returned to first principles and became a convert to economic liberalism, the roots of Thatcher's convictions lay in her upbringing in the Lincolnshire market town of Grantham during the 1920s and 1930s. The values of hard work, self-reliance, thrift and respect for authority were inculcated during her childhood.

So strong was the influence of Thatcher's origins that it sometimes appeared to her closest colleagues that Britain was governed during the 1980s by 'the ghost of Alderman Roberts'. Thatcher's father, Alfred Roberts, owned and ran a family grocery business and lived above the shop. He was a strict Methodist lay preacher and local councillor who approached his duty as chairman of the borough finance committee with Gladstonian rigour. As his daughter would later proudly boast, while he was in charge of Grantham's finances the town was never allowed to get into debt.

'Victorian values' was the catchword that sought to capture Thatcher's approach, but it overlooked the impact of her interwar upbringing. On the economy she was a nineteenth-century Manchester liberal but her social ideal was much closer to the stable and ordered society which prevailed in Britain between the end of the First World War and the mid-1950s. As Patrick Middleton has argued, Thatcher's social values were Georgian rather than Victorian.[2] The reigns of the last two Georges were socially peaceful and saw the 'respectable' values of the Victorian middle class spread through most of the working class.

The years of Thatcher's childhood and youth were a very different period from either the Victorian era, when a large part of the working class 'lived in conditions of economic and moral degradation', or the late 1950s and the 1960s when faster economic growth brought greater social upheaval. By contrast, the thirty-five or so years after 1918 saw working-class people, the majority of whom did not suffer unemployment, enjoy an improvement in their standard of living 'but not in such a rapid and disruptive way as to create social instability'. Steady economic improvement and a greater respect for authority went hand in hand.

Thatcher's Georgian social convictions were demonstrated time and again during the 1980s on law-and-order issues. Reacting to the inner-city riots and suggestions of connection with high levels of unemployment, she drew parallels with the high unemployment of the 1930s and pointed to the lack of violence at the time. Yet her economic radicalism, which by the late 1980s was held by her admirers to have created an 'economic miracle', was incompatible with the restoration of social stability as it had existed between the 1920s and the 1950s.

Although background and upbringing would incline Thatcher to the Tory right and she knew the work of Hayek, her contemporaries at Oxford and in her professional and political life during the 1940s and 1950s attest to her traditional, unremarkable Conservatism. Above all she held an ambition to enter Parliament, which she achieved in 1959. Other members of her intake regarded her as being right of centre in the party without being excessively so. Within two years she accepted appointment as a junior minister in Macmillan's Government, although in July 1963 he was told by his PPS, Knox Cunningham, that Thatcher was one of four junior ministers who were concerned about his leadership and could not be trusted.[3] Yet she survived and would remain a frontbencher in government and opposition until November 1990.

Joseph's espousal of monetarist and market-orientated Conservatism in 1974 rekindled Thatcher's earliest convictions. But her colleagues had not detected any signs of her suffering great crises of conscience before she emerged as one of Joseph's earliest allies. There had been little problem in opposition before 1970, since Heath's 'Selsdon Man' period was associated with more liberal economic policies and a tougher line on law and order. At the time Thatcher was not a fervent advocate of denationalisation, then a rallying cry among *laissez-faire* Conservatives, but she revealed her right-wing economic and social thinking in 1968 when she delivered the prestigious CPC lecture, organised at each year's party conference. The only political philosopher who received a mention was John Stuart Mill. The biblical story of the Good Samaritan was given an interpretation which she would repeat years later as prime minister: 'The point is that even the Good Samaritan had to have the money to help, otherwise he too would have had to pass by on the other side.' The virtues of hard work and personal responsibility were extolled, greater competition was identified as the means to prevent price rises, and monetarism was foreshadowed.

In Heath's cabinet, however, Thatcher accepted the U-turn on economic policy involving the return to government intervention and the imposition of a statutory prices-and-incomes policy. As education secretary, she authorised the abolition of grammar schools and creation of comprehensives by local education authorities on a scale unmatched by her Labour counterparts and, like Joseph at Social Services, demanded extra state spending. In opposition, as shadow environment secretary, she initially resisted Heath's plan to promise during the October 1974 general election that the Tories would limit the interest charge on mortgages for first-time house buyers to 9 per cent. But she acquiesced and advocated the policy, although she was clearly much happier arguing the case for the abolition of the domestic rates — a policy which became a crusade over the next fifteen years.

Little was known about Thatcher when she challenged Heath for the party leadership in the winter of 1974–5, beyond her reputation for administrative competence and a sense that she was on the right of the party with an electorally unappealing middle-class image. She felt that her basic beliefs had been confirmed by the bitter experiences of the Heath Government, but she had also shown herself ready to compromise, albeit after passionately arguing her corner. She was not a resigner. Party came before principle. Heath had even considered appointing her party chairman during 1974. When Joseph told her he would not challenge Heath as party leader she sensed her career and the interests of the party were in conjunction. She later revealed: 'I knew then that I must stand. It had not been a long preconceived ambition, but I knew I just had to.'[4]

Thatcher's election as party leader did not represent any ideological conversion among Tory MPs, Tory activists or Tory peers to the kind of views which would later be termed Thatcherism. Her right-wing sympathies were consciously played down by her campaign team. Her chief strategist, Airey Neave, urged her to make the style of leadership the central issue and not to stray on to ideology. It was a skilful ploy because very few Tory MPs were ready to contemplate rejecting intervention in the economy or to back the kind of moralising to which Thatcher was naturally drawn. A detailed study by Ivor Crewe and Donald Searing of the opinions of Tory MPs on the eve of Thatcher's challenge shows that only an estimated 10–25 per cent of the parliamentary party endorsed the Thatcherite appeal, depending on how strictly the three main criteria of Thatcherism – free enterprise, strong government and social discipline – are applied.[5]

Towards the end of her rule, Thatcher seemed to have tamed her party.
But her impact on the Tories proved to have been more limited.

Thatcher was elected leader because Tory MPs wanted to be rid of Heath. It was not a vote for the emerging economic orthodoxy on the right. There had been little expectation that she would win and no thought about what a Thatcher victory would mean for the party. Thatcher's victory was 'much more peasants' uprising than a religious war'. The result was 'no less than the hijacking of a political party'.[6]

III

Change during the Thatcher years was pushed and guided by Thatcher's compulsive sense of mission. Uniquely for a party leader in modern times, Thatcher was, as Chris Patten has observed, 'more radical in government than in opposition'.[7] But her radicalism was always tempered by an overriding desire that the Conservatives should hold office with her as their leader. The result was a more uneven process of change and patchwork quilt of reform than might be imagined from generalisations about a supposedly consistent ideology called Thatcherism.

Thatcher's principal political legacy is that she asserted the authority of government. There is seeming irony in the fact that the belief in the government's ability to act decisively and effect change should have been restored by a convinced non-interventionist but the irony is more apparent than real. Her refusal to contemplate a prices-and-incomes policy avoided risking a repetition of the defeats inflicted on her predecessors during the 1960s and 1970s. She was determined to stand back and not be drawn into the detailed management of the economy, however great the pressures became. Whatever the economic and social costs – and they were considerable – the political impact of her decision cannot be gainsaid. Thatcher disproved the widely held view that Britain was ungovernable, although it was a close-run thing in the summer of 1981 as the country was assailed by economic slump and inner-city riots.

The real irony is that in her final years Thatcher forgot her own lesson. Her imposition of the poll tax rendered her vulnerable in much the same way that her prime ministerial predecessors were undermined by their imposition of pay policies. The poll tax was seen as unfair and was widely flouted: pay policies had generally been regarded as fair but were eventually broken. Thatcher's authority was eroded by the poll tax as fatally as Heath's and Callaghan's had been by the collapse of their pay policies. But she was brought down by Tory MPs before her government was called to account at the ballot box.

Issues like pay policy and poll tax were aspects of broader themes. Thatcher's wider political legacy stems from the way she ran the economy and dealt with institutions like trade unions and local government which had acted as buffers between central government and individuals. Yet, despite her assertive leadership, she has not had any lasting effect on cabinet government in the manner of Lloyd George, who first established the modern cabinet system, or Attlee, who developed the system of cabinet committees. She increasingly marginalised the cabinet, reducing its full meetings more to a rubber stamp than a collective decision-making body. She preferred to operate through ad hoc meetings with ministers, loyally supported by the courtier-like figures of Bernard Ingham, Charles

Powell and members of her political staff. In the end this highly personalised system helped to cause her downfall. It was immediately reversed by her successor.

Thatcher's style of leadership was her way of combating the constraints which she faced as party leader and prime minister, and from which she could never be entirely free. It partly stemmed from the fact that she was Britain's first woman leader of a major party and first woman prime minister. She simply could not be clubbable in the manner of, say, a Baldwin or a Macmillan. Her male colleagues, particularly in her early years as leader, were still of a society in which women left the table at the end of dinner while the men stayed on to talk politics. But her sex also gave her an advantage. Tory ministers of her generation were not used to arguing politics with a woman, let alone taking orders from one. The chivalry they traditionally extended to women disarmed them in debate with their leader.

It was Thatcher's sense of mission and not solely her gender that set her apart. She always remained an outsider. At times, after she became prime minister, she would refer to the government as though it had nothing to do with her. As Alan Clark, one of her most loyal supporters, commented: 'She was the first prime minister to break with the establishment.'[8] The popular media loved it. Right-wing tabloids regaled their readers with headlines about 'Battling Maggie' while BBC Radio Two's Jimmy Young programme became a regular port of call.

Thatcher was skilfully transformed by her public-relations adviser, Sir Gordon Reece, from the archetypal Home Counties lady who had first appeared in the public eye wearing a forbidding hat at Tory conferences and who had been branded, while education secretary, as the 'milk snatcher'. The development of her populist image and her playing to it was effective, enabling Thatcher with some justification to claim to speak for popular sentiment beyond the shadow cabinet and cabinet table. As the sociologist Professor A. H. Halsey commented:

> One has to wonder about Mrs Thatcher whether she was narrowly or widely based, whether she knew what she was doing or not, but whatever the answers are it is certainly true that there are points of Mrs Thatcher's outlook which go with the grain of ordinary popular aspirations.[9]

Having 'hijacked' the Tory Party in 1975, Thatcher was never able to shake herself completely free from the shackles of her party or her front-bench team. There was little enthusiasm among Tory MPs in 1975 for monetarism and market forces, and there was even less in her shadow cabinet. The key characteristic of Thatcher's four years as leader of the opposition was that by and large her frontbenchers were unsympathetic to her convictions. Her team was remarkably left of centre. Her caution was exemplified by the decision not to appoint Sir Keith Joseph as shadow chancellor, the post going instead to Sir Geoffrey Howe, a co-founder of the Centre for Policy Studies, who was less ideologically motivated than Thatcher or Joseph.

The party's major policy document, published in the autumn of 1976, *The Right Approach*, was moderate in tone and content. But in the autumn of 1977 she exercised her prerogative as leader by refusing to endorse its successor, *The Right Approach to the Economy*, as party policy although it was the work of a group representing both wings of the party including Howe, Joseph and Jim Prior. She objected to the document's view on pay policy, which she regarded as too close to the approach pursued by successive governments since the 1940s. She was unhappy about the suggestion that West German-style 'concerted action', comprising talks between government, employers and unions, had a role to play in Britain as an adjunct to monetary controls, and about the recognition that any government, as a large employer, had to have some view on the level of pay awards. As Prior later acknowledged, her reaction should have warned him of her determination to pursue a radical economic policy once she had won office.[10]

In addition to withholding her endorsement of *The Right Approach to the Economy* as party policy, Thatcher sanctioned a highly confidential examination of policy and presentation after the official party-policy groups had largely completed their work. This exercise, entitled *Stepping Stones*, stemmed from a paper presented to Thatcher by John Hoskyns, a former soldier and founder of a computer company, assisted by Norman Strauss, a management and personnel adviser. They had first approached Joseph through the Centre for Policy Studies, and argued that unless Britain's relative economic decline was reversed the country's decline would become 'absolute'. This collapse could only be prevented through radical policies, principally by a severe reduction in the power of trade unions. But these policies would succeed only if there was a fundamental change in public attitudes towards wealth creation and the welfare state. Hoskyns and Strauss had little obvious effect on policy before the election, but they buttressed Thatcher's arguments and served during the early years of her government in the Number 10 Policy Unit until they left, disillusioned at her failure to reform decision-making at the heart of Whitehall.

Thatcher's conviction that radical change was Britain's only hope of reversing its relative decline created enormous tension within her shadow cabinet. Her tactic of launching personal policy *démarches* in television interviews, as on immigration or her suggestion of holding referendums in the event of national strikes, infuriated colleagues who also found themselves under constant pressure to take a more hawkish line on a range of issues, including trade union reform and the civil war in Rhodesia. But her realisation that her first task was to win control of the levers of power led her to accept the advice of her more moderate colleagues. At the height of the crisis caused by the 'Winter of Discontent' in January 1979, Thatcher's appeal for national unity could have come from the lips of any One Nation paternalist Conservative and in fact had come straight from the pen of Chris Patten, then director of the Conservative Research Department. At the same time, however, Thatcher was pressing Prior, the shadow employment spokesman, to go much further and commit the party to specific changes in the law on the trade unions ahead of the review of the law to which the party was committed. Apart from agreeing to give a pledge that secondary picketing would be made unlawful, Prior was able to resist further commitments.

Although Thatcher's rhetoric foreshadowed radical reform in the event of the Conservatives being returned to office, her 1979 election manifesto was an unexpectedly pragmatic prospectus. Shadow cabinet colleagues could scarcely believe their eyes when they first received draft copies. Its unexceptionable list of tasks scarcely represented an agenda for the Thatcherite revolution. Tory wets thought they would have little trouble gaining the ascendancy in government. They expected to assume an increasingly dominant position as the experience of office taught Thatcher that she had no option but to moderate her stance still further.

Few of her colleagues were taken in by Thatcher's quoting the pacific words attributed to St Francis of Assisi on her arrival in Downing Street in May 1979, but her cabinet appointments initially reassured critics and alarmed loyalists. The overall balance of the cabinet was better than the paternalist and Tory progressives had dared hope: Carrington and Gilmour at the Foreign Office, Whitelaw at the Home Office, Prior at Employment, Walker at Agriculture, Heseltine at Environment, Stevas as Leader of the House, Carlisle at Education, Soames as Lord President and leader in the Lords. However, with the exception of Prior and Walker, Thatcher appointed to the economic portfolios only those ministers whom she regarded as her fellow believers: Howe as chancellor and John Biffen as chief secretary at the Treasury, Joseph at Industry, John Nott at Trade and David Howell at Energy, and outside the cabinet, Nigel Lawson was appointed financial secretary at the Treasury.

It was this Thatcherite stranglehold on the economic departments and the cabinet's economic-strategy committee that enabled her to dismantle the framework of economic management developed over the previous forty years. Labour's adoption of monetarism in 1976 had shifted the emphasis of economic policy-making but their prices-and-incomes policy had perpetuated the paraphernalia of corporatism. Even here, however,

Thatcher's political caution at first moderated her radical instincts, since she had agreed before the 1979 election to honour the public-sector pay increases announced by the pay-comparability commission headed by Professor Clegg. This decision was later criticised because of its impact on public spending but in the early months of 1979 very few Tories were prepared to jeopardise their electoral prospects by refusing to underwrite the pay increases being awarded to millions of public-sector workers.

Yet within Thatcher's first twelve months the die was cast. Howe's first budget signalled radical reform of the tax structure, shifting the burden from income tax to taxes on spending. These changes culminated during Lawson's chancellorship in the late 1980s with a reduction in the basic rate of income tax to 25 per cent compared with 33 per cent when Thatcher came to power and the top rate more than halved to 40 per cent from 83 per cent in 1979. In November 1980, Howe removed the exchange controls which had been in force since wartime, opening the British economy to world market forces for the first time in forty years.

During the winter of 1979–80, Thatcher withstood all pressures to intervene in the national steel strike. It is inconceivable that any previous government since the Second World War would have stood aside as one of the country's basic industries was crippled by a three-month standstill. This action, which also reflected a Thatcherite disregard for Britain's traditional role as a manufacturing economy, signalled more clearly than any other act of policy her determination not to intervene in what she regarded as the details of economic policy.

Thatcher's non-interventionist stance was given strategic effect with the publication at the time of the 1980 budget of the government's first 'Medium Term Financial Strategy'. The MTFS announced the government's intention to concern itself solely with setting the monetary and financial targets and to eschew the interventionist practices of trying to achieve some target rate of economic growth through economic planning or to control inflation through prices-and-incomes policies. Defying widely held expectations to the contrary, Thatcher survived the political pressures caused by rampant inflation in the winter of 1979–80 and soaring unemployment from the summer of 1980. She told Hoskyns, then head of the Number 10 Policy Unit, that she would rather go down fighting than change course, a line which she reiterated publicly at the October 1980 party conference when she declared that 'the lady's not for turning'.

Howe's 1981 budget confirmed Thatcher's rejection of the traditional tools of postwar economic management, further deflating an economy which was already in the deepest recession for half a century. The three most critical ministers in Thatcher's cabinet, derided by her as 'wet', Prior, Gilmour and Walker, met and considered resigning but decided to fight on within the cabinet. In July it seemed that Thatcher was becoming isolated even on the economy when the cabinet rejected Howe's gloomy prognosis and demands for massive cuts in departmental budgets at the start of the annual review of public spending. The only backing for Thatcher and her chancellor came from the recently appointed chief secretary, Leon Brittan, and Joseph. Her erstwhile loyal economic liberals, Biffen and Nott, joined forces with the dissidents.

Thatcher's response came in the autumn 1981 reshuffle, when she asserted her authority in the cabinet, dismissing critics like Gilmour, Soames and Carlisle and exiling Prior to Northern Ireland. In their place came Thatcher loyalists like Norman Tebbit, who replaced Prior at Employment, Lawson, and Lady Young, the only woman to serve in Thatcher's cabinet. The increasingly dissident party chairman, Lord Thorneycroft, a self-confessed victim of 'rising damp', was replaced by Cecil Parkinson, who unlike his predecessor was appointed to the cabinet.

None the less, Thatcher remained vulnerable and her political and economic experiment was still at risk. In the autumn of 1981 she was rated the most unpopular prime minister ever in opinion polls, the Tories trailed third behind the Liberal-SDP Alliance and Labour, and the party lost the hitherto safe Merseyside seat of Crosby to Shirley Williams of the newly formed SDP. There were rumours of a challenge in that year's Tory leadership election, with Geoffrey Rippon, a former minister in Heath's cabinet, suggested as a possible stalking-horse candidate.

But there was no challenge from the opposition. Since the election defeat of 1979, Labour had torn itself apart in an internecine struggle between left and right, and had been weakened by the defection of its social-democratic wing to form the SDP. Labour's election of Michael Foot as their new leader in the autumn of 1980 had also undermined the argument that Thatcher would be certain to lead the Tories to defeat at the next election.

Without an effective opposition, any challenge to Thatcher within the Tory Party was rendered futile. Tory wets were astonished at Labour's low-key response as unemployment passed the 2-million mark and headed remorselessly towards 3 million. They recalled the passionate attacks on the Heath government in 1972 when the headline total had exceeded one million, which had induced the U-turn and retreat from the kind of non-interventionist approach being pursued by Thatcher. And in policy discussions within the government and Tory Party, Thatcher and her supporters were able to point to Britain's relative economic decline during the years when interventionism had held sway.

Mass unemployment reduced the power of the unions, and Tory political prospects revived as the economy began to emerge from recession. Thatcher's 'resolute' image was buoyed by the defeat of General Galtieri in the Falklands in the spring of 1982, although the Argentinian dictator's invasion had followed the withdrawal of HMS *Endurance* from patrol in the South Atlantic as a result of spending cuts. Her rigour as 'Iron Chancellor' inadvertently led her to prove her mettle as the 'Iron Lady'. She had established herself on the world stage. Through her close rapport with President Reagan and later with the new Soviet leader, Mikhail Gorbachev, she appeared in the mid-1980s as a co-equal on the world stage, emulating Macmillan's charade of thirty years earlier in acting as if Britain approximated to superpower status.

Claims by the late 1980s that economic recovery during that decade amounted to a British 'economic miracle' reinforced the impression that a new, Thatcherite consensus on economic management had been established. Yet the reality of policy had increasingly departed from monetarist and market certainties. In 1982 Howe had acknowledged that he would no longer rely on a single measure of the money supply. Lower interest rates, the abolition of hire-purchase controls and deregulation of banks and building societies combined to trigger a distinctly un-Thatcherite credit boom, which fuelled the consumer boom of the 1980s. Growth was fuelled by private borrowing instead of public sector borrowing.

The overall burden of taxation and the level of public spending remained stubbornly higher than when Thatcher had come to office, partly reflecting the cost of unemployment. Ministers increasingly exhorted workers to restrain their pay demands in language redolent of the 1960 and 1970s. And Thatcher's long-serving chancellors, Howe and Lawson, came to the view that exchange-rate stability was essential, in contradiction to Thatcher's faith in market forces.

Increased prosperity among the majority of British voters who remained in work during the early and mid-1980s was sufficient to secure Thatcher's election triumphs in 1983 and 1987. The Tories had reaped the political dividends of a prolonged credit and consumer boom. But by the end of Thatcher's rule the economic costs of Britain's living beyond its means were painfully apparent in high inflation, a huge trade deficit and a looming recession. Despite having had the benefit of North Sea Oil, Thatcher left the underlying economic problems unsolved and the debate on the management of the economy unresolved.

IV

Thatcher's political legacy is the product of the tension between her mission to transform the British economy and society and her political calculation. Her demolition of trade-union power and creation of 'popular capitalism' are the great Thatcherite monuments but they each bear witness to the battle between Thatcher the missionary and Thatcher the pragmatist.

In Thatcher's view, tackling the unions went much further than merely improving Britain's industrial relations. As she told the 1979 Tory Party conference, 'today the conflict is not so much between unions and employers as between unions and the nation'. When it came to reforming the unions, however, Thatcher lost the battle but won the war. She and Howe, who supported her desire to go faster in curbing the legal powers of the unions, were restrained from risking a repetition of Heath's mistake by Prior, her Heathite employment secretary.

Prior held the line for his gradualist and modest 1980 reforms of union elections, the closed shop, secondary picketing and sympathetic action such as blacking by workers not directly involved in a dispute. Thatcherite-inspired back-bench revolts and attacks at party meetings and conferences reached a crescendo during the early months of 1980. Prior's 'step-by-step' approach was only upheld by his mobilising the majority in cabinet against Thatcher and attracting some support from more pragmatic economic liberals like Biffen.

Prior's objective was to retain public support for union reform, never rushing ahead of public opinion and running the risk that union leaders would be able to rally support. On this measure, his gradualist approach worked and ensured public backing for the government's policy. But by the summer of 1981 Prior had made clear in a Green Paper his resistance to Thatcher's demands for a swingeing attack on union immunities. As a result, he was moved from Employment as Thatcher called his bluff, forcing him to climb down and accept his appointment as Northern Ireland secretary. Tebbit, his Thatcherite successor at Employment, maintained Prior's step-by-step approach to reforming the law on trade unions, but the strides went further than Prior had been prepared to contemplate. Union immunities from legal action were pegged back to their position before 1906.

Legal reform, however, would not in itself weaken the industrial muscle of the unions. Thatcher avoided a confrontation with the miners in February 1981 when the recession prompted the National Coal Board to announce an accelerated rate of closure of older pits with poor productivity. Their announcement prompted a spontaneous response from the miners, who were ready to give their moderate president, Joe Gormley, their full backing. As a result, the NCB climbed down. Thatcher agreed to adjust the industry's cash limit to accommodate the cost of the decision, but Tebbit later observed: 'I think there was a note on her pad that things were going to be different.'[11]

Three years later, the NCB instituted a new programme of pit closures.

When the militant president of the National Union of Mineworkers, Arthur Scargill, launched a national dispute without a pithead ballot, he walked into a trap. Scargill had been a bogey of the Tories since 1972 when he organised the picketing which forced the closure of the Saltley cokeworks during the miners' pay dispute. In 1974 the miners' strike had led to the downfall of the Heath government but in 1984 coal stocks were high and the NCB's announcement had been timed for the spring, as the weather was improving. The miners were deeply divided. After a bitter and at times bloody dispute in which neither Scargill nor Thatcher was prepared to compromise, the NUM was defeated. The vanguard of the union movement had been crushed.

Mass unemployment served as the hammer of the unions. In the year after the miners' defeat, the print unions were beaten when they fought News International over the alleged imposition of new working practices in the company's new, high-technology plant at Wapping. The demise of union militants and the rise of a leader like Eric Hammond of the electricians' union, EETPU, who negotiates no-strike deals and accepts working with, rather than against, a market economy, epitomises the transformation in the politics of the unions during the Thatcher years. In the late 1960s, the Labour prime minister Wilson told the engineers' leader Hugh Scanlon to pull the tanks off his lawn, and in the 1970s a Tory government and a Labour government were defeated after the unions had wrecked their pay policies. By the end of Thatcher's rule, talk of trade-union power and of Britain being ungovernable seemed like distant echoes from a bygone age.

When Thatcher entered Number 10, the unions were able to muster 12 million members. This impressive total compared with 3 million shareholders. By 1990 there had been a staggering change, 9 million trade unionists compared with 11 million shareholders. Moreover, between 1979 and 1990 some 3 million more families had become home owners and around 1.3 million public-sector homes had been sold, mainly to former council tenants under the Tories' 'right to buy' legislation. Nearly two-thirds of all homes in Britain are now owner-occupied. 'Popular capitalism' ranks high in the Thatcherite legacy, and, like step-by-step union reforms, generated public support during the 1980s.

Yet the most revolutionary aspect of 'popular capitalism', the privatisation of the great nationalised industries, was not foreseen by the Tories when they returned to office in 1979. This wholesale reversal of one of the most entrenched legacies of Labour governments became Thatcher's 'unexpected crusade'.[12] The 1979 Tory manifesto promised only limited denationalisation. Four years later, privatisation was transformed into a crucial cause in the Thatcherite mission.

After the 1979 election, Thatcher and her fellow economic liberals identified a broad programme of policies to restore a market economy, including decentralisation, contracting out of public-sector work to private firms, greater competition and privatisation. The initial sales of state-owned industries were limited to self-contained companies trading on the fringes of the public sector, such as British Aerospace, Cable & Wireless and the Radiochemical Centre at Amersham. The sale of the National Freight Corporation to its employees raised only £5 million but was proof of the potential attractiveness of share sales to the workforce. With the flotation of Britoil in 1982 and a more radical sales technique, ministers began to realise the potential for a much wider privatisation programme.

The 1983 manifesto lacked a radical edge but the economic liberals managed to include a detailed commitment to privatisation. Thatcher's subsequent appointment of Lawson, a former financial journalist, as chancellor, and John Moore, who had witnessed 'popular capitalism' in the United States in the 1960s, as financial secretary, gave the green light to the development of privatisation as a central plank of policy. Even so, there was scepticism in the government of the likely success of privatisation as an effective means of creating 'popular capitalism'. The numbers owning shares had been dwindling for decades, previous sales had been directed at the financial institutions, and attracting as many as 50,000 investors into a privatisation sale had been reckoned to be good going.

The British Telecom sale proved to be the turning point, attracting over 2 million buyers of whom half had never previously bought a share. Purchasers were able to reap a rapid profit by selling off their shares. The Tories saw an equally attractive political windfall. 'Two million people have put their money on the table,' Lawson declared in a speech to the Institute of Directors, 'and they have put it on the blue square.'

Following the success of the British Telecom sale, as a former Treasury adviser on privatisation has stated, 'a pragmatic shift of opinion occurred within the Government in favour of wider share ownership and it suddenly became attractive to privatise British Gas in its present form rather than to break it up'.[13]

The economic wisdom of creating large private monopolies was doubtful, to say the least, notwithstanding the creation of regulatory agencies. But the political objective was clear, and was spelled out by Walker, the energy secretary, at the Tory Party conference in 1986:

For mean party reasons I delight that the Alliance have bitterly opposed gas privatisation. I delight that the Labour Party have not only opposed it but promised that if they are returned to power they will renationalise it. I look forward to the next election when in something like 12,000 homes in every constituency Labour Party canvassers will be going to the door to persuade those privatised shareholders how essential it is to take back their shares in order that Messrs Hattersley, Meacher and Benn should control such a great industry.

Tory claims to a genuine commitment to 'popular capitalism' were belied by the government's rejection of a fairer allocation of shares in what had been publicly owned industries. Instead, its favoured system of share sales gave a further advantage to the better-off majority of voters. 'Mrs Thatcher has much more of Harold Wilson in her than people realise,' observed Samuel Brittan, a leading proponent of economic liberalism. 'The problem is that she deeply identifies the market economy with the interests of the Tory middle classes, and they're not the same.'[14]

Yet, whatever the wranglings over fairness or the free-market credentials of the privatisers, the policy continued unabated, producing a dramatic redrawing of the boundaries of the mixed economy. The old political football of nationalising or denationalising a few industries, which had been kicked backwards and forwards between Labour and the Tories for decades, was booted out of the park. Thatcher recast the political agenda.

V

The picture for those other bastions on the pre-Thatcherite political landscape, the welfare state and local councils, is less black and white than for the unions or the nationalised industries. Despite Tory claims to have introduced a 'new Beveridge' reform of social security or opponents' accusations that the National Health Service has been destroyed, Thatcher's political legacy in these areas is the result of a perpetual battle to hold down spending, which was never finally won, and an array of specific reforms mainly introduced in the later years of her government.

Issues concerning the future of the welfare state caused Thatcher most difficulty during the 1983 and 1987 elections. The leaking of a government Think Tank report on the NHS had seriously embarrassed the government in the autumn of 1982, and Labour would have been better advised to have pushed much harder their accusations during the 1983 election campaign that the Tories had a 'hidden agenda' for NHS reform. The debate during the Thatcher years focused increasingly on questions of value for money and the cost-effective delivery of services. But this change was less a creation of Thatcherism and more a reflection of a phenomenon which prompted similar shifts in the debate throughout the Western world.

Tory ministers claimed that the poor had done well since 1979, but revised official figures released in July 1990 revealed that income inequality between rich and poor was greater than at any time since the Second World War. The 23 per cent rise in real living standards between 1979 and 1987 was very unequally distributed. Wider pay differentials and increases in profits, dividends and earnings from self-employment boosted the real incomes of the top one per cent of earners by 80 per cent. Cuts in income tax also benefited the better-off while the worse-off were hit by the decision to uprate social security benefits in line with prices instead of earnings, which increased faster in the 1980s. At least 1.3 million people suffered falls of 6 per cent in their real income. The numbers living on below half the average income, the European Community's poverty line, more than doubled from 4.9 million to 10.5 million. Very little economic growth during Thatcher's boom years trickled down to the poor.

Thatcher's distinctive institutional legacy has been her further centralisation of an already centralised state. Traditionally, Conservatives have looked to local education authorities as a guarantee of independence against the kind of state intervention in schooling which they typically identified with the Labour Party. But the national curriculum was imposed by Thatcher's government, not a socialist administration. The attack on local bureaucrats and councillors was extended by enabling schools to opt out of local education authority control and to receive their funding direct from Whitehall.

The assault on local democracy has been unrelenting. Local councils have been subjected to progressively tighter control of their spending. At Thatcher's insistence, the 1983 Tory manifesto pledged abolition of the Greater London Council and the metropolitan county councils, which had long been a thorn in the government's side. They were scrapped in 1986. The imposition of the uniform business rate removed the setting of commercial rates from local councils. Abolition of the domestic rates and their replacement by a poll tax was designed to curb local-authority spending and to make councils more accountable to their electorates.

The poll tax offers a case study in Thatcher's missionary zeal overriding her pragmatism. Having fought for the abolition of the domestic rates at the October 1974 election, she quickly instituted a review of the alternatives after the 1979 election. Her remit to ministers was to devise a fairer system which would make councils more accountable. Both aims could have been achieved by introducing local income tax and proportional representation for council elections, but these options were explicitly ruled out because of the party's overriding commitment to cutting income tax and opposition to electoral reform – stances which Thatcher held as arks of the covenant. Heseltine, then environment secretary, published his Green Paper on alternatives to the rates in 1981, which outlined the difficulties of most options, among them a tax per head, which was called a poll tax and not a 'community charge'.

Heseltine prevented any mention of scrapping the domestic rates in the 1983 manifesto, but Thatcher vetoed a modest package of reforms as inadequate and would not let the matter rest. At the 1984 party conference, Heseltine's successor at Environment, Patrick Jenkin, rejected a motion calling for abolition of the rates but promised another review. At Thatcher's instruction, a junior minister in Jenkin's department, William Waldegrave, was told to find an alternative to the rates which would enable voters to control council spending. Waldegrave's hybrid policy group, comprising departmental officials and outside 'assessors', included Professor Alan Walters, Thatcher's economics adviser, and Lord Rothschild, former head of the government Think Tank. Walters worked on the details of a local sales tax, which was Thatcher's preferred option but which was eventually deemed impractical.

The decision to concentrate on developing the poll tax as the alternative to domestic rates was not taken in the cabinet but was agreed at a meeting called by Thatcher at Chequers in late March 1985, attended by only a small number of cabinet ministers. A few days before the key meeting, Lord Whitelaw, then deputy prime minister, along with the then local government minister, Kenneth Baker, had met Scottish Tories. The rates revaluation north of the border was provoking a political storm, and Whitelaw and Baker were warned that as a result Scots Tories risked becoming an 'endangered species'. As a cabinet minister reportedly commented, 'Scottish revaluation turned the poll tax from the inconceivable into the unavoidable.'

Thatcher opted for the poll tax because she believed that it would force councils to be more financially accountable to voters, despite its being unrelated to ability to pay and difficult to collect. Sir Leon Brittan, then home secretary, raised civil-liberties' objections, and Lawson, then chancellor, opposed it as a bad tax and proposed a property tax. But the poll-tax proposal was approved by cabinet committee in the autumn of 1985, and was published as a Green Paper in January 1986. It was never discussed in full cabinet, but appeared as a firm election pledge in the 1987 Tory manifesto.

The poll tax was the most damaging of Thatcher's political legacies. At the heart of the problem was the erosion of some of the checks and balances of cabinet government which had acted as constraints on Thatcher during her earlier years. The strain on cabinet government had been most dramatically exposed in the Westland crisis of January 1986 when Heseltine resigned because, as he made clear during the 1990 leadership contest, the prime minister claimed that agreement had been reached at a cabinet committee meeting which never took place.

As Thatcher's dominance grew, so the paradox at the heart of her concept of liberty became ever more clear. Lord Jenkins, the former Labour home secretary and SDP leader, encapsulated the problem during the later years of Thatcher's rule: 'This government sees freedom almost entirely in business terms . . . [it] is dedicated to rolling back the state on anything to do with profit but is the bossiest government I've ever known on anything to do with individual conduct and freedom of expression.'[15] Among the instances where Thatcher's hand was most clearly at work were the ban in 1984 on unions at GCHQ, the government's communications (electronic surveillance) headquarters; the ban in 1988 on broadcasting the words of terrorists or their sympathisers, or of any words supporting them; and the ban, also in 1988, on the 'promotion' of homosexuality by local authorities (the so-called Clause 28).

Reasserting the authority of government remains Thatcher's principal political legacy. It is an achievement as welcome to some on the left as it is to Tories. She has radically changed the political landscape. But has she also fundamentally changed attitudes within her party and among the people? Will Thatcherism outlive Thatcher?

VI

Thatcher 'hijacked' her party in 1975 when her views were those of a minority. Although she remained leader for almost sixteen years and led the Tories to three successive election victories, neither she nor her closest allies ever seemed convinced that she had converted a majority of true believers in the country, in her party or even in her government. This state of affairs was reflected in the continual harping on by Thatcherites about whether other Tories or Whitehall officials were 'one of us'. The die-hard loyalists remained a sect who felt themselves to be under siege and feared that they would lose all influence when Thatcher ceased to be leader.

Thatcher's election hat-trick was largely based on the support of the new working class. These converts to the Tory fold were manual workers, typically skilled, who lived in southern England, owned their homes, worked in the private sector and did not belong to a trade union. They were the key element in the coalition of 'winners' who benefited economically from the Thatcher Government's policies.

The importance of the 'new working class' reflects, and is reinforced by, longer-term economic change and an accompanying shift in population towards the southern, more prosperous half of the country. Over the past fifty years, the number of parliamentary seats in the Tory Party's heartland has increased. In 1935, the southern English counties outside London elected 165 MPs. By 1983, they elected 235 MPs, an increase of 40 per cent. And in 1983 and 1987 the British 'first past the post' electoral system heavily benefited the party coming first in a three-horse race – in 1987, 42.3 per cent of the national vote won the Tories 57 per cent of seats in the Commons.

Yet any idea that the Tory trio of triumphs marked a mass conversion to Thatcherism is undermined by a closer look at the results. Her opponents were an enormous asset. The 'Winter of Discontent' in 1978–9 demolished Labour's claim to be able to govern with the unions. In November 1978 Labour had enjoyed a lead of 5 per cent in Gallup's monthly political index; three months later they were trailing by 18 points. All that Thatcher had to do by the spring of 1979 was sit tight and victory was hers. In 1983 and 1987 the Tories' successes were principally attributable to the split within the opposition parties following the defection of Labour's social-democratic wing and its alliance with the Liberals.

In Thatcher's three elections the Tory share of the vote was 43.9 per cent (1979), 42.4 per cent (1983) and 42.3 per cent (1987). This performance compares badly with the three Tory victories of the 1950s, when the party received 48 per cent (1951), 49.7 per cent (1955) and 49.4 per cent (1959). The Tory share of the vote in Thatcher's first election victory was only about half a percentage point higher than the party's share had been in the narrow election defeats of 1950 and 1964. In the 1983 and 1987 victories, the Tory share of the vote was only about half a per cent higher than their share had been when they suffered one of their heaviest defeats, in 1966. Moreover, the 1987 election saw an anti-Tory swing in Scotland, Wales and the north of England. Cities like Bradford, Leicester, Liverpool, Manchester and Newcastle did not elect a single Tory MP.

The Tories chalked up large majorities in the Commons because the opposition vote was split. In 1979 Labour won 37 per cent, the Liberals 13.8 per cent and the others 5.3 per cent. In 1983 the split was 27.6: 25.4 (Alliance): 4.6. In 1987 it was 30.8: 22.6: 4.3. Arguments about lack of support for the winning party in any British election have to be handled with care. Although 57.6 per cent failed to support Thatcher's Tory Party in 1983, 72.4 per cent did not vote for Foot's Labour Party and 74.6 per cent did not back the Jenkins-Steel Alliance. These figures suggest a more plausible perspective on Thatcher's election hat-trick: under her leadership the Tories were regarded as the least bad alternative.

The election figures do not amount to a ringing endorsement of Thatcherism in whichever way they are interpreted. Another possibility, however, is that Thatcherism provided a set of beliefs around which a sizable minority were able to rally to the Tory flag. Winning elections in

Britain depends on mobilising the largest minority – no party has received more than 50 per cent of the popular vote since 1935. On this argument, although Thatcher's Tory Party attracted a smaller share of the national vote than in the 1950s or 1960s, it won because Thatcher's declarations of political faith enabled its potential supporters to identify more strongly with the party.

But this notion is also contradicted by the evidence. In the 1964, 1966 and 1970 elections about half of those voters who identified themselves in surveys as Tory supporters described themselves as 'very strong identifiers'. By 1983, 'very strong' Tory identifiers had fallen to a quarter, which was less than in the Tories' two election defeats of 1974. In short, Thatcherism was not able to reverse the erosion of people's party loyalties which has occurred over the past thirty years.

Broad levels of support for political parties, however, are only a rough guide to people's attitudes on specific issues. Conceivably there might have been greater support for Thatcher's values than would appear to be the case from the overall level of support for the Tories. There are two possibilities. Firstly, that Thatcherism generally brought the Tory Party closer to public opinion. Secondly that Thatcher's leadership persuaded the British people to become more Thatcherite.[16]

A mass of detailed evidence in a range of opinion polls and attitude surveys contradicts any such claims. Thatcherism was never popular and, if anything, it became less so during Thatcher's rule. At the outset, she brought the Tory Party closer than it had been to public opinion in the early 1970s on law-and-order issues, where her emphasis on tougher discipline was also favoured by the electorate. But there was no great support at that stage for denationalisation or rolling back the welfare state.

By 1974, however, the view that the trade unions were too powerful was at its peak and Thatcher's plans to curb the unions were very popular. Union reform became a central strand of Thatcherism, but Heath had introduced wholesale reform in the Industrial Relations Act of 1971. The subsequent debate in the shadow cabinet and cabinet during the late 1970s and early 1980s between the hawks led by Thatcher and the doves led by Prior was about ensuring that union reform was workable, not an argument in principle about whether reform was needed in the first place. Underlying the discussion was a deeper disagreement about the role of the unions in modern Britain and on this question there is no evidence that the Thatcherite contempt for unions was ever popular.

Since the British public were not Thatcherite when Thatcher became Tory leader, to what extent did she succeed in persuading them to adopt Thatcherism? An array of studies of support for Thatcherite positions in public-opinion surveys during her leadership shows that she signally failed. Crewe and Searing suggested that Thatcher 'succeeded in shifting public opinion to the right on only one out of the ten issues [examined] – denationalisation': in 1974, only 24 per cent were in favour of denationalisation but by 1979 this had increased to 40 per cent and to 42 per cent in 1983.[17] By 1990, however, Worcester found that this trend had been reversed and the public were evenly divided on the issue.[18]

On other issues, there is no evidence that Thatcherism has taken hold. On law and order and immigration, where Thatcher's traditionalist support for greater discipline brought the Tory Party closer to the public mood than it had been before 1975, opinion became if anything less authoritarian in the 1980s. Her trade-union reforms during the 1980s received considerable popular support, even from many union members. But this has not translated into support for the tougher Thatcherite view that unions are 'undesirable or unnecessary institutions'. In 1984, at the height of the national coal strike, Thatcher branded Arthur Scargill and other militant trade unionists 'the enemy within' and during 1986 the battle between print unions and newspaper publishers raged at Wapping with scenes on television of violent clashes between the police and pickets. Yet, on the question of whether people feel that generally unions are 'a good thing' or 'a bad thing', Gallup's annual survey in 1986 found only 25 per cent saying that unions were a 'bad thing' compared with 41 per cent in 1979.[19]

At the heart of Thatcherism lay the argument that Britain's economic decline would be reversed only by a fundamental change in the purpose of economic policy. Thatcher argued that the commitment to maintaining full employment in all circumstances should be abandoned and priority given to lower inflation. In 1976 and 1979 around 60 per cent of the public shared this view, but by 1983 only 27 per cent agreed, and this slumped further to 14 per cent in 1986.[20]

This leftward shift in public priorities from prices to jobs no doubt reflected the reduction in inflation to 3 per cent by 1986 and the increase in unemployment to 3 million. But Thatcher's message that eliminating inflation must remain the priority had not been accepted. The considerable public support for putting prices before jobs in the late 1970s was more probably a reflection of the bipartisan rejection of the priority previously accorded by both parties to full employment. In 1976 the Labour government adopted monetarism at the behest of the International Monetary Fund and at that year's party conference Prime Minister Callaghan candidly confessed that the option of printing money to create more jobs no longer existed.

Thatcher's purpose above all was to revive the British economy through incentives and wean the British public away from their dependence on the welfare state. In the late 1970s, the public did give stronger support to the view that social-security benefits had 'gone too far', but by 1983 this had been reversed and the public took a more left-wing position than in 1974. The trade-off between lower taxes and increased spending on state services like health and education is a litmus test showing whether the ethos of Thatcherism has gained at the expense of collectivism. As Crewe and Searing report, the public was evenly divided on the trade-off question between tax-cutters and increased spenders in 1979, but by 1983 the spenders outnumbered the tax-cutters by two to one, and by 1987 the margin had widened to 64 per cent for greater spending against 13 per cent opting for tax cuts.[21]

There is bound to be scepticism about what people say to an opinion pollster and what they actually think as they vote in the privacy of the polling booth, particularly on the question of taxes and government spending. But the large shift in public opinion during the 1980s in favour of higher taxes and higher welfare state spending is striking. The seventh report in the series, British Social Attitudes, had found in 1983 that 54 per cent favoured the existing levels of taxes and spending on health, education and social services, compared with 32 per cent who wanted both taxes and spending to be increased. By 1989, however, the position had been reversed: 37 per cent wanted tax and spending levels to stay the same, while 56 per cent advocated increases.[22]

In April 1989, as Thatcher's tenth anniversary in Number 10 approached, she claimed that people had 'truly moved away from' socialism. Yet an extensive survey of people's values conducted that summer and reported by Jacobs and Worcester in their study, We British, found that more British voters would prefer a 'mainly socialist society' (47 per cent) to a 'mainly capitalist one' (39 per cent).[23] The survey also found that large majorities were in favour of ordinary taxpayers paying more in order to support the elderly, the poor and a better health service. 'The wet tendency was still very much alive and well inside the Tory Party,' Eric Jacobs and Worcester concluded: 73 per cent of Tory supporters favoured higher taxes to boost the health service and 68 per cent backed higher taxes to help the old and the poor. British Social Attitudes also found a substantial increase among Tory supporters favouring more taxes and more welfare state spending between 1983 and 1989.[24]

But the strength of collectivist values did not detract from people's commitment to wealth creation. In 1989, more voters favoured a society which emphasised increased efficiency rather than keeping people in work where this was not very efficient (47 per cent to 42 per cent). And 52 per cent wanted to keep differentials against 40 per cent who favoured a move towards equality.[25] But it is doubtful if Thatcher was responsible for persuading people of the perils of padded payrolls or squeezed differentials – for example, other surveys showed that there had been stronger support in 1979 than there was in 1987 for creating jobs through allowing companies to keep their profits than by the government using taxes.[26]

Thatcher undoubtedly won respect as leader, but it is also clear that even her style of leadership which was an integral part of Thatcherism, failed to have any lasting appeal. As Gallup surveys at the time of the 1983 and 1987 elections demonstrated, the public moved away from a Thatcherite approach. In 1983 more people had agreed than disagreed with the Thatcherite sentiments that 'one should stick firmly to one's beliefs when dealing with political opponents', 'in difficult times, the government should be tough', and 'governments can't do much to create prosperity; it is up to people to help themselves'. But by 1987 the picture had been reversed and more people rejected those sentiments than shared them. Even in 1983, however, there were resounding majorities of around two to one against the Thatcherite notions that 'in dealing with the rest of the world, it is better for Britain to stick resolutely to its own position' and that 'when governments make economic policy, it is better to keep unions and business at arm's length'. The majorities against both statements had increased to around three to one by 1987.[27]

The evidence that neither the public nor Tory supporters have been converted to Thatcherism is compelling. There is equally striking evidence that Tory MPs did not hold to the central tenets of Thatcherism any more strongly at the end of her rule than they did at the beginning. During Thatcher's leadership, estimates of the proportion of the parliamentary party that shared her belief in free-enterprise policies and a traditionalist stance on social and moral issues continued to vary between 10 and 25 per cent.

Categorising Tory MPs according to their stance on issues is fraught with problems, largely because of their non-ideological approach to politics. Only the most rough and ready assumptions can be attempted, and MPs' views change over time. But according to the most detailed and painstaking 'taxonomy' of the Tory parliamentary party undertaken by Philip Norton in 1989, only 19 per cent of Tory MPs were 'Thatcherites'.[28] In all, only 72 Tory MPs, fewer than one in five, shared their leader's views on either the free market or law and order. Of these only 29 MPs (8 per cent) shared Thatcher's commitment to both market forces and capital punishment.

Among the die-hard Thatcherites were Norman Tebbit and John Moore from Thatcher's November 1990 leadership campaign team. Others included No Turning Back members such as Michael Brown and Edward Leigh (who had vainly gone to Number 10 on the morning of Thatcher's announcement of her resignation) and the junior ministers

Michael Fallon, Michael Forsyth and Michael Portillo, who were party to the die-hards' last attempts to dissuade Thatcher from stepping down. The less committed Thatcherites were free-marketeers with libertarian social attitudes, such as John Major's leading supporter, Norman Lamont; the Trade and Industry secretary, Peter Lilley; the former chancellors Sir Geoffrey Howe and Nigel Lawson; the former cabinet minister John Biffen and the Powellite Wolverhampton backbencher Nicholas Budgen. The remaining Thatcherites comprised MPs who possess traditional right-wing views on law and order, including the defence minister, Alan Clark; the former minister Sir Rhodes Boyson; the chairman of the 92 Group, George Gardiner; and the anti-European Community campaigner Teddy Taylor.

As to the varying shades of opinion among the remaining four-fifths of Tory MPs, Norton found that a similar proportion – 18 per cent (67 MPs) – were 'critics' of Thatcher. They represented a combination of traditional and progressive Tories who accepted the need for an interventionist line on the economy, generally took a compassionate, paternalist line on social policy, and supported the European Community. Of the 'critics' 27 MPs were 'wet' and 40 MPs, who tended not to press their opposition as hard, were 'damp'. The wets included the former leader, Edward Heath, the former cabinet minister Sir Ian Gilmour and the challenger to Thatcher's leadership in 1989, Sir Anthony Meyer. The party chairman and leading advocate for Douglas Hurd during the leadership contest, Chris Patten, was designated by Norton as wet, possibly damp. Among the damps were reckoned to be Thatcher's 1990 challenger on the first ballot, Michael Heseltine, the education secretary, Kenneth Clarke, the health secretary, William Waldegrave, and the Foreign Office minister and host of the Catherine Place gathering on the night of the result of the first ballot, Tristan Garel-Jones.

Another 5 per cent of Tory MPs were described as 'populists', generally sharing the public's right-wing line on law and order and its more left-wing line on the economy. These 17 MPs, the so-called awkward squad, included the Birmingham Tory Anthony Beaumont-Dark and the Northampton MP who publicly called on Thatcher to step down before the first ballot, Tony Marlow.

The majority of Tory MPs, however, representing about 58 per cent of the parliamentary party (217 MPs), were categorised as the 'party faithful'. Of these only 20–30 MPs were designated as 'Thatcher loyalists', who were reckoned to have an attachment to Thatcher's style of leadership without any strong ideological commitment. The vast bulk, around 190–200 Tory MPs, were characterised by Norton as being 'loyal to the party rather than to any particular strand of thought within the party'. Writing before Thatcher's demise, Norton added that '[their] loyalty will flow to the leader, albeit on a contingent basis. As long as the leader provides competent – and successful – leadership, with consequent electoral appeal and reward, the loyalty is maintained; if the leader falters, Members start to waver.'

Moreover Thatcherites did not preponderate in Thatcher's Government. Norton's analysis revealed that among ministers, the less committed Thatcherites, the free-marketeer, social libertarians and, even more surprisingly, the damp critics, were over-represented. Furthermore, any notion that Thatcher's influence is stronger among MPs who were first elected during her ascendancy is also demolished. The 1983 intake appears as the most Thatcherite, but even so they only totalled 17 against 53 party faithful. Of the 1987 intake, only 4 MPs were regarded as Thatcherites against 46 party faithful.

The extraordinary conclusion from the detailed research is that Thatcher won despite Thatcherism. She won the leadership of her party and three general elections although she never converted her fellow Tory MPs, Tory supporters or the public to her beliefs. As some of the more cautious Thatcherites appeared to suspect, even by the end of her rule their leader's views still represented only a minority in the country, in her party and even in her government.

Yet Thatcher has had a bigger impact than anybody else over the last decade in fashioning the political landscape in which the majority of non-enthusiasts now have to operate. It is the landscape in which Major has to seek to survive and to restore the Tory Party's political fortunes. But the Tory Party has never judged its leaders by their doctrinal purity. Thatcher has not changed the party one iota in this respect. Her legacy to Major is the consequence of her government's actions, not a strait-jacket of ideology.

8

Major's Challenge

'Politics is like playing dice, you never quite know what's going to turn up but it's very exciting.'

John Major, January 1991

I

Major's longevity as party leader will depend, as it has for his predecessors since the departure of the great election-loser, Lord Derby, more than 120 years ago, on his ability to maintain the Conservatives in office. But what kind of Tory leader is Major? How will he exercise his power? What attitudes will influence his policies? What will his leadership mean for the Conservatives and the country? And how long can he survive?

The most recent precedent for a change of leader after the Tories had already enjoyed a long, unbroken spell in office is discouraging for Major. In October 1963, after twelve years of Tory rule, Douglas-Home became leader with only twelve months remaining at most before he had to call an election. In November 1990, after eleven and a half years of Tory rule, Major was elected leader with a maximum of eighteen months' leeway before an election. When Douglas-Home eventually faced the electorate in October 1964, his government was narrowly defeated. There was a sense of disappointed expectation among the Tories, who had come to believe in their claim to be the natural party of government, similar to that which they had experienced after their defeat in 1906. Unable any longer to resist the pressures on him to go, Douglas-Home quit as leader nine months later. Will Major suffer the same fate?

Douglas-Home, however, had to contend with Wilson, who was a more effective leader than Kinnock. Moreover, the mood of the times was more strongly against the Tories in the early 1960s than it was when Major took over. The 63-year-old Douglas-Home was also of the same political generation as his two immediate predecessors: the Tories only turned to the next generation, by electing the 49-year-old Heath, after they had lost office. But in 1990, it was before the impending election that the party turned to the next generation, choosing a 47-year-old to replace the 65-year-old Thatcher. So how will Major respond to the challenge?

Major entered Number 10 with the least previous ministerial experience of any Tory prime minister since Baldwin replaced Bonar Law in May 1923. Unlike Thatcher or Heath, Major has not served as leader of the opposition, but neither had Douglas-Home in 1963, nor Macmillan in 1957, Eden in 1955, Churchill in 1940, Neville Chamberlain in 1937 nor Baldwin in 1923. Apart from Baldwin, however, these other Tory premiers who emerged from the ministerial ranks had all served in the cabinet longer than Major before attaining the highest office. Major held a marginal edge over Baldwin at the outset of his premiership in terms of cabinet experience and familiarity to the public; his three-year apprenticeship at the cabinet table, including three months at the Foreign Office and a year as chancellor, was better than Baldwin's two-year cabinet tutelage and mere six months at the Exchequer. It is also often forgotten that Macmillan had served only eight months as foreign secretary and a year as chancellor when he became prime minister, but he had greater cabinet experience than Major and had served in the shadow cabinet for six years.

Events and Baldwin's own persona subsequently transformed him into one of the better-known Tory leaders, and ironically it was his predecessor, the unfortunate Bonar Law, who became 'the unknown prime minister'. The Gulf War, which ended in victory within his first hundred days in Number 10, ensured that Major would not be condemned to prime-ministerial anonymity. The Allied bombing of Iraqi targets, which began six weeks into his premiership, suddenly transformed him into a war leader. Each transatlantic phone call conferred new authority on him as Number 10 assiduously assured the media that his conversations with the US president, George Bush, were lasting more than a few minutes.

Major could scarcely have made a better start to his premiership in terms of his personal ratings, largely courtesy of the Gulf War. He chalked up a better rating than Thatcher managed during the Falklands conflict in 1982. Then, 59 per cent of voters said that they were satisfied with Thatcher as prime minister, but 36 per cent of the population was against her. Major's low-key approach, acting in sorrow rather than anger, captured the public mood without antagonising a sizeable minority. Within days of the first Allied air raids on Iraq, 61 per cent said that they were satisfied with him as prime minister and only 15 per cent were dissatisfied.[1]

At the end of January 1991, Major had become the most popular prime minister for thirty years, with 74 per cent saying that he was doing well and only 6 per cent badly.[2] The last prime minister to have enjoyed such ratings was Macmillan in his 'Supermac' heyday in the autumn of 1960, when he deployed gentle humour during his address to the United Nations General Assembly to counter Khrushchev's desk-thumping contest. Major lacks the panache of Macmillan, but displayed similar sang-froid in February 1991, immediately after the IRA mortar attack on Downing Street had blown in the windows: 'Gentlemen, I think we had better start again elsewhere,' he suggested to the war cabinet.

Yet Major the war leader also seems to have reaped a peace dividend of sorts: the peace which came with the end of Thatcher's conviction politics redounded to Major's advantage. The change in prime-ministerial style is a mirror image of the handover from Baldwin to his chancellor, Neville Chamberlain, in 1937, when a conciliator was followed by a combat leader. In 1990, the change was in the opposite direction, but the difference was as great. Whereas Thatcher emulated Chamberlain's hatred for Labour, and seemed happiest hurling insults across the chamber, Major, like Baldwin, recognises that there is another point of view which he respects but with which he does not agree and will argue against, patiently and politely. It scarcely makes for good copy at prime minister's question time, but Major's priority is to demonstrate that he is his own man. It was an impression he created from the moment he entered Number 10 with his immediate replacement of Thatcher's robust press secretary, Bernard Ingham, by Gus O'Donnell, a former economics lecturer who had been his press officer at the Treasury and whose approachable and relaxed manner reflects Major's style.

The contrast in prime-ministerial style between Thatcher and Major follows a pattern: the domineering Lloyd George and, punctuated only by Bonar Law's brief rule, the pacific Baldwin; the magniloquent Churchill and the taciturn Labour premier Attlee; and now the confrontationist Thatcher followed by the more consensual Major. Attlee knew that he could never emulate Churchill's charisma and instead deliberately cultivated an image of being humdrum. Likewise, Major has played to his strengths of being at ease with his ordinary background, displaying emollience and approachability, qualities which were never associated with Thatcher.

Like Attlee, Major rose through the ranks to the highest office as a result of appearing to have done little more than diligently perform his duties. 'Competent', 'reliable', 'unflappable' are the words commonly used by Major's colleagues when they recall his qualities at different stages of his career, and try to explain his success. In Clem Attlee's memoirs, prosaically entitled *As It Happened*, his description of his steady advancement from Independent Labour Party activist to Stepney councillor, to mayor, to MP, to minister and to party leader is remarkably similar to the accounts from Major's friends of his rise to prominence from Lambeth councillor to prime minister. It seemed that Attlee only had to attend a meeting to find himself 'being invited' to take on a new job. So it is with Major.

But Major is not an Attlee when it comes to dealing with his ministers. Attlee's brusque handling allowed cabinet government to function, but the emphasis was on brevity in discussion and the speedy dispatch of government business. Thatcher led from the front, which certainly had the effect in her early days of provoking fierce debate from political contemporaries who were less inclined to accept her authority than her later and younger cabinet appointees. Ministers in Major's cabinet recall only the more submissive Thatcher cabinets and greet innocent queries about whether cabinet meetings are any different since Thatcher's day with a huge grin or laugh. Ministerial taciturnity in the cabinet room is no longer the fashion.

'We're put through our paces much more,' one of Major's senior cabinet ministers commented.[3] He explained that when a minister presented a paper in Thatcher's cabinet and it was endorsed by the Prime Minister, virtually no debate would follow. Whereas Thatcher would declare her own views at the start of any discussion and challenge other ministers to argue, Major is in the tradition of prime ministers who act as chairmen and let the debate between ministers flow before summing up. 'The quality of discussion is now much higher,' a minister observed, claiming that he is now as likely to be questioned in the cabinet by other ministers as by the Prime Minister.[4]

The handover from Thatcher to Major saw one of the biggest ever transformations in the role of cabinet between one prime minister and another. It is the result of both a complete contrast in their characters and approach to decision-making and the sheer length of Thatcher's premiership. By the end of her rule virtually the entire cabinet were her placemen, neither the allies of a former leader whom she dared not risk sacking, nor representatives of some powerful faction within the party that needed to be placated. As some of her younger former cabinet ministers confess, she also dominated by being from a different political generation. She was prime minister in 1979 when Major and Patten were first elected to the Commons, and had already established her authority in the cabinet by the time that Howard and Lilley first became MPs in 1983. Such considerations inevitably affect the chemistry of cabinet debate.

In contrast to Thatcher's pre-eminence by the close of her government,

Major is necessarily first among equals. Most of his cabinet are older than he and many of them have greater political and ministerial experience. His inclination to take opinions and weigh up all the pros and cons has its drawbacks, too, as his closest supporters discovered during the contest for the party leadership. He took longer than was needed to settle who should act as his proposers, and wanted to run his campaign by committee and avoid a hierarchy. One senior minister happily described the result as 'a perfect socialist co-operative',[5] but others were dissatisfied with the consequences. In the end, it was left to members of his team to take the matter in hand and impose some effective chain of command.

Yet Major revealed a hard-nosed approach in his use of patronage, the weapon through which leaders wield their authority. Prime ministers are rated according to whether they are effective 'butchers' or not. Thatcher's 1981 reshuffle established her authority in the cabinet, but that of 1989 raised doubts about her leadership. Like Thatcher in her early years as leader, Major initially had limited scope for change, partly because by the autumn of 1990 the disintegration of Thatcher's cabinet through resignations and retirements had already brought into the cabinet the frontrunners among the next generation of Tory ministers.

Major began consulting colleagues about his proposed changes on the night of his leadership victory, before he had moved into Number 10. Waddington, the home secretary, was persuaded to leave the Commons and lead the government in the Lords to replace the ineffective Lord Belstead. Waddington's reactionary line on law and order had been popular with the party faithful. Major regards him as one of the 'wise old birds' in cabinet: Waddington chairs the home and social policy cabinet committee. But in his place at the Home Office, Major appointed Baker, Thatcher's party chairman, who shares his liberalism on Home Office issues like hanging and race relations. Renton, who had never won Thatcher's complete trust as chief whip and whose close links with Howe had placed him in an awkward position during the entire leadership crisis, was reshuffled to become arts minister.

Major's key appointment was his move of Patten from Environment to become party chairman. Despite Patten's unequivocal support for Hurd, his relationship with Major remained good during the leadership contest. But Patten's posting to Central Office has bound the fate of Major's main rival to his own future: if the Tories win the next election, Major's leadership will be secured for the foreseeable future; if, however, the party is defeated, Major's leadership may come under threat, but Patten will also be damaged. It is little comfort to Patten that the last party chairman who eventually became leader was Neville Chamberlain, more than fifty years ago.

Whatever the precise permutations of the next power struggle in the

Tory Party, Patten's chairmanship ensured that Major has the most able Tory strategist and thinker of his generation in the key position. Despite Thatcher's distrust of Patten's left-wing Toryism, during his years running the Conservative Research Department before the 1979 election, when it was still based in Old Queen Street, separate from Central Office, she had frequently sought his formidable talent as manifesto draftsman and speech-writer. Critics of Patten argue that he prefers to be above the party-political battle. He will not exhibit the bell-ringing exuberance of Hailsham before 1959 nor the partisan excess of Tebbit before 1987, but he realises the need to gear up a poorly prepared organisation and, in the manner of a Butler, to revive the party by demonstrating that it holds the higher ground in the battle of ideas. If that is lost, all is lost.

At the Treasury, the promotion of Lamont, Major's former deputy, to chancellor was to be expected and ensured continuity of approach, although, as Lamont demonstrated during the leadership contest, he is no lapdog and has a determination which could cause Major trouble if their views diverge on either the economy or Europe. The new chief secretary, Mellor, has generally been regarded as more on the left of the party than Major's economically dry supporters like Francis Maude, who remained financial secretary and outside the cabinet. Mellor is, however, renowned as an effective self-publicist and robust advocate: the annual public spending round is likely to be a much more bruising affair than when Major was in charge.

Elsewhere, the distribution of the spoils of office confirmed the impression of Major as a shrewd party manager. The new chief whip, Ryder, was perfect for the job, an ultra-discreet character who has been attuned to the inner thinking of the Tory Party since he had run Thatcher's private office in opposition before 1979. Major seized the opportunity of Parkinson's retirement to move Rifkind from the Scottish Office to Transport, thereby helping to heal the wounds of the civil war that had raged within the Scottish Tory Party between supporters of the die-hard Thatcherite junior minister and former Scottish party chairman, Michael Forsyth, and those of the leftish Rifkind. Ian Lang was an almost automatic choice to succeed Rifkind, although he is unlikely to be as effective or sharp in debate as his predecessor. But there were only ten Scottish Tory MPs from whom Major could choose. Lang was already a junior minister at the Scottish office and had declared support for Major when they happened to have lunch on the day Major formally entered the leadership contest.

The healing of party wounds after the contest was helped by the promotion of Hurd's supporters, like Tim Yeo and Ann Widdecombe, as junior ministers. Although Major pointedly gave no preferment to Heseltine's supporters, his appointment of Heseltine as environment secretary to oversee the reform of local government finance and structure was an astute move. Changing the poll tax had been Heseltine's call to arms against Thatcher. Poll tax rebels were reassured that their champion would be given a largely free hand in devising a replacement, yet the strong anti-Heseltine faction that was still seething at his action in deposing Thatcher thought that he would be hoist by his own petard.

Yet Major blundered over his failure to promote a woman to the cabinet. Thatcher had done little to advance women's interests during her premiership and had failed to bring others of her sex into her cabinet (with the sole exception of Lady Young in the early 1980s), but an all-male cabinet is now woefully anachronistic. The Tories can no longer rely on women voters in the way that they once could, and yet such has been the failure of Tory associations to adopt women candidates that Major was limited in his choice in the Commons to only seventeen Tory women MPs (including Thatcher). Major was maladroit, however, in dealing with Lynda Chalker, the minister for overseas development, the most eligible woman candidate for cabinet rank, asking her to take on extra duties as deputy party chairman without any corresponding promotion. His move to the Treasury of Gillian Shephard as minister of state made some amends for his general oversight. She is in tune with Major's approach to politics. A former social services minister, she had previously served on the Commons social services committee, where she impressed her chairman, Labour's Frank Field, the most knowledgeable MP on social policy issues. Like Ian Lang, the new Scottish secretary, Shephard had lunched with Major on the day of his nomination for the leadership and declared herself a supporter.

Yet one of the most significant of Major's appointments was his choice of Sarah Hogg, former economics editor of the *Daily Telegraph*, to head the Number 10 policy unit. The unit had been created by Wilson in 1974 to provide him with political advice and policy briefings as a counter-weight to the advice generally available to the cabinet through the Cabinet Office and Think Tank, and to the departmental support available to every other minister. Thatcher treated the unit as her revolutionary guard in Whitehall, battling against reluctant ministers and the civil-service establishment.

During Thatcher's premiership, command of the policy unit was entrusted only to ideologically sound Thatcherites like Hoskyns in the early years, and later to the proselytisers of free-market economics, John Redwood, a fellow of All Souls, Oxford, who later became an MP and junior minister, and Professor Brian Griffiths. Ferdinand Mount, the journalist and writer who succeeded Hoskyns in the early 1980s, had been the least warriorlike head of the unit, which contributed to the lack of a detailed Thatcherite agenda in the 1983 election manifesto. Hogg brings to the policy unit an independent-minded approach and technical competence on economics and finance which suggests a preference for specific, workable reform as opposed to policy serving primarily as the arm of pure doctrine.

Major's officials describe him as being insistent that all the facts are marshalled and the arguments explored before he reaches a decision. He will not conclude a briefing session until he is absolutely confident that he has fully understood the issue under discussion. His conscientiousness is coupled with a skill which eases the risk of his being overloaded: he is reckoned in Whitehall to be a past master at getting the best from advisers and officials. In part this reflects his approachable and considerate nature. But a former private secretary recalls Major's unerring ability to 'work the system', detecting which officials would deliver the information he required in the right form and at the right time.

Major's election as leader marked a break with the precedent set by the first two Tory leaders elected by MPs, Heath and Thatcher, who were both 'pro-active', radical prime ministers. Heseltine would have been another inveterate reformer, which is one reason that some die-hard Thatcherites gave him their support.

'Highly political' is the phrase used time and again by advisers, officials and ministers who have worked closely with Major, and in this sense he reflects the Baldwin tradition. But Major is much more methodical in coming to decisions than Baldwin, who would arrive at them through a process of 'sniffing the air', largely by spending a great deal of time around the Commons, and then eventually jumping to a conclusion. Major is closer to Bonar Law's businesslike style of work, which is partly a reflection of his character and partly of his earlier career in banking.

Major's methodical approach is also a result of the demands on a modern prime minister. There is no other way of coping. No present-day premier could spend as much time listening to Commons debates or chatting in the smoking room as Baldwin did. The pressures of modern diplomacy, particularly at the European level, and the modern media, requiring instant responses from government, have ended the days when premiers could be quite as relaxed about their working habits as Baldwin, or even Macmillan.

Major is not in the same league as Baldwin or Macmillan, or, for that matter, Heseltine or Hurd, as a communicator. He appears to be decent and reasonable, but his command and delivery of the spoken word is the most limited of any prime minister in modern times. This is not necessarily a result of his having left school at sixteen: he continued his education by correspondence course and went into banking, where he headed the press office of the Standard Chartered Bank. Moreover, the Labour prime minister Callaghan left school at about the same age and is a better speaker.

Arguably the everyday ordinariness of Major's speech helps confirm his appeal to the average voter. The lengthy expositions of Gladstone or the high-blown rhetoric of Churchill would certainly be inappropriate today. Major's apparent 'safeness' in not saying anything particularly original or colourful, and his calmness and patience when facing hostile questioning – rather like Ken Livingstone, the Labour MP and former leader of the Greater London Council – reveal the man as the epitome of the modern career politician. The end result might not excite or inspire the 'chattering classes' but it is a party professional's dream, minimising the risk of frightening off the voters.

Yet Major's imprecise use of language is his weakest suit. When he launched his bid for the Tory leadership he spoke about achieving a 'classless society' in Britain during the 1990s, but he actually meant creating a more open society with greater social mobility. Laudable as this objective may be, it does not represent a society without class differences. Major is really talking about equality of opportunity, but this inevitably results in new inequalities even if there is greater social mobility. Major may find the new form of inequality more justifiable, but the end result will not be a 'classless society', and subsequently he had to explain more carefully what he had meant.

In the day of the sound bite for television and radio bulletins, when the crisp, punchy comment steals the headlines, Major seems little better than Kinnock in delivering the telling line. More disturbing for the Tories was Major's early gaffe on the poll tax that did not augur well for a closely fought election campaign. During his interview with David Frost in TV-am's *Frost on Sunday* programme in January 1991, Major stated that Heseltine would not recommend abolishing the poll tax in his review of local government finance and structure. Yet Heseltine's line had been that anything should be considered, and Major subsequently sought to pass off his comment as 'a contingent thought'.

Major's undoubted strength, on the other hand, is that he is every bit as unapologetic as his predecessor about his Toryism but at the same time is temperamentally incapable of lacing his advocacy with Thatcher's aggression. Some of the old-style paternalists, as distinct from the self-made Heseltines and Walkers, often sound defensive, their sense of *noblesse oblige* Toryism seeming to be motivated primarily by the Disraelian saw that 'the palace is not safe when the cottage is not happy'. Major is plainly from the cottage, even if it was located in Brixton. His parents' move, necessitated by business failure, from suburban Worcester Park to a small rented flat in a declining area of the inner city gave Major no privileges and no thought of needing to be defensive about his Toryism.

Major, however, has not assumed the cocky assertiveness of some self-made Tories who, like him, have risen from the back streets. Brixton man is not 'Essex man', the aggressively right-wing working-class and upwardly mobile voters in new towns and suburbs on London's northeastern fringe, whom Tebbit epitomises. Major's inspiration comes from an incomparably more civilised, though no less partisan, quarter.

II

In conversation, Major eschews talk of political heroes. Nor is he a philosopher politician in the mould of Balfour, Butler or, in today's Tory Party, Patten. Yet he does express great admiration for Iain Macleod, the 'One Nation' Tory of the 1950s and 1960s, who occupies a unique place in the pantheon of left-wing Tories.[6] He vividly recalls the moment when he first heard of Macleod's death in July 1970, in the way that most people remember exactly what they were doing when they learned of Kennedy's assassination. Major was staying at the home of his wife's mother, a few months before he and Norma were married, and was deeply shocked when he saw the morning headlines announcing that Macleod, then chancellor, had died of a heart attack at Number 11.

Yet Major's style of leadership has prompted other Tories, including both Hurd and Biffen, to detect signs in Major of another Baldwin, the paternalist Tory leader of the 1920s and 1930s. Certainly, like Baldwin, Major appears as a Tory through attitude and general approach, rather than somebody consciously seeking to apply a carefully thought-out philosophy. Baldwin is revered by Tory consolidators, yearning for a period of calm after Thatcher's permanent revolution, and is abhorred in equal measure by Tory radicals.

Baldwin and Macleod are two of the least likely models that it would be possible to imagine for a man who was portrayed during the leadership contest as Thatcher's heir presumptive. It therefore comes as little surprise that Thatcherite die-hards soon began to evince disillusion with Major's leadership. For the most part, however, Thatcherite moderates remain confident, as do some on the left of the party, that Major was the best choice. What is to be made of these conflicting impressions?

Major's admiration for Macleod has been the subject of much speculation. Does it suggest that Major is a closet left-wing Tory? Macleod, after all, was an acolyte of Rab Butler's from his days in the Conservative Research Department; was a founder member of the One Nation group; and served in Conservative governments and shadow cabinets when the Tories accepted the postwar settlement based on the welfare state and the mixed economy, and sought to make it work more efficiently than under Labour, as opposed to trying to demolish it as Thatcher sought to do.

But others have seen in Macleod a more radical Tory who would not have been unhappy with some of the reforms introduced during Thatcher's leadership. They point to Macleod's advocacy, with Enoch Powell, of selectivity in the social services, his tough stand against the transport worker's union in the London bus strike of 1958 and, as shadow chancellor after 1965, his opposition to prices and incomes policies and his support for market-style solutions in the 1970 Conservative manifesto.

A further suggestion is that in his youth Major was simply spellbound by Macleod's oratory and has remained awe-struck ever since, with little realisation of where Macleod stood in the party. Macleod attracted many young people of Major's generation into the Tory Party. It is easy now to forget his impact after Macmillan appointed him colonial secretary in October 1959, following the Tory landslide election victory. At the time, the sixteen-year-old Major was spending his first autumn after leaving Rutlish grammar school in Merton, South London, earning some money and helping support his family. For the next two years, Macleod was barely out of the headlines as he hastened independence in Britain's African colonies where white settlers were strongest, notably Kenya, Nyasaland (now Malawi), Tanganyika (Tanzania) and Northern Rhodesia (Zambia).

Macleod expressed in Britain, as far as many young Tories like Major were concerned, what the youthful Kennedy articulated in the United States when he was elected president in the autumn of 1960: an enlightened, socially liberal alternative to either stuffy conservatism on the one hand or state socialism on the other. It was a vision exemplified in Macleod's 'brotherhood of man' speech at the Tory Party conference in October 1961. Macleod's rapport with the Young Conservatives had been strengthened shortly before that year's party conference when Macmillan had appointed him party chairman, in addition to making him Leader of the House. His resignation in the 1963 leadership crisis led to his being ostracised in the Commons smoking room but confirmed him as the favourite of young Tories who despaired at the leadership's grouse-moor image. The Greater London Young Conservatives, whom Major joined, were Macleod's staunchest supporters.

Major first saw and heard Macleod, 'the last of the orators in the Tory Party' in Macmillan's phrase, in full flow at party conferences from the mid-1960s, and at Young Conservative gatherings in London. Listening to him, either on a public platform or in conversation, was, in Major's memory, an uplifting experience, and, like everybody else in the audience, he recalls that he always left feeling better. He was struck by Macleod's concern, bordering on nervousness, even when addressing only small gatherings of Young Conservatives, that he should deliver a rousing speech. But what is most striking about Major's impressions of Macleod, in view of his own unapologetic but unbrutal Toryism, is his sense that whatever Macleod argued in his speeches 'seemed to be said with total conviction, both moral and intellectual'. Major thus draws inspiration from Macleod as a 'conviction politician', but one 'who had a particular affinity for young people because he appealed to the better side of public nature'.

Moreover, Major admires Macleod's readiness to take his convictions to the point of resignation. 'If he thought something was wrong and he couldn't tolerate it, he wouldn't be part of it,' recalls Major: 'one always knew that was the case, and indeed at one point he proved it.' This view sets Major apart from many other Tories, who tend to judge the 1963 leadership crisis principally by the traditional Tory yardstick of loyalty to the leader; Macleod and Powell are condemned for their refusal to serve, and Douglas-Home is now recast as the wounded hero. Major sees Macleod's resignation as an act which deserves praise, not repudiation, although he has great affection and respect for Douglas-Home.

At the root of Macleod's resignation lay the cause that Major shares. It also explains why so many of Macleod's contemporaries were infuriated and why, even today, many Tories can never forgive him. The cause was Macleod's attack on the privileged elite who ran the Tory Party. In his damning indictment of 'the magic circle', Macleod did what many Tories found, and some still find, inexcusable: not only did he criticise the self-selecting control of the party leadership by a closely knit inner group, but he also drew attention to their social background, commenting that eight of the nine men in the 'magic circle' who effectively settled the leadership of the party, 'went to Eton'.

As a meritocrat Macleod had a particular detestation of what had happened in the Tory Party in October 1963. In a curious way, Major's election as leader appears as the meritocrats' revenge: Hurd was the hapless victim, whose old Etonian background became a handicap in 1990. Whoever would have thought in 1963 that that would ever have happened in the Tory Party? Certainly not the old Etonian members of the 'magic circle', nor probably even Macleod.

In a number of speeches during the mid-1960s Macleod developed his meritocratic ideals, advocating what he saw as the need for 'the pursuit of excellence'. He wanted to break down the old barriers of a class-ridden society, which were so wasteful of talent and skill, and which he believed were a root cause of Britain's malaise. Patently, the Tory Party would be in no position to lead this crusade while a 'magic circle' mentality persisted.

Interestingly, it was in this respect that Thatcher was also most similar to Macleod. She too was a card-carrying meritocrat, but unlike Macleod with his 'pursuit of excellence' or Major with his talk of 'opportunity', she contrived to emphasise its negative connotations. She almost seemed to embrace the unavoidable inequalities in a meritocratic society. Hers was a reaction to the political battles of the 1970s, and particularly the debate about the future of Britain's schooling, when she saw the trend towards egalitarianism as the great dragon which had to be slain.

Macleod's more positive meritocratic message in the mid-1960s had already struck a chord with the former grammar-school boy from Brixton. It still remains the lodestar of Major's political belief. 'You will never fill a book of philosophy about John's political thinking,' one of Major's closest friends commented, 'but if there's one thing which he feels passionately about it's opportunity, the right of people to have the chance to get on and make something of their lives, whatever their background.'[1] It was a conviction that formed the centrepiece of his campaign for the leadership.

'As long as I am privileged to lead our party it will never become an exclusive club,' Major told his audience at the formal party meeting when he was presented as the new Tory leader. The words might well have been Macleod's, had he ever succeeded in grasping the Tory crown. Anybody who heard Major's ad-libbed comment at the opening of his speech at the party conference in Bournemouth less than two months earlier would have been aware that he believes that the Tory Party must practise what it preaches. Prompted by a contribution to the debate on the economy from John Horam, the former Labour MP, Major responded with an off-the-cuff assertion that the Tory Party should always remain open to everybody, whatever their background.

There are shades of Baldwin here, as well as Macleod. It was Baldwin who told the Tory Party conference in 1924 of his ambition that 'a ladder' would be set up within the Tory Party, which would help 'the working men of this country' as effectively as 'the ladder which exists today in the Labour Party, by which a man, whatever his means or his origin, may hope, by the exercise of his natural ability, to render service to his country into whatsoever office he may be called'. In terms of his own background, Major can be seen as both heir and beneficiary of Baldwin's and Macleod's ambitions for the Tory Party.

Major was equally impressed by Macleod's socially liberal 'conviction politics'. In October 1969, Macleod volunteered his public support for Nigel Fisher, the Tory MP and a long-time friend, who came under threat of deselection from right-wing activists – the 'skinheads of Surbiton', as Wilson dubbed them – because of his liberal views on race relations. As Major recalls, many politicians would have kept quiet on an issue which would make Macleod unpopular with many in the party at the time.

Less than eighteen months earlier, in April 1968, Heath had sacked

Enoch Powell from his shadow cabinet after his 'Rivers of Blood' speech. That spring, like many other Young Conservative hopefuls, the 25-year-old Major was fighting his first election as a Tory candidate in the London borough elections. Contemporaries still recall the huge impact of Powell's speech in the kind of inner-city ward which Major was contesting on Lambeth Council. The Ferndale ward was in Clapham, an area with high immigration, where Powell attracted strong, in some cases impassioned, support among white working-class voters. A vocal minority of party activists took up the Powellite crusade, notably in nearby Vauxhall. Major was not of their number. After his election in a great landslide victory in which 57 Tories were elected to a 60-strong council which Labour had controlled for forty years, Major would have no truck with the minority of Powellite councillors and along with other Tories ensured their virtual isolation.

A great influence on Major's first experience as a practising politician was Bernard Perkins, leader of the Tories on Lambeth Council. Perkins also worked in the Wandsworth finance department, and is remembered as a living embodiment of the motto which used to hang above the desk of the former Tory Party chairman, Lord Woolton, and which Macleod used to quote approvingly: 'We not only cope, we care.' It was Perkins who appointed Major vice-chairman and then chairman of the borough housing committee, which also included among its members Sir George Young, who became a Tory MP in 1974 and whom, in 1990, Major appointed as housing minister. Lambeth's director of housing during Major's chairmanship was another humane and liberal man, Harry Simpson, who later headed the Northern Ireland housing executive.

Lambeth Council became a trail-blazer in housing policy, rejecting the conventional wisdom that the planners knew best. They reversed the wholesale redevelopment policies which had become the vogue through-out British cities in the 1960s and had gone far beyond the original aim of slum clearance, entailing the loss of housing stock and the destruction of working-class communities. They put a stop to the building of tower blocks, and priority was given to renovation instead of demolition. They pioneered housing-advice centres. The Major–Simpson duumvirate were committed to government intervention on a big scale, but they were motivated by social considerations in a reaction against grandiose plans. The Tories, and Major, were defeated in 1971 as the political pendulum swung back in Labour's favour, but, as friends at the time realised, he had been 'bitten by the political bug'.

But what of Major's views on the economy? Can the acolyte of Macleod, and Thatcher's chief secretary and chancellor, be the same person? Or has he undergone a political conversion akin to Joseph's in the mid-1970s? The circle is partly squared by recalling that the Macleod whom the young Major heard during the late 1960s was in opposition. It was not the time to give intellectual justification for the interventionist, consensus-style Keynesianism of Tory rule between 1951 and 1964. Instead, at party conferences and Young Conservatives' meetings, Macleod's first task as the Tories' most effective debater and orator was to pillory the economic record of Wilson and Callaghan, the hapless chancellor until the Labour government's devaluation in late 1967, and to rouse the party faithful. 'Macleod rallies the Tories,' the party conference headlines would proclaim, year in, year out. 'He was a very sharp-edged politician indeed,' Major recollects. 'He certainly didn't scruple to attack his opponents, very savagely and with great effect.'[8]

But Major also recalls that during those years Macleod set out his package of tax reforms, including a shift from tax on earnings to tax on spending in the form of value-added tax. Restoring incentives was presented as part and parcel of Macleod's 'pursuit of excellence'. Moreover, Macleod wanted to extend the property-owning democracy and realise Eden's great vision of a truly 'capital-owning democracy', in which many more people, not just the rich, would have the ability and inclination to build up capital.

Major believes that a capital-owning democracy will increasingly be created as a result of the property-owning democracy: more people than ever before will inherit a house or flat in middle age. But he does not believe that enough has yet been done. In advocating his objective, Major deliberately seeks to paraphrase Macleod, saying: 'we want people actually to build up their own savings for the independence and security that savings will give them.' Close colleagues of Major's identify his introduction of the TESSA scheme in his 1990 budget as quintessentially Major's policy. Whereas Lawson's tax cuts gave greatest help to the highest-paid, Major's principal reform sought to encourage savings by the ordinary taxpayer.

Yet the most fascinating insight of all is provided by Major's reflections on the loss suffered by the Tory Party when Macleod died: 'Macleod had that rare gift of instinct for what the British people regard as fair. They will take a great deal that they don't like provided they regard it as fair, and he had as fine an instinct for what people regard as fair as anyone I recall.'

Major avers that there is no difference between the principles that Macleod enunciated and the policies that the Tories have pursued since 1979. But fairness is not a concept which readily sprang to the lips of his predecessor in Number 10. Its rehabilitation under Major's leadership would mark a significant change.

Major's response on specific social problems suggests at least a change of tone. Thatcher was inclined to remain obdurate against small increases in spending to help resolve some of the most sensitive issues, despite the political hue and cry. As a result, if she did eventually capitulate, as in the case of extra payments to war widows, she gained little political credit because it seemed that the money had had to be prised from her grasp. Yet on issues like compensation to haemophiliacs given AIDS-infected blood, homelessness in Britain's cities and the speedy extension of cold-weather payments, Major has seen that for very little cost the government can appear fairer and gain political credit. It is an equation of which Macleod, a liberal and shrewd politician would have approved. But are there likely to be significant changes in policy?

III

'When John came to inspect the policy files he found quite a lot of blank sheets,' revealed a cabinet minister in Major's administration.[9] Policy work had been due to begin when the leadership crisis developed, but this revelation is ironic in view of Thatcherite die-hard worries only weeks after Major became leader that Thatcherism was being abandoned.

The Tories were perilously close to appearing to have run out of steam, and Major was left with very little time to make policy before an election. Despite the Thatcherite mutterings, however, he was well placed to dictate the terms. The Thatcherite old guard form only a minority, albeit a vociferous one, within the parliamentary party, and an impending election generally unites the Tory Party behind its leader. If, however, Major should lead his party to defeat, he will face much greater disunity and, on the Tory Party's track record, a challenge to his leadership.

'Thatcherism ended a couple of years ago,' a former minister commented during the 1990 leadership contest. As a dry Tory on economic policy, he had in mind the increased spending sanctioned by the cabinet, notably on transport and welfare, in the last couple of years of the Thatcher government. Her cabinet 'had already spent the money which John Smith [the shadow chancellor] had earmarked for the first two years of a Labour government,' he observed.[10]

The sense that Thatcherism was over, or had stalled, was in large part testimony to the number of far-reaching reforms which had been introduced during Thatcher's premiership. She had profoundly recast the British political landscape. The unions, the nationalised industries, local councils, the NHS, social security and schools had all experienced radical restructuring. There was a limit to how much more change was feasible in the near future, notwithstanding the exhortations of the No Turning Back group.

During the leadership crisis, a former Thatcher adviser confided that further reforms of the welfare state would be politically unacceptable, since the government had kept saying that there was no hidden agenda: any new schemes would immediately provoke an outcry. Moreover, tax cuts had gone far enough: it was time to channel more help to the family. Talk of that kind from a dyed-in-the-wool Thatcher loyalist suggested the emergence of a potential consensus on policy. His thoughts were not too dissimilar from those voiced by Patten, the party chairman: 'We have to establish a rhythm for our radicalism which matches the prevailing mood. I don't think people just want a quiet life and no change, but they want to feel that the government is setting about change in a deliberate and considered way.'[11]

What then are the main themes of the Major premiership? The Gulf War and deepening economic recession dominated its first hundred days, and their impact – one positive, the other negative – on Major's and the government's standing in the public-opinion polls will largely settle the outcome of the election. The main areas of policy debate involve fleshing out Major's rallying cry of the 'opportunity society' and what that entails in terms of education and training; reforming the poll tax and local government; tackling incentives and disincentives for the lower paid; dealing with the quality of service in the public sector; and trying to resolve the questions raised by European economic and political union. Family policy, the role of women, the encouragement of wider owner-ship, and the environment are also likely to feature on Major's agenda.

'I want the 1990s to become a Decade of Opportunity,' Major told the party meeting in December 1990 when he was officially adopted as party leader. From the day he launched his leadership campaign, Major has put education at the top of his political agenda. It reflects the man's genuine commitment to a meritocratic society. It also amounts to an admission that the Thatcher government failed in this area. The collapse in the morale of the teaching profession was one of the greatest follies of government policy during the 1980s, and Major has promised to reverse this mistake.

The Thatcher years saw a considerable increase in private education, which represents, on any objective measure, an entrenchment of in-equality: the creation of a class-ridden, not a classless, society. Moreover, one factor underlying wage and salary awards during the 1980s was not militant trade unionism, which Thatcher had slain, but continued skill shortages. Ministers point to an array of initiatives and schemes in education and training during the 1980s, but they were never accorded the priority which was needed to prepare Britain for competing within the single European market from 1992.

'Where's the beef?' is the challenge that Major must meet in his policies for an 'opportunity society'. Education policy is to Major what housing was to the Tories when they returned to office in 1951: it is the social policy on which his government will be judged. The housing minister, Macmillan, never looked back. Major's education secretary, Kenneth Clarke, having been appointed initially by Thatcher, now finds himself facing a similar political challenge.

The Thatcher government's basic reforms of the national curriculum and testing in schools are likely to stay in place. The thrust of policy looks set to enshrine the local management of schools, removing them from local-authority control, but this will necessitate effective quality control. Major and Clarke share the view that one of the reasons some parents are prepared to spend a fortune on school fees is that the private sector provides a formalised and disciplined approach in which children are stretched to their limits, which many parents feel no longer exists in much of the state sector. 'I want the most rigorous standards applied in teacher training,' Major told the Young Conservatives' conference in February 1991, envisaging an emphasis on training teachers in the subjects they are going to teach, rather than in 'the theory of education'.

If the policy is to realise Major's objectives, there has to be a revolution in provision for the 70 per cent or so of young people who do not proceed to traditional higher or further education. This requires motivating the vast majority of non-academic young people to continue in vocational education. Training in industry is unlikely to be sufficiently effective unless firms are required to contribute to the cost: exhortation is an inadequate means of revolutionising Britain's deep-rooted neglect of technical training.

The reforms of education for the non-academic will require more government spending if Major's objective of an 'opportunity society' is to remain anything other than an attractive but distant aspiration. The Treasury, however, will be resistant to demands for substantial extra spending at a time of economic recession and when unforeseen bills from the Gulf War have to be met. The work on the new policies has sought to minimise costs, for Clarke is a political realist, but Major faces a difficult trade-off between giving substance to his ambition and dashing people's expectations of much better opportunities.

Yet it is on the vexed issue of local-government finance that Major faced the most immediate political challenge. Ministers in Thatcher's government were well aware that despite the unpopularity of domestic rates, almost any reform would create large numbers of people who would be worse off. So it is with changing the poll tax: any new system is bound to create new groups of losers. Ministers agonised over the best method of reform. And however fair Heseltine's new proposals may seem, Major has the awkward problem of explaining why the Tory government inflicted the poll tax on people in the first place.

Potentially the most divisive policy in the Tory Party for Major is the issue of European economic and political union. This was an issue which Thatcher had signally failed to resolve. She appeared to confuse a loss of national sovereignty with a loss of national identity, refusing to acknowledge that sovereignty was already diminished, as the impact on British economic policy of the Bundesbank's decisions on interest rates has repeatedly demonstrated. And although she persisted in making plain her deep-seated opposition to closer union and whipped up anti-European sentiment in her own party, she conceded at every stage.

Major made the clearest possible statement of the difference between his approach on Europe and that of his predecessor, when he addressed German Christian Democrats in Bonn in March 1991. Thatcher's singularly ill-timed comments, on the eve of Major's visit to Bonn, about her fears of German domination in a united Europe served to heighten the contrast. Major, however, declared that he wanted to see Britain 'where we belong. At the very heart of Europe'. And whereas Thatcher's intransigence had isolated Britain in the European Community and had ultimately proved self-defeating, Major's aim is to try to exert greater influence over decisions by affirming unequivocally Britain's commitment to Europe and showing his readiness to co-operate in talks on closer union.

Major's problem is that in Europe there is a considerable head of steam, generated principally by the German government, for closer economic and political union, while in his own party anti-European feeling was strengthened by the divergences in Europe at the outset of the Gulf War. There is little Major can do about the pressures for union on the continent: Britain is now a middle-ranking European power, and will largely have to react to events. The crucial question will be the extent to which the Germans press for giving more formal powers to the European Community institutions, which would require amending the Treaty of Rome, or whether some less formal mechanism, possibly involving co-operation through the intergovernmental conferences, will satisfy them.

European union has the potential to split the Tory Party. Major is not a Peel, nor is he a Balfour, although he may find himself in a similar predicament to the latter. The crucial factor will be whether the Tories remain in office or not, as leading opponents of closer European union acknowledge. If Major succeeds in maintaining the Tories in office, rebellion over closer, more formal European union would be limited to a hard core of back-bench critics. If, however, the Tories are driven into opposition, the party could be split three ways between the anti-Europeans, pro-Europeans and a centre group, loyal to the leader, who will be trying to effect some compromise; the relative strengths of these groups would depend on the impact of election losses on the parliamentary party. Major's situation could resemble Balfour's in the early 1900s, when the party was split between free-traders, tariff reformers and centrists, and was denied office for a decade.

Yet Europe impinges more immediately through Major's decision in the autumn of 1990 that sterling should join the European Exchange-Rate Mechanism. At the time, he won plaudits for resolving the issue which had divided Thatcher and Lawson, and his decisive action helped him when the leadership contest suddenly occurred. But as the recession deepened during the winter of 1990–91, it seemed that Major's critics at the time of entry had been right. The effect was to drive the economy deeper into recession as interest rates stayed high. As a result, Major came under pressure from outright opponents of British membership, including Thatcher's former economics adviser, Sir Alan Walters, and five other economists who wrote to *The Times* in February 1991, arguing that without an immediate 2 per cent cut in interest rates, which would effectively entail withdrawal from the ERM, British industry would face a tougher squeeze than in 1980–81.

Major stuck to his line about 'loathing' inflation, maintaining that membership of the ERM was evidence of his commitment to sustaining a low level of inflation in the longer term. Barely an interview or speech passed without ministers of all shades of opinion in the Tory Party intoning the central plank of Thatcherism, the defeat of inflation. This begs the question of who allowed it to rise into double digits.

There is, however, another reason for ministers to emphasise repeatedly the need to defeat inflation. They know that over the months before the election, inflation is one of the few main economic indicators likely to improve – not a difficult achievement when the economy is shrinking instead of growing. Rather in the way that Labour ministers selected the balance of trade as their yardstick before the 1970 election, Tory ministers are using inflation to measure their success. The ploy backfired on Labour when the figures for the month before the election suddenly seemed bad.

In many ways, the advent of Major appeared to usher a return to the traditional concerns of economic policy. This largely reflects the ending of the illusion of an 'economic miracle' at the end of the 1980s. In March 1991, an all-party Lords' committee reported that there had been virtually no net investment in British manufacturing industry during the previous decade. Moreover, the finance and service sectors, the success stories of Thatcher's boom, were being badly hit by the recession. And the government is again becoming a borrower. A return to a fixed exchange rate, albeit a system which allows for periodic devaluation and revaluation of currencies within the ERM, will also inevitably renew concern with the issues that dominated the debate about the management of the economy over twenty years ago, notably the balance of payments and regional policy.

Similarly, the notion that Britain should now emulate the German 'social market' economy suggests a return to a political debate more redolent of the 1950s and 1960s. 'For too long we have tolerated public services that are just not good enough,' Major proclaims.[12] He could easily be responding to the charge of 'private affluence and public squalor' made thirty years ago. Major and his ministers emphasise value for money as opposed to increased spending on the public services, but, as many companies appreciate, changes in working practices or new investment which increase efficiency often initially involve extra spending.

Moreover, the use of the phrase 'social market' economy overlooks the fact that the German system was based on the assumptions about the mixed economy which were prevalent after the Second World War. The Germans were more successful at organising their institutions and economic policies, but in essence it is no different from the approach with which any 1950s Tory like Butler or Macleod would have agreed. Patten has said of Germany's Christian Democrats that 'they've constructed a political philosophy which works and delivers not only in terms of the prosperity which it helps to produce but also in terms of – to use a rather Christian Democrat word – the solidarity which it establishes'.[13] Why not use a rather Tory phrase and say 'One Nation'?

When Major launched his campaign for the Tory leadership, he deliberately chose, as chancellor, to emphasise that the next general election would be fought on the battle-ground of the economy. His succession and the Gulf War have not changed the Tories' underlying concern that the economic cycle is out of kilter with the electoral timetable, an anxiety which intensified as the recession deepened. But Labour has an electoral mountain to climb after its shattering defeats in 1983 and 1987. Merely to draw level in popular support with the Tories since 1987, Labour needs a swing in its favour of 5.8 per cent, which would set a record for any election since the end of the Second World War. Moreover, the country has polarised socially since the early 1970s: fewer mixed communities means fewer marginal seats. In order to win an overall majority of seats, Labour must achieve a swing of 8.5 per cent since 1987.[14]

In 1983 and 1987, however, the Liberal–SDP Alliance won 25.4 and 22.6 per cent of the popular vote respectively. At the next election, the Liberal Democrats are likely to be nearer to the 14 to 19 per cent range won by the Liberals in 1974 and 1979 notwithstanding their remarkable victories in by-elections at Eastbourne and Ribble Valley. The Tory lead over Labour in 1979 was 6.9 per cent of the total vote and the overall majority in the Commons was 43 seats. Major should regard those figures as more accurate starting posts.

The next election will be decided by the voters' judgement of the Government's record, of the policies on offer, of the competence of the leaders and their frontbench teams to govern, and perceptions of the parties' images. As regards competence to govern, Labour's weakness is that it has failed to convince the voters that it can be trusted to manage the economy. In terms of image, Major appears an asset as Tory leader. Ordinary people can readily identify with him. He looks like a respectable pillar of any local community who might easily be seen at a Rotary Club dinner; sipping a half-pint at the golf-club; or sitting behind the desk in the bank manager's office. In February 1991, his breakfast of bacon and eggs, with brown sauce, which he enjoyed at the Happy Eater motorway cafeteria at Doncaster on his way to the Young Conservatives' conference, became the stuff of tabloid legend.

In the longer term, however, assuming that Major continues as prime minister, he will face the problem which confronts all modern leaders: power insulates as much as it corrupts. The demands on their time, coupled with the exigencies of tight security against the terrorist threat, inevitably risk cutting them off from both party and public. Although Baldwin became one of the most familiar figures of the 1920s and 1930s, he enjoyed the freedom denied to modern premiers of walking alone about London and travelling on public transport. Thatcher had been able once to persuade people that in some ways she was in touch with them. But it was an impression that vanished as she became increasingly preoccupied on the international stage. Her 'power-dressing' from the 1980s came to symbolise not only her domination, but also her growing isolation. Major, the consummate political operator, is unlikely to sacrifice the opportunity for other exploits similar to the brown-sauce breakfast, but the schedule of international diplomacy, round-the-clock meetings and security constraints threaten, over time, to make him seem more distant and out of touch.

As Tory leader, Baldwin was able to call upon the sense among the party faithful that he had risen from their ranks. 'There is nothing I ask you to do that I have not done myself,' he told the 1928 Tory Party conference in words which might just as easily be spoken by Major today. 'I have marked off polling cards. I have addressed envelopes (laughter), and I have shepherded the last batch of voters from the public house (cheers, and laughter). I gained my experience in an old borough and there is nothing you can teach me.' Major conveys the same impression of having risen from the ranks, and he has an advantage over Baldwin in that local party workers were able to exert some influence in his selection, through their consultations with their MPs during the weekend before the

"REMEMBER YOU SAID MAGGIE'S PRESENCE WOULD NEVER REALLY LEAVE DOWNING STREET.....?"

second ballot in the 1990 leadership contest.

But at the end of the day the challenge facing Major is to meet his party's expectation of electoral success. After the shock defeat in 1929, many activists turned against Baldwin. In Major's case, party expectations have been heightened by his predecessor's hat-trick of election triumphs. The paradox for Major is that although he benefited from a widespread relief at Thatcher's demise, she was a hard act to follow. As other Tory Party leaders have discovered, if he disappoints his party's expectations and fails to maintain the Tories in office, he is unlikely to be easily forgiven.

Notes

Chapter 1: He Who Wields the Dagger

1. In April 1990 Thatcher broke her own record, which she had first set in the autumn of 1981, for being the most unpopular prime minister since Gallup polls in 1938 first asked people about their satisfaction with the premier. But as Peter Kellner has noted (*The Independent*, 30 November 1990), Thatcher's satisfaction rating was always higher than that of her Government. Although her rating sometimes dipped below the level of support for the Conservatives, this gap was exaggerated: satisfaction ratings are calculated for the electorate as a whole whereas voting intention figures include only those naming a party – when the Tories fell to 35 per cent in the polls, their support among the electorate as a whole was only about 30 per cent, not much higher than Thatcher's satisfaction rating at the time of around 25–30 per cent.

2. Bernard Ingham, Thatcher's press secretary, Charles Powell, her private secretary, Peter Morrison, her parliamentary private secretary, Gerry Neale and Michael Neubert, members of her campaign team, and George Gardiner of the right-wing 92 Group were subsequently knighted, but in the text, which refers to events before they received their honours, they appear without their titles.

Chapter 2: The Queen Is Dead

1. MacGregor's cabinet colleagues continue to be puzzled by reports of his precise figures, which he has not revealed. The confusion was not as great as over Dilhorne's figures in October 1963: the reports of MacGregor's estimates all indicated that a clear majority were opposed to Thatcher contesting the second ballot. As there were 22 ministers in the cabinet, including the Prime Minister, the commonly quoted estimate of 14–7 includes everybody except Thatcher. Another reported figure of 12–7 appears to have been derived by eliminating the two members of the Lords –

Mackay, the Lord Chancellor, and Belstead, leader of the Government in the Lords – presumably since they had no vote in the leadership election, although they were able to vote in the consultation of Tory peers which is part of the selection procedure. MacGregor did not consult Hurd or Major because they were Thatcher's proposers and their support was taken for granted. Of the seven ministers who were said to have been counted as supporting Thatcher's fighting on, only Baker and Parkinson were unqualified supporters.

2. *A Week In Politics*, Channel 4 Television, November 1990.
3. *The Thatcher Factor*, Channel 4 Television, April 1989.

Chapter 3: Long Live the King

1. *Frost on Sunday*, TV-am, 6 January 1991.
2. Interview with the author, spring 1987.
3. *The Guardian*, December 1990.
4. The problem had not arisen in 1975 because Thatcher had won outright in the second ballot. In the first ballot in 1965, Edward Heath established such a commanding lead over his rivals that although he had not secured the requisite majority they withdrew. None the less, Heath submitted his nomination for the second ballot and was declared to be the duly elected leader only when the deadline for nominations had passed and no other candidates had stepped forward. There was no precedent for 1990, but the rules state that in the event of there being no outright winner in the second ballot, all candidates automatically proceed to a third ballot.

Chapter 4: Tory Democracy

1. Gilmour, 1969, p. 78.
2. Beer, 1969, p. 14.
3. Ibid, p. 15.
4. Cited ibid, p. 12.
5. Cited ibid, p. 10.
6. 3 November 1774.
7. Cited in Blake, 1985, pp. 40–41. I acknowledge a particular debt to Blake's invaluable 'Commentary upon the history of the party'.
8. Cited in Blake, 1985, p. 41.
9. Blake, 1985, p. 111.
10. Hills (editor), 1990, pp. 338–41.
11. Amery, 1953, p. 21.
12. Gash, 1972, p. 37, and Blake, 1985, p. 6.
13. Feuchtwanger, 1968, p. 130, cited in Blake, 1985, p. 146.
14. McKenzie, 1963, p. 146.
15. Adelman, 1970, p. 30.
16. Quoted in *The Times*, 16 November 1990.

17. Maxwell-Fyfe, 1948 and 1949, p. 29.
18. Kilmuir, 1964, p. 324.
19. Ball, 1990, provides a detailed history of the formative years of the 1922 Committee.
20. *Dictionary of National Biography*.
21. Interview with author, January 1991.

Chapter 5: Coups and Crises

1. Southgate, 1974, p. 5.
2. Ibid, p. 159.
3. Ibid, p. 154.
4. Ramsden, 1978, p. 14.
5. Southgate, 1974, p. 156.
6. Dugdale, 1936, vol. ii, p. 23.
7. Dugdale, 1936, vol. ii, p. 25.
8. Ramsden, 1978, pp. 25–6.
9. Ibid, p. 32.
10. Dutton, 1985, p. 88.
11. McKenzie, 1963, pp. 81–2.
12. Ibid, p. 82.
13. Southgate, 1974, p. 170.
14. McKenzie, 1963, p. 81.
15. Chamberlain, 1936, p. 384.
16. Petrie, 1939, vol. i, p. 295.
17. Chamberlain, 1936, p. 387.
18. Thorpe, 1980, pp. 46–7.
19. Ibid, p. 47.
20. Ibid, p. 49.
21. Chamberlain, 1936, p. 396.
22. McKenzie, 1963, p. 81.
23. Ramsden, 1978, p. 67.
24. Ibid, p. 75.
25. Rhodes James, 1969, pp. 103–4.
26. Cited in McKenzie, 1963, p. 31.
27. Ramsden, 1978, pp. 150–1.
28. McKenzie, 1963, p. 89.
29. Thorpe, 1980, pp. 67–8.
30. McKenzie, 1963, p. 92.
31. Ibid, pp. 92–3.
32. Ibid, p. 92.
33. Dutton, 1985, p. 192.
34. Thorpe, 1980, pp. 71–2.
35. McKenzie, 1963, p. 98.
36. Thorpe, 1980, pp. 73–4.
37. Ibid, p. 74.

38. McKenzie, 1963, pp. 103–4.
39. Ibid, p. 104.
40. Ibid, p. 102.
41. Thorpe, 1980, p. 75.
42. Dutton, 1985, p. 199.
43. Ibid.
44. Rhodes James, 1969, p. 117.
45. Blake, 1985, pp. 211–13.
46. Thorpe, 1980, pp. 149–50.
47. Blake, 1985, p. 213.
48. Thorpe, 1980, p. 150.
49. Ramsden, 1978, p. 178.
50. Ibid.
51. Ibid, p. 182.
52. Ibid, p. 189.
53. McKenzie, 1963, p. 117.
54. Young, 1952, p. 73.
55. Williamson, 1982, pp. 385–7.
56. Ibid, pp. 400–8.
57. Macleod, 1961, p. 138.
58. Ibid.
59. Ibid, pp. 139–41.
60. Ibid, p. 142.
61. Middlemas and Barnes, 1969, p. 590.
62. Macleod, 1961, p. 143.
63. *The Times*, 18 March 1931.
64. *The Times*, 1 June 1937.
65. Macleod, 1961, p. 162.
66. Harvey, 1970, p. 21.
67. *The Times*, 1 June 1937.
68. Macleod, 1961, p. 203.
69. Shepherd, 1988, p. 109.
70. Ibid, p. 111.
71. Ibid, p. 292.
72. Howard, 1987, p. 93.
73. Shepherd, 1988, p. 293.
74. Ibid.
75. Ibid, p. 297.

Chapter 6: The Magic Circle and After

1. Seldon, 1981, pp. 39–40, who adds that when Churchill suggested persevering with the idea he was opposed by other ministers, including Harold Macmillan, the housing minister, and James Stuart, the Scottish Secretary.
2. Gilbert, 1988, p. 253.

3. Seldon, 1981, p. 39.
4. Lord Camrose, quoted in Gilbert, 1988, p. 244.
5. Gilbert, 1988, p. 341.
6. Seldon, 1981, p. 43.
7. Gilbert, 1988, p. 960.
8. Ibid, p. 990.
9. Ibid, p. 1039.
10. Ibid, p. 1064.
11. Seldon, 1981, p. 50.
12. Lord Home, quoted in Hennessy, 1986, p. 51.
13. Gilbert, 1988, p. 1086.
14. Ibid, p. 1107.
15. Ibid, p. 1115.
16. Quoted in Fisher, 1977, p. 72.
17. Rhodes James, 1986, pp. 590–1.
18. Howard, 1987, p. 244.
19. Kilmuir, 1964, pp. 283–4.
20. Rhodes James, 1986, p. 593.
21. Kilmuir, 1964, pp. 283–4.
22. Rhodes James, 1986, p. 595.
23. Ibid, p. 597.
24. Kilmuir, 1964, p. 285.
25. Ibid.
26. Rhodes James, 1986, p. 599.
27. Howard, 1987, p. 247.
28. Horne, 1988, p. 460.
29. Kilmuir, 1964, p. 285.
30. Rhodes James, 1986, p. 600.
31. Howard, 1987, pp. 248–9.
32. Ibid, p. 244.
33. Ibid, pp. 244–5.
34. Carlton, 1981, and Scott-Lucas, 1987, suggest that Eisenhower had a hand in Eden's downfall, but Lamb, 1987, and Reynolds, 1989, emphasise that the problems faced by Eden's government were largely self-inflicted.
35. Carlton, 1981, p. 463.
36. Lamb, 1987, p. 57.
37. Horne, 1988, p. 488.
38. Ibid.
39. Ibid, pp. 529–30.
40. Higgins, 1984, p. 145.
41. Hailsham, 1990, p. 342.
42. Author's interview with Julian Amery, November 1990, and Horne, 1989, p. 536.
43. Horne, 1989, p. 539, and Hailsham, 1990, p. 350.
44. Young, 1970, pp. 161–2.
45. Horne, 1989, p. 451.
46. Macleod's article, entitled simply 'The Tory Leadership' was written as a

review of Randolph Churchill's book, *The Fight for the Tory Leadership*, which drew heavily on Macmillan's version of events.

47. Horne, 1989, pp. 544–5.
48. Ibid, p. 545.
49. Howard, 1987, p. 310.
50. Hailsham, 1990, p. 352.
51. Ibid, and Walters, 1989, p. 124.
52. BBC Television, 13 June 1963.
53. Article in *The Times* by David Wood, 10 March 1980, and author's interview with Sir Harry Boyne, June 1990.
54. Butler, 1982, p. 96.
55. Howard, 1987, p. 313.
56. Thorpe, 1989, pp. 374–5.
57. Prior, 1986, p. 33.
58. Hailsham, 1990, pp. 354–5.
59. Horne, 1989, p. 555.
60. Ibid, p. 556–7.
61. Ibid, p. 559.
62. Ibid.
63. Prior, 1986, pp. 32–3.
64. Horne, 1989, pp. 559–60.
65. Ibid, 560–62.
66. *Spectator*, 17 January 1964.
67. Butler, M., 1987, p. 81, and Walters, 1989, pp. 131–43.
68. *Spectator*, 17 January 1964.
69. Howard, 1987, p. 318.
70. Ibid, p. 317.
71. *Spectator*, 17 January 1964.
72. Ibid.
73. Howard, 1987, pp. 318–19.
74. Thorpe, 1989, p. 379.
75. *Spectator*, 17 January 1964.
76. *Reputations*, BBC 2, presented by Anthony Howard, 13 July 1983, Powell quoted Macleod.
77. *The Day Before Yesterday*, Thames Television, October 1970.
78. *Spectator*, 17 January, 1964.
79. *Spectator*, October 1990.
80. *Spectator*, 17 January 1964.
81. Thorpe, 1989, p. 393.
82. Prior, 1986, p. 36.
83. Private information.
84. Cosgrave, 1989, p. 206.
85. The estimate of George Hutchinson, the political journalist and biographer, cited in Fisher, 1977, p. 126.
86. Prior, 1986, p. 44.
87. Ibid.
88. Ibid, p. 98.

89. Fisher, 1977, p. 151. Their earlier meeting at Edward du Cann's city office caused them to be dubbed 'the Milk Street Mafia'. Brock and Wapshott, 1980, and Young, 1989, also provide details of the 1974–75 leadership crisis.
90. Fisher, 1977, p. 163.
91. Ibid, p. 164.
92. Ibid, p. 169.
93. Tebbit, 1988, p. 141.
94. Prior, 1986, p. 100.

Chapter 7: Thatcher's Impact

1. See, for example, Hall and Jacques, 1983.
2. Middleton, 1986.
3. Horne, 1989, p. 532.
4. *A Week In Politics*, Channel 4 Television, February 1985.
5. Crewe and Searing, 1988, p. 371.
6. Keegan, 1984, p. 33.
7. Young and Sloman, 1986, p. 135.
8. *The Thatcher Factor*, Channel 4 Television, December 1990.
9. Ibid.
10. Prior, 1986, pp. 109–10.
11. *The Thatcher Factor*, Channel 4 Television, December 1990.
12. Grimstone, 1987.
13. Ibid.
14. *The Thatcher Factor*, Channel 4 Television, April 1989.
15. Ibid, December 1990.
16. Crewe and Searing, 1988, p. 371.
17. Ibid, pp. 375–6.
18. Worcester, citing MORI opinion polls, December 1990.
19. Crewe and Searing, p. 377.
20. Ibid.
21. Ibid.
22. British Social Attitudes, 1990. p. 2.
23. Jacobs and Worcester, 1990, p. 25.
24. British Social Attitudes, 1990. p. 2.
25. Jacobs and Worcester, 1990, p. 27.
26. British Social Attitudes, 1990. p. 2.
27. Gallup surveys, 1983 and 1987, cited in Butler and Kavanagh, 1988, p.6.
28. Norton, 1990.

Chapter 8: Major's Challenge

1. MORI survey, 18–21 January 1991, for the *Sunday Times*, cited in *British Public Opinion Newsletter*, January–February 1991.

2. NOP survey, 9–13 February 1991, for the *Independent* and BBC2's *Newsnight*.
3. Interview with the author, January 1991.
4. Interview with the author, January 1991.
5. Interview with the author, December 1990.
6. The author interviewed Major about his impressions of Macleod while Major was chancellor. His comments quoted in this section are taken from that interview, unless otherwise indicated.
7. Interview with the author, January 1991.
8. *Frost on Sunday*, TV-am, 6 January 1991. This programme is also the source of the quote at the head of the chapter.
9. Interview with the author, February 1991.
10. Interview with the author, November 1990.
11. Interviewed by David Marquand in *Marxism Today*, February 1991.
12. Speech to Young Conservatives conference, Scarborough, February 1991.
13. Interviewed by David Marquand in *Marxism Today*, February 1991.
14. Professor Anthony King, 'The twin peaks still to climb' in the *Sunday Telegraph*, 2 December 1990.

Select Bibliography

The following books and articles are those referred to in the notes for each chapter, and are given in alphabetical order by author. I have also included a few other books that are of special interest.

Chapter 4

Leo Amery in *Thoughts on the Constitution* (Oxford University Press, 1953) presents a Tory rationale of Britain's evolutionary and imperfect democracy, and an insight into the origins of a much mythologised Tory institution is provided by Stuart Ball, 'The 1922 Committee: The Formative Years 1922–45', in *Parliamentary History* (1990). Samuel H. Beer, *Modern British Politics* (Faber and Faber, 1969) remains invaluable as a guide to the ideological roots of British political debate. Analysis of recent change in the Tory Party is provided in Robert Behrens, *The Conservative Party from Heath to Thatcher* (Saxon House, 1980), while Robert Blake, *The Conservative Party from Peel to Thatcher* (Fontana, 1985) stands as the classic commentary on the party's history, enlivened by its author's personal knowledge and lifetime study of his subject. Philip W. Buck (editor), *How Conservatives Think* (Pelican, 1975) provides a well-judged guide. Edmund Burke, *Reflections on the Revolution in France* (Pelican 1973) is the definitive statement of evolutionary and pragmatic conservatism, which is made accessible to the modern reader by Conor Cruise O'Brien's introduction and editing. Lord Butler (editor), *The Conservatives: a History from their Origins to 1965* (Allen and Unwin, 1977) includes contributions by distinguished historians and Butler's own defence of moderate Toryism. Bruce Coleman, *Conservatism and the Conservative Party in the Nineteenth Century* (Edward Arnold, 1988) presents an excellent analysis of the party's first sixty years and incorporates recent research, while F. J. Feuchtwanger, *Disraeli, Democracy and the Conservative Party* (Oxford University Press, 1968) is instructive on party organisation.

Michael Foot, *Debts of Honour* (Picador, 1980) includes a fascinating essay which presents Disraeli as the most extraordinary of all Tory leaders. The party's response to the challenge of winning office in a modern democracy is analysed in Andrew Gamble, *The Conservative Nation* (Routledge and Kegan Paul, 1974). Norman Gash, *Mr Secretary Peel* (Longman, 1961) and *Sir Robert Peel* (Longman, 1972) are compelling and beautifully written studies of the first leader of the modern Conservative Party, and the same author surveys society at the time of the party's formation in *Aristocracy and People: Britain 1815–1865* (Edward Arnold, 1979). Ian Gilmour, *The Body Politic* (Hutchinson, 1969) offers an astute study of British politics and parties, and his enlightened paternalism is elegantly presented in *Inside Right: A Study of Conservatism* (Hutchinson, 1977). Sir Philip Goodhart, *The 1922 Committee* (Macmillan, 1973) offers a narrative account, written to mark the '22's fiftieth anniversary by its then honorary secretary. Richard N. Kelly, *Conservative Party Conferences: the hidden conference system* (Manchester University Press, 1989), questions the notion that Tory Party conferences have no influence on the leadership. A useful study of the party and its leaders from the end of the First World War to the Party's 1970 election victory is to be found in T. F. Lindsay and M. Harrington, *The Conservative Party, 1918–1970* (Macmillan, 1974). John P. Mackintosh, *The British Cabinet* (Methuen, 1968) includes illuminating insights on Tory premiers and their cabinets, and concise taxonomy of the different ideological strands in the modern Tory Party is given in Vincent McKee, 'Conservative Factions' in *Contemporary Record* (Autumn 1989).

Robert McKenzie, *British Political Parties* (Heinemann, 1963) is the classic study of party organisation, although it should now be read in conjunction with later research. The starting point for any study of working-class Tory voters is Robert McKenzie and A. Silver, *Angels in Marble* (Heinemann, 1968). The upsurge of Tory backbench rebellions during Heath's leadership is examined in Philip Norton, *Conservative Dissidents: Dissent within the Parliamentary Conservative Party, 1970–74* (Temple Smith, 1978). Philip Norton and Arthur Aughey, *Conservatives and Conservatism* (Temple Smith, 1981) updates McKenzie (1963). Frank O'Gorman, *British Conservatism* (Longman, 1986) offers an illuminating insight into Tory thinking, supported with well-chosen examples. John Ramsden, *The Making of Conservative Party Policy: The Conservative Research Department since 1929* (Longman, 1980) is a detailed and revealing study, which draws on privileged access to the department's papers. R. J. White (editor), *The Conservative Tradition* (Nicholas Kaye, 1950) remains a helpful guide. D. G. Wright, *Democracy and Reform 1815–1885* (Longman, 1970) provides a useful brief analysis and relevant documents.

Chapter 5

Analysis and key texts are provided in Paul Adelman, *Gladstone, Disraeli and Later Victorian Politics* (Longman, 1970). Stuart Ball, *Baldwin and the Conservative Party: the Crisis of 1929–31* (Yale University Press, 1988) delivers an important re-evaluation of the Tory leader who has often been caricatured as a pig-stroking, indolent failure, while Baldwin's predecessor, Bonar Law, is best depicted in Robert (now Lord) Blake, *The Unknown Prime Minister* (Eyre and Spottiswoode, 1955), and the same author's *Disraeli* (Eyre and Spottiswoode, 1966) is the definitive study. Robert Blake and H. Cecil (editors) *Salisbury: the Man and his Policies* (Macmillan, 1987) is also a valuable guide. Sir Austen Chamberlain, *Politics From the Inside* (Cassell, 1936), is self-revealing of the Tory leader who never became prime minister. The life of his brother is given detailed scrutiny up to the end of his period as a reforming Minister of Health in David Dilks, *Neville Chamberlain: Pioneering and Reform, 1869–1929* (Cambridge University Press, 1984). Blanche Dugdale, *Arthur James Balfour* (Hutchinson, 1936), a niece of her subject, provides some interesting insights. David Dutton, *Austen Chamberlain: Gentleman in Politics* (Ross Anderson Publications, 1985) offers a modern re-assessment. Keith Feiling, *Life of Neville Chamberlain* (Macmillan, 1946), remains the most detailed full-length biography. Nigel Fisher, *The Tory Leaders: Their Struggle for Power* (Weidenfeld and Nicolson, 1977) surveys the party's leaders, and as a senior backbencher at the time provides insight into the 1975 leadership contest. The champion of Tory democracy is profiled in R. F. Foster, *Lord Randolph Churchill* (Oxford University Press, 1981). E. H. H. Green, 'Radical Conservatism: the Electoral Genesis of Tariff Reform', in the *Historical Journal* (1985) tackles an area often misunderstood by other historians and examines the electoral appeal of tariff reform. John Harvey (editor), *The Diplomatic Diaries of Oliver Harvey, 1937–1940* (Collins, 1970) reveals an inside view from the beleaguered Foreign Office during Chamberlain's premiership. The champion of this policy is assessed in Richard Jay, *Joseph Chamberlain: A Political Study* (Oxford University Press, 1981) and Dennis Judd, *Radical Joe* (Hamish Hamilton, 1977), and both books contain useful information on the Liberal Unionists. Roy Jenkins, *Baldwin* (Collins, 1987) offers an elegant and rewarding biographical essay.

Iain Macleod, *Neville Chamberlain* (Frederick Muller, 1961) did not satisfy its author, but it brings to its subject an understanding of how politicians operate and think. Similarly, Harold Macmillan, *The Past Masters* (Macmillan, 1975) surveys earlier leaders with the insight provided by a practitioner's eye. Peter Marsh, *The Discipline of Popular Government: Lord Salisbury's Domestic Statecraft* (Harvester, 1978) leads the field on Salisbury in office, and Keith Middlemas and John Barnes, *Baldwin* (Weidenfeld and Nicolson, 1969) remains useful. Sir Charles Petrie's *Walter Long and his Times* (Hutchinson, 1936) and *The Life and Letters of Sir Austen Chamberlain* (Cassell, 1939) contain helpful material on the rival, but eventually unsuccessful, contenders to succeed Balfour in 1911. Enoch Powell, *Joseph Chamberlain* (Thames and Hudson, 1977) casts his subject's unionism as the centre-piece of his political career. John Ramsden, *The Age of Balfour and Baldwin 1902–40* (Longman, 1978) provides an excellent and thorough analysis of Tory leaders and their impact on the party in the first forty years of the twentieth century. Robert Rhodes James, *Memoirs of a Conservative* (Weidenfeld and Nicolson, 1969) presents the edited diaries of J. C. C. Davidson, and contains important information on Bonar Law, Baldwin and the party in the 1920s. Robert Shepherd, *A Class Divided* (Macmillan, 1988) deals with the debate in the 1930s over appeasement and Munich, ending with Chamberlain's resignation and Churchill becoming prime minister in May 1940. Donald Southgate, *The Conservative Leadership 1832–1932* (Macmillan, 1974) includes chapters on the party leaders from Peel to Baldwin.

The early history of the party is fully examined in Robert Stewart, *The Politics of Protection* (Cambridge University Press, 1971) and *The Foundation of the Conservative Party, 1830–67* (Longman, 1978). The party's problems when it was denied office before the First World War are reviewed in Alan Sykes, 'The Radical Right and the Crisis of Conservatism before the First World War', in the *Historical Journal* (1983). D. R. Thorpe, *The Uncrowned Prime Ministers* (Dark Horse, 1980) incorporates three biographies in one book, presenting assiduously researched studies of Tories who narrowly failed to become prime minister: Austen Chamberlain, Lord Curzon and Rab Butler. Philip Williamson, ' "Safety First": Baldwin, the Conservative Party, and the 1929 General Election', in the *Historical Journal* (1982) offers a positive interpretation of Baldwin's famously unsuccessful appeal to the voters. G. M. Young, *Stanley Baldwin* (Rupert Hart-Davis, 1952) and Kenneth Young, *Arthur James Balfour* (G. Bell and Sons, 1963) are helpful biographies of previous leaders.

Chapter 6

Lord Butler, *The Art of the Possible* (Hamish Hamilton, 1971) is an elegantly written autobiography. His posthumously published *The Art of Memory: Friends in Perspective* (Hodder and Stoughton, 1982) contains a chapter on his acolyte, Iain Macleod. Mollie Butler, *August and Rab: A Memoir* (Weidenfeld and Nicolson, 1987) is a moving portrait of Rab Butler by his second wife and sheds further light on why he failed to become prime minister. David Carlton, *Anthony Eden* (Allen Lane, 1981) is thorough and highly critical of its subject, but loses from its brief coverage of Eden's earlier life. Randolph Churchill, *The Fight for the Tory Leadership* (Heinemann, 1964) reflects Macmillan's version of events in the 1963 leadership crisis and probably reveals more than its author or principal source realised. A rewarding study of Macleod's fellow rebel in 1963 is presented by Patrick Cosgrave, *The Lives of Enoch Powell* (The Bodley Head, 1989), and the same author's *R. A. Butler, an English Life* (Quartet, 1981) also covers the 1963 crisis. The events leading up to the leadership crisis of 1956–7 are examined in Howard J. Dooley, 'Great Britain's Last Battle in the Middle East', in *International History Review* (August 1989). The leader whose career was ruined by Suez rationalises the crisis in Sir Anthony Eden, *Full Circle* (Cassell, 1960).

Nigel Fisher, *Iain Macleod* (Andre Deutsch, 1973) is a sympathetic study of a complex character, and the same author's *Harold Macmillan* (Weidenfeld and Nicolson, 1982) portrays another Tory of Scottish highland ancestry. Martin Gilbert, *'Never Despair': Winston S. Churchill, 1945–65* (Heinemann, 1988) provides the fascinating, final narrative in his mammoth biography. Lord Hailsham, *A Sparrow's Flight: Memoirs* (Collins, 1990) reveals the views of Macmillan's initial choice as his successor in 1963. Peter Hennessy's *Cabinet* (Basil Blackwell, 1986), and Hennessy and Anthony Seldon (editors), *Ruling Performance* (Basil Blackwell, 1987) present fascinating studies of British governments from Attlee to Thatcher. Sydney Higgins, *The Benn Inheritance* (Weidenfeld and Nicolson, 1984) includes useful background on the Peerage Act 1963, which allowed peers to disclaim their titles and which had such a profound impact on the Tory leadership. The two-volume study, Alastair Horne, *Macmillan: 1894–1957* (Macmillan, 1988) and *Macmillan: 1957–1986* (Macmillan, 1989) provides an official biography of an intriguing leader, and draws heavily on diaries and interviews with the subject. The man whom Macmillan blocked from the leadership is well portrayed in Anthony Howard, *Rab: The Life of R. A. Butler* (Jonathan Cape, 1987).

A useful study of a difficult subject is provided by George Hutchinson,

Edward Heath: a Personal and Political Biography (Longman, 1978) and the same author presents a well-drawn profile of Macmillan in *The Last Edwardian at No. 10* (Quartet, 1980). An inside view of the Heath premiership is presented by his former political secretary, Douglas Hurd in *An End to Promises: Sketch of a Government, 1970–74* (Collins, 1979). The Earl of Kilmuir, *Political Adventure* (Weidenfeld and Nicolson, 1964), is a self-important account of his role in events, but none the less contains valuable information on Macmillan's succession to Eden in 1957. Richard Lamb, *The Failure of the Eden Government* (Sidgwick and Jackson, 1987) is an excellent study, which draws extensively on the official papers. Harold Macmillan's memoirs published between 1966 and 1973, and those dealing with his leadership are *Riding the Storm 1956–59* (Macmillan, 1971), *Pointing the Way 1959–61* (Macmillan, 1972) and *At the End of the Day 1961–63*. Iain Macleod, 'The Tory Leadership', in the *Spectator*, 17 January 1964, was one of the most powerful pieces of political journalism for a long time. Reginald Maudling, *Memoirs* (Sidgwick and Jackson, 1978), covers Tory politics from his days in the Conservative Research Department during Churchill's leadership to Thatcher's shadow cabinet.

David Reynolds, 'Eden the Diplomatist', in *History* (1989) reviews the books on Eden and presents a well-informed analysis of the Suez crisis. Robert Rhodes James, *Anthony Eden* (Weidenfeld and Nicolson, 1986), is a fine, official biography, and W. Scott Lucas, 'Suez, the Americans and the Overthrow of Anthony Eden,' in *LSE Quarterly* (August 1987) has a self-explanatory title and largely follows the thesis presented by Carlton (1981). A detailed analysis of the Churchill government of 1951–5 is provided in Anthony Seldon, *Churchill's Indian Summer* (Hodder and Stoughton, 1981). Norman Tebbit, *Upwardly Mobile* (Weidenfeld and Nicolson, 1988) is a less than inspired autobiography from an ardent Thatcherite. D. R. Thorpe, *Selwyn Lloyd* (Jonathan Cape, 1989) is a thoroughly researched study of another Tory politician who never became leader, but who played an important part in Home succeeding Macmillan in 1963. Dennis Walters, *Not Always with the Pack* (Constable, 1989) provides fresh insight into the 1963 crisis from a former aide of Hailsham, and is a highly readable memoir by a Tory backbencher. Kenneth Young, *Sir Alec Douglas-Home: A Biography* (Dent, 1978) profiles the last Tory leader to have 'evolved' as opposed to having been elected.

Chapter 7

Samuel Brittan, *A Restatement of Economic Liberalism* (Macmillan,

1988), lucidly demonstrates the chasm between the economic philosophy to which Thatcher paid lip-service and the highly selective version that she pursued as Tory leader. Jock Bruce-Gardyne, *Mrs Thatcher's First Administration: The Prophets Confounded* (Macmillan, 1984) and *Ministers and Mandarins* (Sidgewick and Jackson, 1986) are finely written accounts by a former minister in Thatcher's government. The Nuffield general election studies by David Butler and Dennis Kavanagh for 1979, 1983 and 1987 provide basic source material on Thatcher's hat-trick of election victories. Michael Cockerell, *Live From Number 10* (Faber and Faber, 1988) presents a well-informed account of prime ministers and the broadcast media. Michael Cockerell, Peter Hennessy and David Walker, *Sources Close to the Prime Minister* (Macmillan, 1984) probes the lobby system, an indispensable weapon in a leader's news management. John Cole, *The Thatcher Years* (BBC Books, 1987) is a readable and well-informed account of the collapse of consensus in British politics in the 1980s. Patrick Cosgrave, *Margaret Thatcher: a Tory and her Party* (Hutchinson, 1978) is a profile by a former adviser.

Ivor Crewe and Martin Harrop, *Political Communications: the General Election Campaign of 1987* (Cambridge University Press, 1987) offers an understanding of Thatcher's third election triumph, and the impact of Thatcher on people's political attitudes is extensively surveyed in Ivor Crewe and Donald Searing, 'Ideological Change in the British Conservative Party', in *American Political Science Review* (June 1988). Lawrence Freedman, *Britain and the Falklands War* (Basil Blackwell, 1988) presents a balanced assessment of the 1982 conflict in the south Atlantic. Andrew Gamble, *The Free Economy and the Strong State* (Macmillan, 1987) assesses the politics of Thatcher's leadership, and Cosmo Graham and Tony Prosser, *Waiving the Rules* (Open University Press, 1988) examines her government's impact on the constitution. The insight of a former civil servant is provided in Gerry Grimstone, 'Privatisation: the Unexpected Crusade', in *Contemporary Record* (spring 1987). Stuart Hall and Martin Jacques (editors), *The Politics of Thatcherism* (Penguin, 1983) incorporates a Marxist analysis of Thatcher's electoral appeal. Robert Harris, *Good and Faithful Servant* (Faber and Faber, 1990) is the 'unauthorised' biography of Sir Bernard Ingham, Thatcher's press secretary. A detailed study of why people voted Tory during Thatcher's leadership is offered by Anthony Heath, Roger Jowell and John Curtice, *How Britain Votes* (Pergamon, 1985). Peter Hennessy, *Whitehall* (Secker and Warburgh, 1989) is a classic study of British government, and John Hills (editor), *The State of Welfare* (Clarendon Press, 1990) presents an exhaustive study of social policy since 1974. Martin Holmes, *The First Thatcher Government 1979–83* (Wheatsheaf, 1985) emphasises Thatcher's economic record. A lively and illuminating survey of public attitudes at the close of the Thatcher era is presented in Eric Jacobs and Robert Worcester, *We British* (Weidenfeld and Nicolson, 1990).

Peter Jenkins, *Mrs Thatcher's Revolution* (Jonathan Cape, 1987) is a lively account of the Thatcher years, drawing on his store of conversations and interviews with key actors in the drama. R. J. Johnston, C. J. Pattie, and J. G. Allsopp, *A Nation Dividing?* (Longman, 1988) assesses Britain's changing political geography, a key element in Thatcher's success. Sir Keith Joseph, *Reversing the Trend* (Barry Rose, 1975), contains his key speeches from his personal road to Damascus during 1974. Roger Jowell, Sharon Witherspoon and Lindsay Brook (editors), *British Social Attitudes* (7th ed, Gower, 1990) continues the series on public attitudes towards social issues. Dennis Kavanagh, *Thatcherism and British Politics* (Oxford University Press, 1987), *Politics and Personalities* (Oxford University Press, 1990) and Dennis Kavanagh and Anthony Seldon (editors), *The Thatcher Effect: A Decade of Change* (Clarendon Press, 1989) all provide valuable insights on recent political change. William Keegan *Mrs Thatcher's Economic Experiment* (Allen Lane, 1984), *Britain Without Oil* (Penguin, 1985), and *Mr Lawson's Gamble* (Hodder and Stoughton, 1989) provide lucidly written and authoritative analysis of the failures of economic policy during the Thatcher years. Anthony King (editor), *The British Prime Minister* (2nd ed, Macmillan, 1985) offers an updated analysis of the role and power of the highest office. A perceptive analysis of Thatcher's attitudes towards social issues is provided in Patrick Middleton, 'For "Victorian" read "Georgian": Mrs Thatcher Corrected', in *Encounter* (July/August 1986). Philip Norton, '"The Lady's Not for Turning" But What About the Rest?', and 'Choosing a Leader', in *Parliamentary Affairs* (Hamish Hamilton, 1990) presents a detailed analysis of the ideological sympathies of Tory MPs at the close of the Thatcher era.

Jim Prior, *A Balance of Power* (Hamish Hamilton, 1986) provides a paternalist's view of life at the heart of the Tory Party in the Heath and Thatcher years, and Francis Pym, *The Politics of Consent* (Hamish Hamilton, 1985) offers a paternalist's political credo. Peter Riddell, *The Thatcher Government* (Martin Robertson, 1985) and *The Thatcher Decade* (Blackwell, 1989) are assiduously researched and readable accounts, and Robert Skidelsky (editor), *Thatcherism* (Chatto and Windus, 1988) contains excellent analysis. The 1987 election campaign is chronicled in an inside story provided in Rodney Tyler, *Campaign* (Grafton, 1987). Nicholas Wapshott and George Brock, *Thatcher* (Macdonald, 1983) is a good biography, particularly on the early years. Lord Whitelaw, *The Whitelaw Memoirs* (Aurum Press, 1989) is disappointingly bland. Robert M. Worcester, 'The End of Thatcherism', in

British Public Opinion Newsletter, December 1990, provides further evidence of Thatcher's limited effect on attitudes. Hugo Young, *One of Us* (Macmillan, 1989) is the best biography of Thatcher, and Hugo Young and Anne Sloman, *The Thatcher Phenomenon* (BBC Books, 1986) contains many illuminating insights about the former Tory leader.

Chapter 8

Chris Patten, *The Tory Case* (Longman, 1983) and his interview by David Marquand, in *Marxism Today* (February 1991) provide eloquent testimony to the thinking of Major's party chairman.

Illustration
Acknowledgements

The publishers and the author would like to thank the following for their kind permission to reproduce the illustrations in this book: Camera Press/Tom Blau (plate 6 *bottom*); the Centre for the Study of Cartoons and Caricature, University of Kent at Canterbury (pp. 144, 158); *Illustrated London News* (pp. 85, 108, 122); *The Independent*/Nicholas Garland (pp. 16, 45, 177); Hulton Picture Company (plates 1 *top left, bottom*, 2 *bottom left*, 3 *bottom*); Hulton/Central Press (plates 4 *top right*, 6 *top*); Hulton/Evening Standard Collection (plate 5 *top left*); Hulton Fox Photos (plate 4 *bottom*); Hulton/Keystone Collection (plate 5 *top right, bottom left*); Hulton/Topical Press (plate 4 *top left*); Tom Johnston (p. 221); the Mansell Collection (plate 3 *top left*); National Portrait Gallery (plate 2 *top*); Network/Mike Abrahams (plate 7 *top*); Network/John Sturrock (plate 7 *middle*); Network/Homer Sykes (plate 8 *top*); *New Statesman*/Vicky (p. 144); *Observer*/Dod Miller (plate 8 *middle*); *Observer*/Gavin Smith (plate 8 *bottom*); Popperfoto (plates 1 *bottom*, 3 *top right*); *Sunday Telegraph*/John Jensen (p. 158); Topham/Associated Press (plates 5 *bottom right*, 7 *bottom*).

Index